Stoddart

By Joan Didion

AFTER

JOAN

HENRY

DIDION

First published in 1992 by
Stoddart Publishing Co. Limited
34 Lesmill Road
Toronto, Canada
M3B 2T6

Published in the United States in 1992 by
Simon & Schuster

ISBN 0-7737-5528-4

Printed and bound in the United States

Acknowledgments

"In the Realm of the Fisher King", "Insider Baseball", Shooters Inc.", "Girl of the Golden West", and "Sentimental Journeys" appeared originally in *The New York Review of Books*. "Los Angeles Days", "Down at City Hall", "L.A. Noir", "Fire Season", "Times Mirror Square", and part of "Pacific Distances" appeared originally as "Letters from Los Angeles" in *The New Yorker*. Most of "Pacific Distances" and the introductory piece, "After Henry", appeared originally in *New West*, which later became *California* and eventually folded. I would like to thank my editors at all three magazines, Jon Carroll at *New West*, Robert Gottlieb at *The New Yorker*, and most especially, since he has put up with me over nineteen years and through many long and eccentric projects, Robert Silvers at *The New York Review*.

This book is dedicated to Henry Robbins
and to Bret Easton Ellis,
each of whom did time
with its publisher.

Contents

AFTER HENRY

After Henry

IN THE SUMMER of 1966 I was living in a borrowed house in Brentwood, and had a new baby. I
had published one book, three years before. My husband was writing his first. Our daybook for those
months shows no income at all for April, $305.06 for
May, none for June, and, for July, $5.29, a dividend
on our single capital asset, fifty shares of Transamer-
ica stock left to me by my grandmother. This 1966
daybook shows laundry lists and appointments with
pediatricians. It shows sixty christening presents received and sixty thank-you notes written, shows the
summer sale at Saks and the attempt to retrieve a
fifteen-dollar deposit from Southern Counties Gas,
but it does not show the date in June on which we
first met Henry Robbins.

This seems to me now a peculiar and poignant
omission, and one that suggests the particular frac-
tures that new babies and borrowed houses can cause
in the moods of people who live largely by their wits.
Henry Robbins was until that June night in 1966 an
abstract to us, another New York editor, a stranger at
Farrar, Straus & Giroux who had called or written

and said that he was coming to California to see some writers. I thought so little of myself as a writer that summer that I was obscurely ashamed to go to dinner with still another editor, ashamed to sit down again and discuss this "work" I was not doing, but in the end I did go: in the end I put on a black silk dress and went with my husband to the Bistro in Beverly Hills and met Henry Robbins and began, right away, to laugh. The three of us laughed until two in the morning, when we were no longer at the Bistro but at the Daisy, listening over and over to "In the Midnight Hour" and "Softly As I Leave You" and to one another's funny, brilliant, enchanting voices, voices that transcended lost laundry and babysitters and prospects of $5.29, voices full of promise, *writers'* voices.

In short we got drunk together, and before the summer was out Henry Robbins had signed contracts with each of us, and, from that summer in 1966 until the summer of 1979, very few weeks passed during which one or the other of us did not talk to Henry Robbins about something which was amusing us or interesting us or worrying us, about our hopes and about our doubts, about work and love and money and gossip; about our news, good or bad. On the July morning in 1979 when we got word from New York that Henry Robbins had died on his way to work a few hours before, had fallen dead, age fifty-one, to the floor of the 14th Street subway station, there was only one person I wanted to talk to about it, and that one person was Henry.

"Childhood is the kingdom where nobody dies" is a line, from the poem by Edna St. Vincent Millay, that has stuck in my mind ever since I first read it, when I was in fact a child and nobody died. Of course people did die, but they were either very old or died unusual deaths, died while rafting on the Stanislaus or loading a shotgun or doing 95 drunk: death was construed as either a "blessing" or an exceptional case, the dramatic instance on which someone else's (never our own) story turned. Illness, in that kingdom where I and most people I knew lingered long past childhood, proved self-limiting. Fever of unknown etiology signaled only the indulgence of a week in bed. Chest pains, investigated, revealed hypochondria.

As time passed it occurred to many of us that our benign experience was less than general, that we had been to date blessed or charmed or plain lucky, players on a good roll, but by that time we were busy: caught up in days that seemed too full, too various, too crowded with friends and obligations and children, dinner parties and deadlines, commitments and overcommitments. "You can't imagine how it is when everyone you know is gone," someone I knew who was old would say to me, and I would nod, uncomprehending, yes I can, I can imagine; would even think, God forgive me, that there must be a certain peace in outliving all debts and claims, in being known to no one, floating free. I believed that days would be too full forever, too crowded with friends there was no time to see. I believed, by way of contemplating the future, that we would all be around for one another's funerals. I was wrong. I had failed to imagine, I had not understood. Here was the way it was going to be: I would be around for Henry's funeral, but he was not going to be around for mine.

The funeral was not actually a funeral but a memorial service, in the prevailing way, an occasion for all of us to meet on a tropical August New York morning in the auditorium of the Society for Ethical Culture at 64th and Central Park West. A truism about working with language is that other people's arrangements of words are always crowding in on one's actual experience, and this morning in New York was no exception. "Abide with me: do not go away" was a line I kept hearing, unspoken, all through the service; my husband was speaking, and half a dozen other writers and publishers who had been close to Henry Robbins—Wilfrid Sheed, Donald Barthelme, John Irving, Doris Grumbach; Robert Giroux from Farrar, Straus & Giroux; John Macrae from Dutton—but the undersongs I heard were fragments of a poem by Delmore Schwartz, dead thirteen years, the casualty of another New York summer. *Abide with me: do not go away*, and then:

> *Controlling our pace before we get old,*
> *Walking together on the receding road,*
> *Like Chaplin and his orphan sister.*

Five years before, Henry had left Farrar, Straus for Simon and Schuster, and I had gone with him. Two years after that he had left Simon and Schuster and gone to Dutton. This time I had not gone with him, had stayed where my contract was, and yet I remained Henry's orphan sister, Henry's writer. I remember that he worried from time to time about whether we had enough money, and that he would sometimes, with difficulty, ask us if we needed some. I remember that he did not like the title *Play It As It Lays* and I remember railing at him on the telephone from a hotel room in Chicago because my husband's novel *True Confessions* was not yet in the window at Kroch's & Brentano's and I remember a Halloween night in New York in 1970 when our children went trick-or-treating together in the building on West 86th Street in which Henry and his wife and their two children then lived. I remember that this apartment on West 86th Street had white curtains, and that on one hot summer evening we all sat there and ate chicken in tarragon aspic and watched the curtains lift and move in the air off the river and our world seemed one of considerable promise.

I remember arguing with Henry over the use of the second person in the second sentence of *A Book of Common Prayer*. I remember his actual hurt and outrage when any of us, any of his orphan sisters or brothers, got a bad review or a slighting word or even a letter that he imagined capable of marring our most inconsequential moment. I remember him flying to California because I wanted him to read the first 110 pages of *A Book of Common Prayer* and did not want to send them to New York. I remember him turning up in Berkeley one night when I needed him in 1975; I was to lecture that night, an occasion freighted by the fact that I was to lecture many members of the English department who had once lectured me, and I was, until Henry arrived, scared witless, the sacrificial star of my own exposure dream. I remember that he came first to the Faculty Club, where I was staying, and walked me down the campus to 2000 LSB, where I was to speak. I remember him telling me that it would go just fine. I remember believing him.

I always believed what Henry told me, except about two things, the title *Play It As It Lays* and the use of the second person in the second sentence of *A Book of Common Prayer*, believed him even when time and personalities and the difficulty of making a living by either editing books or writing them had complicated our relationship. What editors do for writers is mysterious, and does not, contrary to general belief, have much to do with titles and sentences and "changes". Nor, my railing notwithstanding, does it have much to do with the window at Kroch's & Brentano's in Chicago. The relationship between an editor and a writer is much subtler and deeper than that, at once so elusive and so radical that it seems almost parental: the editor, if the editor was Henry Robbins, was the person who gave the writer the idea of himself, the idea of herself, the image of self that enabled the writer to sit down alone and do it.

This is a tricky undertaking, and requires the editor

not only to maintain a faith the writer shares only in intermittent flashes but also to like the writer, which is hard to do. Writers are only rarely likeable. They bring nothing to the party, leave their game at the typewriter. They fear their contribution to the general welfare to be evanescent, even doubtful, and, since the business of publishing is an only marginally profitable enterprise that increasingly attracts people who sense this marginality all too keenly, people who feel defensive or demeaned because they are not at the tables where the high rollers play (not managing mergers, not running motion picture studios, not even principal players in whatever larger concern holds the paper on the publishing house), it has become natural enough for a publisher or an editor to seize on the writer's fear, reinforce it, turn the writer into a necessary but finally unimportant accessory to the "real" world of publishing. Publishers and editors do not, in the real world, get on the night TWA to California to soothe a jumpy midlist writer. Publishers and editors in the real world have access to corporate G-3s, and prefer cruising the Galápagos with the raiders they have so far failed to become. A publisher or editor who has contempt for his own class position can find solace in transferring that contempt to the writer, who typically has no G-3 and can be seen as dependent on the publisher's largesse.

This was not a solace, nor for that matter a contempt, that Henry understood. The last time I saw him was two months before he fell to the floor of the 14th Street subway station, one night in Los Angeles

21

when the annual meeting of the American Booksellers Association was winding to a close. He had come by the house on his way to a party and we talked him into skipping the party, staying for dinner. What he told me that night was indirect, and involved implicit allusions to other people and other commitments and everything that had happened among us since that summer night in 1966, but it came down to this: he wanted me to know that I could do it without him. That was a third thing Henry told me that I did not believe.

WASHINGTON

In the Realm
of the Fisher King

PRESIDENT RONALD REAGAN, we were later
told by his speechwriter Peggy Noonan, spent his off-
camera time in the White House answering fifty letters a week, selected by the people who ran his mail
operation, from citizens. He put the family pictures
these citizens sent him in his pockets and desk draw-
ers. When he did not have the zip code, he apologized
to his secretary for not looking it up himself. He
sharpened his own pencils, we were told by Helene
von Damm, his secretary first in Sacramento and then
in Washington, and he also got his own coffee.

In the post-Reagan rush to establish that we knew
all along about this peculiarity in that particular White
House, we forgot the actual peculiarity of the place,
which had to do less with the absence at the center
than with the amount of centrifugal energy this absence left spinning free at the edges. The Reagan
White House was one in which great expectations
were allowed into play. Ardor, of a kind that only
rarely survives a fully occupied Oval Office, flourished unchecked. "You'd be in someone's home and
on the way to the bathroom you'd pass the bedroom

and see a big thick copy of Paul Johnson's *Modern Times* lying half open on the table by the bed," Peggy Noonan, who gave Ronald Reagan the boys of Pointe du Hoc and the *Challenger* crew slipping the surly bonds of earth and who gave George Bush the thousand points of light and the kinder, gentler nation, told us in *What I Saw at the Revolution: A Political Life in the Reagan Era.*

"Three months later you'd go back and it was still there," she wrote. "There were words. You had a notion instead of a thought and a dustup instead of a fight, you had a can-do attitude and you were in touch with the zeitgeist. No one had intentions they had an agenda and no one was wrong they were fundamentally wrong and you didn't work on something you broke your pick on it and it wasn't an agreement it was a done deal. All politics is local but more to the point all economics is micro. There were phrases: personnel is policy and ideas have consequences and ideas drive politics and it's a war of ideas . . . and to do nothing is to endorse the status quo and roll back the Brezhnev Doctrine and there's no such thing as a free lunch, especially if you're dining with the press."

Peggy Noonan arrived in Washington in 1984, thirty-three years old, out of Brooklyn and Massapequa and Fairleigh Dickinson and CBS Radio, where she had written Dan Rather's five-minute commentaries. A few years later, when Rather told her that in lieu of a Christmas present he wanted to make a donation to her favorite charity, the charity she specified was The William J. Casey Fund for the Nicaraguan Resistance. She did not immediately, or for some months after, meet the man for whose every public utterance she and the other staff writers were responsible; at the time she checked into the White House, no speechwriter had spoken to Mr. Reagan in more than a year. "We wave to him," one said.

In the absence of an actual president, this resourceful child of a large Irish Catholic family sat in her office in the Old Executive Office Building and invented an ideal one: she read Vachel Lindsay (particularly "I brag and chant of Bryan Bryan Bryan / Candidate for President who sketched a silver Zion") and she read Franklin Delano Roosevelt (whom she pictured, again ideally, up in Dutchess County "sitting at a great table with all the chicks, eating a big spring lunch of beefy red tomatoes and potato salad and mayonnaise and deviled eggs on the old china with the flowers almost rubbed off") and she thought "this is how Reagan should sound". What Miss Noonan had expected Washington to be, she told us, was "Aaron Copland and 'Appalachian Spring' ". What she found instead was a populist revolution trying to make itself, a crisis of raised expectations and lowered possibilities, the children of an expanded middle class determined to tear down the established order and what they saw as its repressive liberal orthodoxies: "There were libertarians whose girlfriends had just given birth to their sons, hoisting a Coors with social conservatives who walked into the party with a wife who bothered to be warm and a son who carried a Mason jar of something daddy grew in the backyard. There were Protestant fundamentalists hoping they wouldn't be dismissed by neocon intellectuals from Queens and neocons talking to fundamentalists thinking: I wonder if when they look at me they see what Annie Hall's grandmother saw when she looked down the table at Woody Allen."

She stayed at the White House until the spring of 1986, when she was more or less forced out by the refusal of Donald Regan, at that time chief of staff, to approve her promotion to head speechwriter. Regan thought her, according to Larry Speakes, who did not have a famous feel for the romance of the revolution, too "hard-line", too "dogmatic", too "right-wing", too much "Buchanan's protégée". On the occasion of her resignation she received a form letter from the president, signed with the auto-pen. Donald Regan said that there was no need for her to have what was referred to as "a good-bye moment", a farewell shakehands with the president. On the day Donald Regan himself left the White House, Miss Noonan received this message, left on her answering machine by a friend at the White House: "Hey, Peggy, Don Regan didn't get his good-bye moment." By that time she was hearing the "true tone of Washington" less as "Appalachian Spring" than as something a little more raucous, "nearer," she said, "to Jefferson Starship and 'They Built This City on Rock and Roll' ".

The White House she rendered was one of considerable febrility. Everyone, she told us, could quote Richard John Neuhaus on what was called the collapse of the dogmas of the secular enlightenment. Everyone could quote Michael Novak on what was called the collapse of the assumption that education is or should be "value-free". Everyone could quote George Gilder on what was called the humane nature of the free market. Everyone could quote Jean-François Revel on how democracies perish, and everyone could quote Jeane Kirkpatrick on authoritarian versus totalitarian governments, and everyone spoke of "the movement", as in "he's movement from way back", or "she's good, she's hard-core".

They talked about subverting the pragmatists, who believed that an issue could not be won without the *Washington Post* and the networks, by "going over the heads of the media to the people". They charged one another's zeal by firing off endless letters, memos, clippings. "Many thanks for Macedo's new monograph; his brand of judicial activism is more principled than Tribe's," such letters read. "If this gets into the hands of the Russians, it's curtains for the free world!" was the tone to take on the yellow Post-It attached to a clipping. "Soldier on!" was the way to sign off. Those PROF memos we later saw from Robert McFarlane to Lieutenant Colonel Oliver North ("Roger Ollie. Well done—if the world only knew how many times you have kept a semblance of integrity and gumption to US policy, they would make you Secretary of State. But they can't know and would complain if they did—such is the state of democracy in the late 20th century. . . . Bravo Zulu") do not seem, in this context, quite so unusual.

"Bureaucrats with soft hands adopted the clipped laconic style of John Ford characters," Miss Noonan noted. "A small man from NSC was asked at a meeting if he knew of someone who could work up a statement. Yes, he knew someone at State, a paid pen who's pushed some good paper." To be a moderate was to be a "squish", or a "weenie", or a "wuss". "He got rolled," they would say of someone who had lost the day, or, "He took a lickin' and kept on tickin'." They walked around the White House wearing ties ("slightly stained," according to Miss Noonan, "from the mayonnaise that fell from the sandwich that was wolfed down at the working lunch on judicial reform") embroidered with the code of the movement: eagles, flags, busts of Jefferson. Little gold Laffer curves identified the wearers as "free-market purists". Liberty bells stood for "judicial restraint".

The favored style here, like the favored foreign policy, seems to have been less military than paramilitary, a matter of talking tough. "That's not off my disk," Lieutenant Colonel Oliver North would snap by way of indicating that an idea was not his. "The fellas", as Miss Noonan called them, the sharp, the smooth, the inner circle and those who aspired to it, made a point of not using seat belts on Air Force One. The less smooth flaunted souvenirs of action on the far borders of the Reagan doctrine. "Jack Wheeler came back from Afghanistan with a Russian officer's belt slung over his shoulder," Miss Noonan recalls. "Grover Norquist came back from Africa rubbing his eyes from taking notes in a tent with Savimbi." Miss Noonan herself had lunch in the White House mess with a "Mujahadeen warrior" and his public relations man. "What is the condition of your troops in the field?" she asked. "We need help," he said. The Filipino steward approached, pad and pencil in hand. The mujahadeen leader looked up. "I will have meat," he said.

This is not a milieu in which one readily places Nancy Reagan, whose preferred style derived from the more structured, if equally rigorous, world from which she had come. The nature of this world was not very well understood. I recall being puzzled, on visits to Washington during the first year or two of the Reagan administration, by the tenacity of certain misapprehensions about the Reagans and the men generally regarded as their intimates, that small group of industrialists and entrepreneurs who had encouraged and financed, as a venture in risk capital, Ronald Reagan's appearances in both Sacramento and Washington. The president was above all, I was told repeatedly, a Californian, a Westerner, as were the acquaintances who made up his kitchen cabinet; it was the "Westernness" of these men that explained not only their rather intransigent views about America's mission in the world but also their apparent lack of interest in or identification with Americans for whom the trend was less reliably up. It was "Westernness", too, that could explain those affronts to the local style so discussed in Washington during the early years, the overwrought clothes and the borrowed jewelry and the Le Cirque hair and the wall-to-wall carpeting and the table settings. In style and substance alike, the Reagans and their friends were said to display what was first called "the California mentality", and then, as the administration got more settled and the social demonology of the exotic landscape more specific, "the California Club mentality".

I recall hearing about this "California Club mentality" at a dinner table in Georgetown, and responding with a certain atavistic outrage (I was from California, my own brother then lived during the week at the California Club); what seems curious in retrospect is that many of the men in question, including the president, had only a convenient connection with California in particular and the West in general. William Wilson was actually born in Los Angeles, and Earle Jorgenson in San Francisco, but the late Justin Dart was born in Illinois, graduated from Northwestern, married a Walgreen heiress in Chicago, and did not move United Rexall, later Dart Industries, from Boston to Los Angeles until he was already its president. The late Alfred Bloomingdale was born in New York, graduated from Brown, and seeded the Diners Club with money from his family's New York store. What these men represented was not "the West" but what was for this century a relatively new kind of monied class in America, a group devoid of social responsibilities precisely because their ties to any one place had been so attenuated.

Ronald and Nancy Reagan had in fact lived most of their adult lives in California, but as part of the entertainment community, the members of which do not belong to the California Club. In 1964, when I first went to live in Los Angeles, and for some years later, life in the upper reaches of this community was, for women, quite rigidly organized. Women left the table after dessert, and had coffee upstairs, isolated in the bedroom or dressing room with demitasse cups and rock sugar ordered from London and cinnamon sticks in lieu of demitasse spoons. On the hostess's dressing table there were always very large bottles of Fracas and Gardenia and Tuberose. The dessert that preceded this retreat (a soufflé or mousse with raspberry sauce) was inflexibly served on Flora Danica plates, and was itself preceded by the ritual of the finger bowls and the doilies. I recall being repeatedly told a cautionary tale about what Joan Crawford had said to a young woman who removed her finger bowl but left the doily. The details of exactly what Joan Crawford had said and to whom and at whose table she had said it differed with the teller, but it was always Joan Crawford, and it always involved the doily; one of the reasons Mrs. Reagan ordered the famous new china was because, she told us in her own account of life in the Reagan White House, *My Turn*, the Johnson china had no finger bowls.

These subtropical evenings were not designed to invigorate. Large arrangements of flowers, ordered from David Jones, discouraged attempts at general conversation, ensuring that the table was turned on schedule. Expensive "resort" dresses and pajamas were worn, Pucci silks to the floor. When the women rejoined the men downstairs, trays of white crème de menthe were passed. Large parties were held in tents, with pink lights and chili from Chasen's. Lunch took place at the Bistro, and later at the Bistro Garden and at Jimmy's, which was owned by Jimmy Murphy, who everyone knew because he had worked for Kurt Niklas at the Bistro.

These forms were those of the local *ancien régime*, and as such had largely faded out by the late sixties, but can be examined in detail in the photographs Jean Howard took over the years and collected in *Jean Howard's Hollywood: A Photo Memoir*. Although neither Reagan appears in Miss Howard's book (the people she saw tended to be stars or powers or famously amusing, and the Reagans, who fell into hard times and television, were not locally thought to fill any of these slots), the photographs give a sense of the rigors of the place. What one notices in a photograph of the Joseph Cottens' 1955 Fourth of July lunch, the day Jennifer Jones led the conga line into the pool, is not the pool. There are people in the pool, yes, and even chairs, but most of the guests sit decorously on the lawn, wearing rep ties, silk dresses, high-heeled shoes. Mrs. Henry Hathaway, for a day in the sun at Anatole Litvak's beach house, wears a strapless dress of embroidered and scalloped organdy, and pearl ear-rings. Natalie Wood, lunching on Minna Wallis's lawn with Warren Beatty and George Cukor and the Hathaways and the Minnellis and the Axelrods, wears a black straw hat with a silk ribbon, a white dress, black and white beads, perfect full makeup, and her hair pinned back.

This was the world from which Nancy Reagan went in 1966 to Sacramento and in 1980 to Washington, and it is in many ways the world, although it was vanishing *in situ* even before Ronald Reagan was elected governor of California, she never left. *My Turn* did not document a life radically altered by later experience. Eight years in Sacramento left so little imprint on Mrs. Reagan that she described the house in which she lived there—a house located on 45th Street off M Street in a city laid out on a numerical and alphabetical grid running from 1st Street to 66th Street and from A Street to Y Street—as "an English-style country house in the suburbs".

She did not find it unusual that this house should have been bought for and rented to her and her husband (they paid $1,250 a month) by the same group of men who gave the State of California eleven acres on which to build Mrs. Reagan the "governor's mansion" she actually wanted and who later funded the million-dollar redecoration of the Reagan White House and who eventually bought the house on St. Cloud Road in Bel Air to which the Reagans moved when they left Washington (the street number of the St. Cloud house was 666, but the Reagans had it changed to 668, to

35

avoid an association with the Beast in Revelations); she seemed to construe houses as part of her deal, like the housing provided to actors on location. Before the kitchen cabinet picked up Ronald Reagan's contract, the Reagans had lived in a house in Pacific Palisades remodeled by his then sponsor, General Electric.

This expectation on the part of the Reagans that other people would care for their needs struck many people, right away, as remarkable, and was usually characterized as a habit of the rich. But of course it is not a habit of the rich, and in any case the Reagans were not rich: they, and this expectation, were the products of studio Hollywood, a system in which performers performed, and in return were cared for. "I preferred the studio system to the anxiety of looking for work in New York," Mrs. Reagan told us in *My Turn*. During the eight years she lived in Washington, Mrs. Reagan said, she "never once set foot in a supermarket or in almost any other kind of store, with the exception of a card shop at 17th and K, where I used to buy my birthday cards", and carried money only when she went out for a manicure.

She was surprised to learn ("Nobody had told us") that she and her husband were expected to pay for their own food, dry cleaning, and toothpaste while in the White House. She seemed never to understand why it was imprudent of her to have accepted clothes from their makers when so many of them encouraged her to do so. Only Geoffrey Beene, whose clothes for Patricia Nixon and whose wedding dress for Lynda Bird Johnson were purchased through stores at retail prices, seemed to have resisted this impulse. "I don't quite understand how clothes can be 'on loan' to a woman," he told the *Los Angeles Times* in January of 1982, when the question of Mrs. Reagan's clothes was first raised. "I also think they'll run into a great deal of trouble deciding which of all these clothes are of museum quality. . . . They also claim she's helping to 'rescue' the American fashion industry. I didn't know it was in such dire straits."

The clothes were, as Mrs. Reagan seemed to construe it, "wardrobe"—a production expense, like the housing and the catering and the first-class travel and the furniture and paintings and cars that get taken home after the set is struck—and should rightly have gone on the studio budget. That the producers of this particular production—the men Mrs. Reagan called their "wealthier friends", their "very generous" friends—sometimes misunderstood their own role was understandable: Helene von Damm told us that only after William Wilson was warned that anyone with White House credentials was subject to a full-scale FBI investigation (Fred Fielding, the White House counsel, told him this) did he relinquish Suite 180 of the Executive Office Building, which he had commandeered the day after the inauguration in order to vet the appointment of the nominal, as opposed to the kitchen, cabinet.

"So began my stewardship," Edith Bolling Wilson wrote later about the stroke that paralyzed Woodrow

Wilson in October of 1919, eighteen months before he left the White House. The stewardship Nancy Reagan shared first with James Baker and Ed Meese and Michael Deaver and then less easily with Donald Regan was, perhaps because each of its principals was working a different scenario and only one, James Baker, had anything approaching a full script, considerably more Byzantine than most. Baker, whose ultimate role in this White House was to preserve it for the established order, seems to have relied heavily on the tendency of opposing forces, let loose, to neutralize each other. "Usually in a big place there's only one person or group to be afraid of," Peggy Noonan observed. "But in the Reagan White House there were two, the chief of staff and his people and the First Lady and hers—a pincer formation that made everyone feel vulnerable." Miss Noonan showed us Mrs. Reagan moving through the corridors with her East Wing entourage, the members of which were said in the West Wing to be "not serious", readers of *W* and *Vogue*. Mrs. Reagan herself was variously referred to as "Evita", "Mommy", "The Missus", "The Hairdo with Anxiety". Miss Noonan dismissed her as not "a liberal or a leftist or a moderate or a détentist" but "a Galanoist, a wealthy well-dressed woman who followed the common wisdom of her class".

In fact Nancy Reagan was more interesting than that: it was precisely "her class" in which she had trouble believing. She was not an experienced woman. Her social skills, like those of many women trained in the insular life of the motion picture community, were strikingly undeveloped. She and Raisa Gorbachev had "little in common", and "completely different outlooks on the world". She and Betty Ford "were different people who came from different worlds". She seems to have been comfortable in the company of Michael Deaver, of Ted Graber (her decorator), and of only a few other people. She seems not to have had much sense about who goes with who. At a state dinner for José Napoleón Duarte of El Salvador, she seated herself between President Duarte and Ralph Lauren. She had limited social experience and apparently unlimited social anxiety. Helene von Damm complained that Mrs. Reagan would not consent, during the first presidential campaign, to letting the fund-raisers call on "her New York friends"; trying to put together a list for the New York dinner in November of 1979 at which Ronald Reagan was to announce his candidacy, Miss von Damm finally dispatched an emissary to extract a few names from Jerry Zipkin, who parted with them reluctantly, and then said, "Remember, don't use my name."

Perhaps Mrs. Reagan's most endearing quality was this little girl's fear of being left out, of not having the best friends and not going to the parties in the biggest houses. She collected slights. She took refuge in a kind of piss-elegance, a fanciness (the "English-style country house in the suburbs"), in using words like "inappropriate". It was "inappropriate, to say the least" for Geraldine Ferraro and her husband to leave the dais and go "down on the floor, working the crowd" at a 1984 Italian-American Federation dinner at which the candidates on both tickets were speaking. It was "uncalled for—and mean" when, at the time John Koehler had been named to replace Patrick Buchanan as director of communications and it was learned that Koehler had been a member of Hitler Youth, Donald Regan said "blame it on the East Wing".

Mrs. Gorbachev, as Mrs. Reagan saw it, "condescended" to her, and "expected to be deferred to". Mrs. Gorbachev accepted an invitation from Pamela Harriman before she answered one from Mrs. Reagan. The reason Ben Bradlee called Iran-contra "the most fun he'd had since Watergate" was just possibly because, she explained in *My Turn*, he resented her relationship with Katharine Graham. Betty Ford was given a box on the floor of the 1976 Republican National Convention, and Mrs. Reagan only a skybox. Mrs. Reagan was evenhanded: Maureen Reagan "may have been right" when she called this slight deliberate. When, on the second night of that convention, the band struck up "Tie a Yellow Ribbon Round the Ole Oak Tree" during an ovation for Mrs. Reagan, Mrs. Ford started dancing with Tony Orlando. Mrs. Reagan was magnanimous: "Some of our people saw this as a deliberate attempt to upstage me, but I never thought that was her intention."

Michael Deaver, in his version of more or less the same events, *Behind the Scenes*, gave us an arresting account of taking the Reagans, during the 1980 campaign, to an Episcopal church near the farm on which they were staying outside Middleburg, Virginia. After advancing the church and negotiating the subject of the sermon with the minister (Ezekiel and the bones rather than what Deaver called "reborn Christians", presumably Christian rebirth), he finally agreed that the Reagans would attend an eleven o'clock Sunday service. "We were not told," Deaver wrote, "and I did not anticipate, that the eleven o'clock service would also be holy communion," a ritual he characterized as "very foreign to the Reagans". He described "nervous glances", and "mildly frantic" whispers about what to do, since the Reagans' experience had been of Bel Air Presbyterian, "a proper Protestant church where trays are passed containing small glasses of grape juice and little squares of bread." The moment arrived: ". . . halfway down the aisle I felt Nancy clutch my arm. . . . *'Mike!'* she hissed. *'Are those people drinking out of the same cup?'* "

Here the incident takes on elements of "I Love Lucy". Deaver assures Mrs. Reagan that it will be acceptable to just dip the wafer in the chalice. Mrs. Reagan chances this, but manages somehow to drop the wafer in the wine. Ronald Reagan, cast here as Ricky Ricardo, is too deaf to hear Deaver's whispered instructions, and has been instructed by his wife to "do exactly as I do". He, too, drops the wafer in the wine, where it is left to float next to Mrs. Reagan's. "Nancy was relieved to leave the church," Deaver reports. "The president was chipper as he stepped into the sunlight, satisfied that the service had gone quite well."

41

I had read this account several times before I realized what so attracted me to it: here we had a perfect
model of the Reagan White House. There was the
aide who located the correct setting ("I did some quick
scouting and found a beautiful Episcopal church"),
who anticipated every conceivable problem and handled it adroitly (he had "a discreet chat with the minister", he "gently raised the question"), and yet who
somehow missed, as in the visit to Bitburg, a key
point. There was the wife, charged with protecting
her husband's face to the world, a task requiring, she
hinted in *My Turn*, considerable vigilance. This was a
husband who could be "naive about people". He had
for example "too much trust" in David Stockman. He
had "given his word" to Helmut Kohl, and so felt
"duty-bound to honor his commitment" to visit Bitburg. He was, Mrs. Reagan disclosed during a "Good
Morning America" interview at the time *My Turn* was
published, "the softest touch going" when it came to
what she referred to as (another instance of somehow
missing a key point) "the poor". Mrs. Reagan understood all this. She handled all this. And yet there she
was outside Middleburg, Virginia, once again the victim of bad advance, confronted by the "foreign" communion table and rendered stiff with apprehension
that a finger bowl might get removed without its
doily.

And there, at the center of it all, was Ronald Reagan, insufficiently briefed (or, as they say in the White
House, "badly served") on the wafer issue but moving
ahead, stepping "into the sunlight" satisfied with his

own and everyone else's performance, apparently oblivious of (or inured to, or indifferent to) the crises being managed in his presence and for his benefit. What he had, and the aide and the wife did not have, was the story, the high concept, what Ed Meese used to call "the big picture", as in "he's a big-picture man". The big picture here was of the candidate going to church on Sunday morning; the details obsessing the wife and the aide—what church, what to do with the wafer—remained outside the frame.

From the beginning in California, the principal in this administration was operating on what might have seemed distinctly special information. He had "feelings" about things, for example about the Vietnam War. "I have a feeling that we are doing better in the war than the people have been told," he was quoted as having said in the *Los Angeles Times* on October 16, 1967. With the transforming power of the presidency, this special information that no one else understood— these big pictures, these high concepts—took on a magical quality, and some people in the White House came to believe that they had in their possession, sharpening his own pencils in the Oval Office, the Fisher King himself, the keeper of the grail, the source of that ineffable contact with the electorate that was in turn the source of the power.

There were times, we know now, when this White House had fairly well absented itself from the art of the possible. McFarlane flying to Teheran with the

43

cake and the Bible and ten falsified Irish passports did
not derive from our traditional executive tradition.
The place was running instead on its own supersti-
tion, on the reading of bones, on the belief that a
flicker of attention from the president during the presentation of a plan (the ideal presentation, Peggy
Noonan explained, was one in which "the president
was forced to look at a picture, read a short letter, or
respond to a question") ensured the transfer of the
magic to whatever was that week exciting the ardor of
the children who wanted to make the revolution—to
SDI, to the mujahadeen, to Jonas Savimbi, to the
contras.

Miss Noonan recalled what she referred to as "the
contra meetings", which turned on the magical notion
that putting the president on display in the right setting (i.e., "going over the heads of the media to the
people") was all that was needed to "inspire a commitment on the part of the American people". They sat
in those meetings and discussed having the president
speak at the Orange Bowl in Miami on the anniversary
of John F. Kennedy's Orange Bowl speech after the
Bay of Pigs, never mind that the Kennedy Orange
Bowl speech had become over the years in Miami the
symbol of American betrayal. They sat in those meetings and discussed having the president go over the
heads of his congressional opponents by speaking in
Jim Wright's district near the Alamo: ". . . something
like '*Blank* miles to the north of here is the Alamo,' "
Miss Noonan wrote in her notebook, sketching out
the ritual in which the magic would be transferred.

" '. . . Where brave heroes *blank*, and where the commander of the garrison wrote during those terrible last days *blank* . . .' "

But the Fisher King was sketching another big picture, one he had had in mind since California. We have heard again and again that Mrs. Reagan turned the president away from the Evil Empire and toward the meetings with Gorbachev. (Later, on NBC "Nightly News," the San Francisco astrologer Joan Quigley claimed a role in influencing both Reagans on this point, explaining that she had "changed their Evil Empire attitude by briefing them on Gorbachev's horoscope".) Mrs. Reagan herself allowed that she "felt it was ridiculous for these two heavily armed superpowers to be sitting there and not talking to each other" and "did push Ronnie a little".

But how much pushing was actually needed remains in question. The Soviet Union appeared to Ronald Reagan as an abstraction, a place where people were helpless to resist "communism", the inanimate evil which, as he had put it in a 1951 speech to a Kiwanis convention and would continue to put it for the next three and a half decades, had "tried to invade our industry" and been "fought" and eventually "licked". This was a construct in which the actual citizens of the Soviet Union could be seen to have been, like the motion picture industry, "invaded"—in need only of liberation. The liberating force might be the appearance of a Shane-like character, someone to "lick" the evil, or it might be just the sweet light of reason. "A people free to choose will always choose peace," as President Reagan told students at Moscow State University in May of 1988.

In this sense he was dealing from an entirely abstract deck, and the opening to the East had been his card all along, his big picture, his story. And this is how it went: what he would like to do, he had told any number of people over the years (I recall first hearing it from George Will, who cautioned me not to tell it because conversations with presidents were privileged), was take the leader of the Soviet Union (who this leader would be was another of those details outside the frame) on a flight to Los Angeles. When the plane came in low over the middle-class subdivisions that stretch from the San Bernardino mountains to LAX, he would direct the leader of the Soviet Union to the window, and point out all the swimming pools below. "Those are the pools of the capitalists," the leader of the Soviet Union would say. "No," the leader of the free world would say. "Those are the pools of the workers." *Blank* years further on, when brave heroes *blanked*, and where the leader of the free world *blank*, accidental history took its course, but we have yet to pay for the ardor.

—1989

Insider Baseball

1

IT OCCURRED to me during the summer of 1988, in California and Atlanta and New Orleans, in the course of watching first the California primary and then the Democratic and Republican national conventions, that it had not been by accident that the people with whom I had preferred to spend time in high school had, on the whole, hung out in gas stations. They had not run for student body office. They had not gone to Yale or Swarthmore or DePauw, nor had they even applied. They had gotten drafted, gone through basic at Fort Ord. They had knocked up girls, and married them, had begun what they called the first night of the rest of their lives with a midnight drive to Carson City and a five-dollar ceremony performed by a justice still in his pajamas. They got jobs at the places that had laid off their uncles. They paid their bills or did not pay their bills, made down payments on tract houses, led lives on that social and economic edge referred to, in Washington and among those whose preferred locus is Washington, as "out there". They were never destined to be, in other words, communicants in what we have come to call, when we want to indicate the traditional ways in which power is exchanged and the status quo maintained in the United States, "the process".

"The process today gives everyone a chance to participate," Tom Hayden, by way of explaining "the difference" between 1968 and 1988, said to Bryant Gumbel on NBC at 7:50 A.M. on the day after Jesse Jackson spoke at the 1988 Democratic convention in Atlanta. This was, at a convention that had as its controlling principle the notably nonparticipatory idea of "unity", demonstrably not true, but people inside the process, constituting as they do a self-created and self-referring class, a new kind of managerial elite, tend to speak of the world not necessarily as it is but as they want people out there to believe it is. They tend to prefer the theoretical to the observable, and to dismiss that which might be learned empirically as "anecdotal". They tend to speak a language common in Washington but not specifically shared by the rest of us. They talk about "programs", and "policy", and how to "implement" them or it, about "trade-offs" and constituencies and positioning the candidate and distancing the candidate, about the "story", and how it will "play". They speak of a candidate's performance, by which they usually mean his skill at circumventing questions, not as citizens but as professional insiders, attuned to signals pitched beyond the range of normal hearing: "I hear he did all right this afternoon," they were saying to one another in the press section of the

Louisiana Superdome in New Orleans on the evening in August of 1988 when Dan Quayle was or was not to be nominated for the vice presidency. "I hear he did OK with Brinkley." By the time the balloons fell that night the narrative had changed: "Quayle, zip," the professionals were saying as they brushed the confetti off their laptops.

These were people who spoke of the process as an end in itself, connected only nominally, and vestigially, to the electorate and its possible concerns. "She used to be an issues person but now she's involved in the process," a prominent conservative said to me in New Orleans by way of suggesting why an acquaintance who believed Jack Kemp was "speaking directly to what people out there want" had nonetheless backed George Bush. "Anything that brings the process closer to the people is all to the good," George Bush had declared in his 1987 autobiography, *Looking Forward*, accepting as given this relatively recent notion that the people and the process need not automatically be on convergent tracks.

When we talk about the process, then, we are talking, increasingly, not about "the democratic process", or the general mechanism affording the citizens of a state a voice in its affairs, but the reverse: a mechanism seen as so specialized that access to it is correctly limited to its own professionals, to those who manage policy and those who report on it, to those who run the polls and those who quote them, to those who ask and those who answer the questions on the Sunday shows, to the media consultants, to the columnists, to the issues advisers, to those who give the off-the-record breakfasts and to those who attend them; to that handful of insiders who invent, year in and year out, the narrative of public life. "I didn't realize you were a political junkie," Martin Kaplan, the former *Washington Post* reporter and Mondale speechwriter who was married to Susan Estrich, the manager of the Dukakis campaign, said when I mentioned that I planned to write about the campaign; the assumption here, that the narrative should be not just written only by its own specialists but also legible only to its own specialists, is why, finally, an American presidential campaign raises questions that go so vertiginously to the heart of the structure.

What strikes one most vividly about such a campaign is precisely its remoteness from the actual life of the country. The figures are well known, and suggest a national indifference usually construed, by those inside the process, as ignorance, or "apathy", in any case a defect not in themselves but in the clay they have been given to mold. Only slightly more than half of those eligible to vote in the United States did vote in the 1984 presidential election. An average 18.5 percent of what Nielsen Media Research calls the "television households" in the United States tuned into network coverage of the 1988 Republican convention in New Orleans, meaning 81.5 percent did not. An average 20.2 percent of these "television households" tuned into network coverage of the 1988 Democratic

convention in Atlanta, meaning 79.8 percent did not.
The decision to tune in or out ran along predictable
lines: "The demography is good even if the households are low," a programming executive at Bozell,
Jacobs, Kenyon & Eckhardt told the *New York Times*
in July of 1988 about the agency's decision to buy
"campaign event" time for Merrill Lynch on both
CBS and CNN. "The ratings are about nine percent
off 1984," an NBC marketing vice president allowed,
again to the *New York Times*, "but the upscale target
audience is there."

When I read this piece I recalled standing, the day
before the California primary, in a dusty Central California schoolyard to which the leading Democratic
candidate had come to speak one more time about
what kind of president he wanted to be. The crowd
was listless, restless. There were gray thunderclouds
overhead. A little rain fell. "We welcome you to Silicon Valley," an official had said by way of greeting
the candidate, but this was not in fact Silicon Valley:
this was San Jose, and a part of San Jose particularly
untouched by technological prosperity, a neighborhood in which the lowering of two-toned Impalas remained a central activity.

"I want to be a candidate who brings people together," the candidate was saying at the exact moment
a man began shouldering his way past me and through
a group of women with children in their arms. This
was not a solid citizen, not a member of the upscale
target audience. This was a man wearing a down vest
and a camouflage hat, a man with a definite little glit-

51

ter in his eyes, a member not of the 18.5 percent and not of the 20.2 percent but of the 81.5, the 79.8. "I've got to see the next president," he muttered repeatedly. "I've got something to tell him."

". . . Because that's what this party is all about," the candidate said.

"Where is he?" the man said, confused. "Who is he?"

"Get lost," someone said.

". . . Because that's what this country is all about," the candidate said.

Here we had the last true conflict of cultures in America, that between the empirical and the theoretical. On the empirical evidence this country was about two-toned Impalas and people with camouflage hats and a little glitter in their eyes, but this had not been, among people inclined to the theoretical, the preferred assessment. Nor had it even been, despite the fact that we had all stood together on the same dusty asphalt, under the same plane trees, the general assessment: this was how Joe Klein, writing a few weeks later in *New York* magazine, had described those last days before the California primary:

> Breezing across California on his way to the nomination last week, Michael Dukakis crossed a curious American threshold. . . . The crowds were larger, more excited now; they seemed to be searching for reasons to love him. They cheered eagerly, almost without provocation. People reached out to touch him—not to shake hands, just to

touch him. . . . Dukakis seemed to be making an almost subliminal passage in the public mind: he was becoming presidential.

Those June days in 1988 during which Michael Dukakis did or did not cross a curious American threshold had in fact been instructive. The day that ended
in the schoolyard in San Jose had at first seemed,
given that it was the day before the California primary, underscheduled, pointless, three essentially
meaningless events separated by plane flights. At Taft
High School in Woodland Hills that morning there
had been little girls waving red and gold pom-poms in
front of the cameras; "Hold that tiger," the band had
played. "Dream . . . maker," the choir had crooned.
"Governor Dukakis . . . this is . . . Taft High," the
student council president had said. "I understand that
this is the first time a presidential candidate has come
to Taft High," Governor Dukakis had said. "Is there
any doubt . . . under those circumstances . . . who
you should support?"

"Jackson," a group of Chicano boys on the back
sidewalk shouted in unison.

"That's what it's all about," Governor Dukakis had
said, and "health care", and "good teachers and good
teaching".

This event had been abandoned, and another materialized: a lunchtime "rally", in a downtown San
Diego office plaza through which many people were
passing on their way to lunch, a borrowed crowd but

a less than attentive one. The cameras focused on the balloons. The sound techs picked up "La Bamba". "We're going to take child-support enforcement seriously in this country," Governor Dukakis had said, and "tough drug enforcement here and abroad". "Tough choices," he had said, and "we're going to make teaching a valued profession in this country".

Nothing said in any venue that day had seemed to have much connection with anybody listening ("I want to work with you and with working people all over this country," the candidate had said in the San Diego office plaza, but people who work in offices in San Diego do not think of themselves as "working people"), and late that afternoon, on the bus to the San Jose airport, I had asked a reporter who had traveled through the spring with the various campaigns (among those who moved from plane to plane it was agreed, by June, that the Bush plane had the worst access to the candidate and the best food, that the Dukakis plane had average access and average food, and that the Jackson plane had full access and no time to eat) if the candidate's appearances that day did not seem a little off the point.

"Not really," the reporter said. "He covered three major markets."

Among those who traveled regularly with the campaigns, in other words, it was taken for granted that these "events" they were covering, and on which they were in fact filing, were not merely meaningless but deliberately so: occasions on which film could be shot and no mistakes made ("They hope he won't make any big mistakes," the NBC correspondent covering George Bush kept saying the evening of the September 25, 1988, debate at Wake Forest College, and, an hour and a half later, "He didn't make any big mistakes"), events designed only to provide settings for those unpaid television spots which in this case were appearing, even as we spoke, on the local news in California's three major media markets. "On the fishing trip, there was no way for the television crews to get videotapes out," the *Los Angeles Times* noted a few weeks later in a piece about how "poorly designed and executed events" had interfered with coverage of a Bush campaign "environmental" swing through the Pacific Northwest. "At the lumber mill, Bush's advance team arranged camera angles so poorly that in one setup only his legs could get on camera." A Bush adviser had been quoted: "There is no reason for camera angles not being provided for. "We're going to sit down and talk about these things at length."

Any traveling campaign, then, was a set, moved at considerable expense from location to location. The employer of each reporter on the Dukakis plane the day before the California primary was billed, for a total flying time of under three hours, $1,129.51; the billing to each reporter who happened, on the morning during the Democratic convention in Atlanta when Michael Dukakis and Lloyd Bentsen met with Jesse Jackson, to ride along on the Dukakis bus from the Hyatt Regency to the World Congress Center, a distance of perhaps ten blocks, was $217.18. There was the hierarchy of the set: there were actors, there were directors, there were script supervisors, there were grips.

There was the isolation of the set, and the arrogance, the contempt for outsiders. I recall pink-cheeked young aides on the Dukakis campaign referring to themselves, innocent of irony and therefore of history, as "the best and the brightest". On the morning after the Wake Forest debate, Michael Oreskes of the *New York Times* gave us this memorable account of Bush aides crossing the Wake Forest campus:

> The Bush campaign measured exactly how long it would take its spokesmen to walk briskly from the room in which they were watching the debate to the center where reporters were filing their articles. The answer was three and a half minutes—too long for Mr. Bush's strategists, Lee Atwater, Robert Teeter, and Mr. Darman. They ran the course instead as young aides cleared students and other onlookers from their path.

There was also the tedium of the set: the time spent waiting for the shots to be set up, the time spent waiting for the bus to join the motorcade, the time spent waiting for telephones on which to file, the time spent waiting for the Secret Service ("the agents", they were called on the traveling campaigns, never the Secret Service, just "the agents", or "this detail", or "this rotation") to sweep the plane.

It was a routine that encouraged a certain passivity. There was the plane, or the bus, and one got on it. There was the schedule, and one followed it. There was time to file, or there was not. "We should have had a page-one story," a *Boston Globe* reporter complained to the *Los Angeles Times* after the Bush campaign had failed to provide the advance text of a Seattle "environment" speech scheduled to end only twenty minutes before the departure of the plane for California. "There are times when you sit up and moan, 'Where is Michael Deaver when you need him?' " an ABC producer said to the *Times* on this point.

A final victory, for the staff and the press on a traveling campaign, would mean not a new production but only a new location: the particular setups and shots of the campaign day (the walk on the beach, the meet-and-greet at the housing project) would dissolve imperceptibly, isolation and arrogance and tedium intact, into the South Lawns, the Oval Office signings, the arrivals and departures of the administration day. There would still be the "young aides". There would still be "onlookers" to be cleared from the path. Another location, another stand-up: "We already shot a tarmac departure," they say on the campaign planes. "This schedule has two Rose Gardens," they say in the White House pressroom. Ronald Reagan, when asked by David Frost how his life in the Oval Office had differed from his expectations of it, said this: "—I was surprised at how familiar the whole routine was—the fact that the night before I would get a schedule telling me what I'm going to do all day the next day and so forth."

American reporters "like" covering a presidential campaign (it gets them out on the road, it has balloons, it has music, it is viewed as a big story, one that leads to the respect of one's peers, to the Sunday shows, to lecture fees and often to Washington), which is one reason why there has developed among those who do it so arresting an enthusiasm for overlooking the contradictions inherent in reporting that which occurs only in order to be reported. They are willing, in exchange for "access", to transmit the images their sources wish transmitted. They are even willing, in exchange for certain colorful details around which a "reconstruction" can be built (the "kitchen table" at which the Dukakis campaign conferred on the night Lloyd Bentsen was added to the 1988 Democratic ticket, the "slips of paper" on which key members of the 1988 Bush campaign, aboard Air Force Two on their way to New Orleans, wrote down their own guesses for vice president), to present these images not as a story the campaign wants told but as fact. This was *Time*, reporting from New Orleans on George Bush's reaction when Dan Quayle came under attack:

> Bush never wavered in support of the man he had lifted so high. "How's Danny doing?" he asked several times. But the Vice President never felt the compulsion to ques-

tion Quayle face-to-face. The awkward investigation was left to Baker. Around noon, Quayle grew restive about answering further questions. "Let's go," he urged, but Baker pressed to know more. By early afternoon, the mood began to brighten in the Bush bunker. There were no new revelations: the media hurricane had for the moment blown out to sea.

This was Sandy Grady, reporting from Atlanta:

Ten minutes before he was to face the biggest audience of his life, Michael Dukakis got a hug from his 84-year-old mother, Euterpe, who chided him, "You'd better be good, Michael." Dukakis grinned and said, "I'll do my best, Ma."

"Appeal to the media by exposing the [Bush campaign's] heavy-handed spin-doctoring," William Safire advised the Dukakis campaign on September 8, 1988. "We hate to be seen being manipulated."

"Periodically," the *New York Times* reported in March 1988, "Martin Plissner, the political editor of CBS News, and Susan Morrison, a television producer and former political aide, organize gatherings of the politically connected at their home in Washington. At such parties, they organize secret ballots asking the assembled experts who will win. . . . By November 1, 1987, the results of Mr. Dole's organizing efforts were apparent in a new Plissner-Morrison poll . . ."

The symbiosis here was complete, and the only out-sider was the increasingly hypothetical voter, who was seen as responsive not to actual issues but to their adroit presentation: "At the moment the Republican message is simpler and more clear than ours," the Democratic chairman for California, Peter Kelly, said to the *Los Angeles Times* on August 31, 1988, complain-ing, on the matter of what was called the Pledge of Allegiance issue, not that it was a false issue but that Bush had seized the initiative, or "the symbolism".

"Bush Gaining in Battle of TV Images," the *Wash-ington Post* headlined a page-one story on September 10, 1988, and quoted Jeff Greenfield, the ABC News political reporter: "George Bush is almost always out-doors, coatless, sometimes with his sleeves rolled up, and looks ebullient and Happy Warrior–ish. Mike Dukakis is almost always indoors, with his jacket on, and almost always behind a lectern." The Bush cam-paign, according to that week's issue of *Newsweek*, was, because it had the superior gift for getting film shot in "dramatic settings—like Boston Harbor", win-ning "the all-important battle of the backdrops". A CBS producer covering the Dukakis campaign was quoted complaining about an occasion when Gover-nor Dukakis, speaking to students on a California beach, had faced the students instead of the camera. "The only reason Dukakis was on the beach was to get his picture taken," the producer had said. "So you might as well see his face." Pictures, *Newsweek* had concluded, "often speak louder than words."

This "battle of the backdrops" story appeared on

page twenty-four of the *Newsweek* dated September 12, 1988. On page twenty-three of the same issue there appeared, as illustrations for the lead National Affairs story ("Getting Down and Dirty: As the mud-slinging campaign moves into full gear, Bush stays on the offensive—and Dukakis calls back his main street-fighting man"), two half-page color photographs, one of each candidate, which seemed to address the very concerns expressed on page twenty-four and in the *Post*. The photograph of George Bush showed him indoors, with his jacket on, and behind a lectern. That of Michael Dukakis showed him outdoors, coatless, with his sleeves rolled up, looking ebullient, about to throw a baseball on an airport tarmac: something had been learned from Jeff Greenfield, or something had been told to Jeff Greenfield. "We talk to the press, and things take on a life of their own," Mark Siegel, a Democratic political consultant, said to Elizabeth Drew.

About this baseball on the tarmac. On the day that Michael Dukakis appeared at the high school in Woodland Hills and at the rally in San Diego and in the schoolyard in San Jose, there was, although it did not appear on the schedule, a fourth event, what was referred to among the television crews as a "tarmac arrival with ball tossing". This event had taken place in late morning, on the tarmac at the San Diego airport, just after the chartered 737 had rolled to a stop and the candidate had emerged. There had been a

61

moment of hesitation. Then baseball mitts had been produced, and Jack Weeks, the traveling press secretary, had tossed a ball to the candidate. The candidate had tossed the ball back. The rest of us had stood in the sun and given this our full attention, undeflected even by the arrival of an Alaska Airlines 767: some forty adults standing on a tarmac watching a diminutive figure in shirtsleeves and a red tie toss a ball to his press secretary.

"Just a regular guy," one of the cameramen had said, his inflection that of the "union official" who confided, in an early Dukakis commercial aimed at blue-collar voters, that he had known "Mike" a long time, and backed him despite his not being "your shot-and-beer kind of guy".

"I'd say he was a regular guy," another cameraman had said. "Definitely."

"I'd sit around with him," the first cameraman said.

Kara Dukakis, one of the candidate's daughters, had at that moment emerged from the 737.

"You'd have a beer with him?"

Jack Weeks had tossed the ball to Kara Dukakis.

"I'd have a beer with him."

Kara Dukakis had tossed the ball to her father. Her father had caught the ball and tossed it back to her.

"OK," one of the cameramen had said. "We got the daughter. Nice. That's enough. Nice."

The CNN producer then on the Dukakis campaign told me, later in the day, that the first recorded ball tossing on the Dukakis campaign had been outside a bowling alley somewhere in Ohio. CNN had shot it.

When the campaign realized that only one camera had it, they had restaged it.

"We have a lot of things like the ball tossing," the producer said. "We have the Greek dancing for example."

I asked if she still bothered to shoot it.

"I get it," she said, "but I don't call in anymore and say, 'Hey, hold it, I've got him dancing.' "

This sounded about right (the candidate might, after all, bean a citizen during the ball tossing, and CNN would need film), and not until I read Joe Klein's version of these days in California did it occur to me that this eerily contrived moment on the tarmac at San Diego could become, at least provisionally, history. "The Duke seemed downright jaunty," Joe Klein reported. "He tossed a baseball with aides. He was flagrantly multilingual. He danced Greek dances . . ." In the July 25, 1988, issue of *U.S. News & World Report*, Michael Kramer opened his cover story, "Is Dukakis Tough Enough?", with a more developed version of the ball tossing:

> The thermometer read 101 degrees, but the locals guessed 115 on the broiling airport tarmac in Phoenix. After all, it was under a noonday sun in the desert that Michael Dukakis was indulging his truly favorite campaign ritual—a game of catch with his aide Jack Weeks. "These days," he has said, "throwing the ball around when we land somewhere is about the only exercise I get." For 16 minutes, Dukakis shagged flies and

threw strikes. Halfway through, he rolled
up his sleeves, but he never loosened his tie.
Finally, mercifully, it was over and time to
pitch the obvious tongue-in-cheek question:
"Governor, what does throwing a ball
around in this heat say about your mental
stability?" Without missing a beat, and without a trace of a smile, Dukakis echoed a sen-
timent he has articulated repeatedly in
recent months: "What it means is that I'm
tough."

Nor was this the last word. On July 31, 1988, in the
Washington Post, David S. Broder, who had also been
with the Dukakis campaign in Phoenix, gave us a
third, and, by virtue of his seniority in the process,
perhaps the official version of the ball tossing:

Dukakis called out to Jack Weeks, the handsome, curly-haired Welshman who good-
naturedly shepherds us wayward pressmen
through the daily vagaries of the campaign
schedule. Weeks dutifully produced two
gloves and a baseball, and there on the tarmac, with its surface temperature just below
the boiling point, the governor loosened up
his arm and got the kinks out of his back by
tossing a couple hundred 90-foot pegs to
Weeks.

What we had in the tarmac arrival with ball tossing,
then, was an understanding: a repeated moment wit-

nessed by many people, all of whom believed it to be a setup and yet most of whom believed that only an outsider, only someone too "naive" to know the rules of the game, would so describe it.

2

THE NARRATIVE is made up of many such un-derstandings, tacit agreements, small and large, to overlook the observable in the interests of obtaining a dramatic story line. It was understood, for example, that the first night of the 1988 Republican National Convention in New Orleans should be for Ronald Reagan "the last hurrah". "Reagan Electrifies GOP" was the headline the next morning on page one of *New York Newsday;* in fact the Reagan appearance, which was rhetorically pitched not to a live audience but to the more intimate demands of the camera, was, inside the Superdome, barely registered. It was understood, similarly, that Michael Dukakis's acceptance speech on the last night of the 1988 Democratic National Convention in Atlanta should be the occasion on which his "passion", or "leadership", emerged. "Could the no-nonsense nominee reach within himself to discover the language of leadership?" *Time* had asked. "Could he go beyond the pedestrian promise of 'good jobs at good wages' to give voice to a new Dem-ocratic vision?"

The correct answer, since the forward flow of the narrative here demanded the appearance of a genuine contender (a contender who could be seventeen points "up", so that George Bush could be seventeen points "down", a position from which he could rise to "claim" his own convention), was yes: "The best speech of his life," David Broder reported. Sandy Grady found it "superb", evoking "Kennedyesque echoes" and showing "unexpected craft and fire". *Newsweek* had witnessed Michael Dukakis "electrifying the convention with his intensely personal acceptance speech". In fact the convention that evening had been electrified, not by the speech, which was the same series of nonsequential clauses Governor Dukakis had employed during the primary campaign ("My friends . . . son of immigrants . . . good jobs at good wages . . . make teaching a valued and honored profession . . . it's what the Democratic Party is all about"), but because the floor had been darkened, swept with laser beams, and flooded with "Coming to America", played at concert volume with the bass turned up.

It is understood that this invented narrative will turn on certain familiar elements. There is the continuing story line of the "horse race", the reliable daily drama of one candidate falling behind as another pulls ahead. There is the surprise of the new poll, the glamour of the one-on-one colloquy on the midnight plane, a plot point (the nation sleeps while the candidate and his confidant hammer out its fate) pioneered by Theodore H. White. There is the abiding if unexamined faith in the campaign as personal odyssey, and in the spiritual benefits accruing to those who undertake it. There is, in the presented history of the candidate, the crucible event, the day that "changed the life".

Robert Dole's life was understood to have changed when he was injured in Italy in 1945. George Bush's life is understood to have changed when he and his wife decided to "get out and make it on our own" (his words, or rather those of his speechwriter, Peggy Noonan, from the "lived the dream" acceptance speech at the 1988 convention, suggesting action, shirtsleeves, privilege cast aside) in west Texas. For Bruce Babbitt, "the dam just kind of broke" during a student summer in Bolivia. For Michael Dukakis, the dam was understood to have broken not during his student summer in Peru but after his 1978 defeat in Massachusetts; his tragic flaw, we read repeatedly during the 1988 campaign, was neither his evident sulkiness at losing that earlier election nor what many saw later as a rather dissociated self-satisfaction ("We're two people very proud of what we've done," he said on NBC in Atlanta, falling into a favorite speech pattern, "very proud of each other, actually . . . and very proud that a couple of guys named Dukakis and Jackson have come this far"), but the more attractive "hubris".

The narrative requires broad strokes. Michael Dukakis was physically small, and had associations with Harvard, which suggested that he could be cast as an "intellectual"; the "immigrant factor", on the other hand, could make him tough (as in "What it means is

67

that I'm tough"), a "streetfighter". "He's cool, shrewd and still trying to prove he's tough," the July 25, 1988, cover of *U.S. News & World Report* said about Dukakis. "Toughness is what it's all about," one of his advisers was quoted as having said in the cover story. "People need to feel that a candidate is tough enough to be president. It is the threshold perception."

George Bush had presented a more tortured narrative problem. The tellers of the story had not understood, or had not responded to, the essential Bush style, which was complex, ironic, the diffident edge of the Northeastern elite. This was what was at first identified as "the wimp factor", which was replaced not by a more complicated view of the personality but by its reverse: George Bush was by late August no longer a "wimp" but someone who had "thrown it over", "struck out" to make his own way: no longer a product of the effete Northeast but someone who had thrived in Texas, and was therefore "tough enough to be president".

That George Bush might have thrived in Texas not in spite of being but precisely because he was a member of the Northeastern elite was a shading that had no part in the narrative: "He was considered back at the time one of the most charismatic people ever elected to public office in the history of Texas," Congressman Bill Archer of Houston said. "That charisma, people talked about it over and over again." People talked about it, probably, because Andover and Yale and the inheritable tax avoidance they suggested were, during the years George Bush lived in

Texas, the exact ideals toward which the Houston and
Dallas establishment aspired, but the narrative called
for a less ambiguous version: "Lived in a little shotgun
house, one room for the three of us," as Bush, or
Peggy Noonan, had put it in the celebrated no-
subject-pronoun cadences of the "lived the dream" acceptance speech. "Worked in the oil business, started
my own. . . . Moved from the shotgun to a duplex
apartment to a house. Lived the dream—high school
football on Friday night, Little League, neighborhood
barbecue . . . pushing into unknown territory with
kids and a dog and a car . . ."

All stories, of course, depend for their popular interest upon the invention of personality, or "character", but in the political narrative, designed as it is to
maintain the illusion of "consensus" by obscuring
rather than addressing actual issues, this invention
served a further purpose. It was by 1988 generally if
unspecifically agreed that the United States faced certain social and economic realities that, if not intracta-
ble, did not entirely lend themselves to the kinds of
policy fixes people who run for elected office, on
whatever ticket, were likely to undertake. We had not
yet accommodated the industrialization of parts of the
third world. We had not yet adjusted to the economic
realignment of a world in which the United States was
no longer the principal catalyst for change. "We really
are in an age of transition," Brent Scowcroft, Bush's
leading foreign policy adviser, told Robert Scheer
of the *Los Angeles Times* in the fall of 1988, "from a
postwar world where the Soviets were the enemy,

where the United States was a superpower and trying to build up both its allies and its former enemies and help the third world transition to independence. That whole world and all of those things are coming to an end or have ended, and we are now entering a new and different world that will be complex and much less unambiguous than the old one."

What continued to dominate the rhetoric of the 1988 campaign, however, was not this awareness of a new and different world but nostalgia for an old one, and coded assurance that symptoms of ambiguity or change, of what George Bush called the "deterioration of values", would be summarily dealt with by increased social control. It was not by accident that the word "enforcement", devoid of any apparent awareness that it had been tried before, kept coming up in this campaign. A problem named seemed, for both campaigns, a problem solved. Michael Dukakis had promised, by way of achieving his goal of "no safe haven for dope dealers and drug profits anywhere on this earth", to "double the number" of Drug Enforcement Administration agents, not a promising approach. George Bush, for his part, had repeatedly promised the death penalty, and not only the Pledge of Allegiance but prayer, or "moments of silence", in the schools. "We've got to change this entire culture," he said in the Wake Forest debate; the polls indicated that the electorate wanted "change", and this wish for change had been translated, by both campaigns, into the wish for a "change back", a regression to the "gentler America" of which George Bush repeatedly spoke.

To the extent that there was a "difference" between the candidates, the difference lay in just where on the time scale this "gentler America" could be found. The Dukakis campaign was oriented to "programs", and the programs it proposed were similar to those that had worked (the encouragement of private sector involvement in low-cost housing, say) in the boom years following World War II. The Bush campaign was oriented to "values", and the values to which it referred were those not of a postwar but of a prewar America. In neither case did "ideas" play a part: "This election isn't about ideology, it's about competence," Michael Dukakis had said in Atlanta. "First and foremost, it's a choice between two persons," one of his senior advisers, Thomas Kiley, had told the *Wall Street Journal*. "What it all comes down to, after all the shouting and the cheers, is the man at the desk," George Bush had said in New Orleans. In other words, what it was "about", what it came "down to", what was wrong or right with America, was not a historical shift largely unaffected by the actions of individual citizens but "character", and if "character" could be seen to count, then every citizen—since everyone was a judge of character, an expert in the field of personality—could be seen to count. This notion, that the citizen's choice among determinedly centrist candidates makes a "difference", is in fact the narrative's most central element, and also its most fictive.

3

THE DEMOCRATIC National Convention of 1968, during which the process was put to a popular vote on the streets of Chicago and after which it was decided that what had occurred could not be allowed to recur, is generally agreed to have prompted the multiplication of primaries, and the concomitant coverage of those primaries, which led to the end of the national party convention as a more than ceremonial occasion. Early in 1987, as the primary campaigns got under way for the 1988 election, David S. Broder, in the *Washington Post*, offered this compelling analysis of the power these "reforms" in the nominating procedure had vested not in the party leadership, which is where this power of choice ultimately resides, but in "the existing communications system", by which he meant the press, or the medium through which the party leadership sells its choice:

> Once the campaign explodes to 18 states, as it will the day after New Hampshire, when the focus shifts to a super-primary across the nation, the existing communications system simply will not accommodate more than two or three candidates in each party. Neither the television networks, nor newspapers nor magazines, have the resources of people, space and time to describe and analyze the dynamics of two simultaneous half-national elections among Republicans and Democrats. That task is simply beyond us. Since we cannot reduce the number of states vot-

ing on Super Tuesday, we have to reduce the number of candidates treated as serious contenders. Those news judgments will be arbitrary—but not subject to appeal. Those who finish first or second in Iowa and New Hampshire will get tickets from the mass media to play in the next big round. Those who don't, won't. A minor exception may be made for the two reverends, Jesse L. Jackson and Marion G. (Pat) Robertson, who have their own church-based communications and support networks and are less dependent on mass-media attention. But no one else.

By the time the existing communications system set itself up in July and August of 1988 in Atlanta and New Orleans, the priorities were clear. "NOTICE NOTICE NOTICE," read the typed note given to some print reporters when they picked up their credentials in Atlanta. "Because the National Democratic Convention Committee permitted the electronic media to exceed specifications for their broadcast booths, your assigned seat's sight line to the podium and the convention floor was obliterated." The network skyboxes, in other words, had been built in front of the sections originally assigned to the periodical press. "This is a place that was chosen to be, for all intents and purposes, a large TV studio, to be able to project our message to the American people and a national audience," Paul Kirk, the chairman of the Democratic National Committee, said by way of explaining why the podium and the skyboxes had so

73

reduced the size of the Omni Coliseum in Atlanta that some thousand delegates and alternates had been, on the evening Jesse Jackson spoke, locked out. Mayor Andrew Young of Atlanta apologized for the lockout, but said that it would be the same on nights to follow: "The one hundred and fifty million people in this country who are going to vote have got to be our major target." Still, convention delegates were seen to have a real role: "The folks in the hall are so important for how it looks," Lane Venardos, senior producer in charge of convention coverage for CBS News, said to the *New York Times* about the Republican convention. The delegates, in other words, could be seen as dress extras.

During those eight summer evenings in 1988, four in Atlanta and four in New Orleans, when roughly 80 percent of the television sets "out there" were tuned somewhere else, the entire attention of those inside the process was directed toward the invention of this story in which they themselves were the principal players, and for which they themselves were the principal audience. The great arenas in which the conventions were held became worlds all their own, constantly transmitting their own images back to themselves, connected by skywalks to interchangeable structures composed not of floors but of "levels", mysteriously separated by fountains and glass elevators and escalators that did not quite connect.

In the Louisiana Superdome in New Orleans as in the Omni Coliseum in Atlanta, the grids of lights blazed and dimmed hypnotically. Men with rifles patrolled the high catwalks. The nets packed with balloons swung gently overhead, poised for that instant known as the "money shot", the moment, or "window", when everything was working and no network had cut to a commercial. Minicams trawled the floor, fishing in Atlanta for Rob Lowe, in New Orleans for Donald Trump. In the NBC skybox Tom Brokaw floated over the floor, adjusting his tie, putting on his jacket, leaning to speak to John Chancellor. In the CNN skybox Mary Alice Williams sat bathed in white light, the blond madonna of the skyboxes. On the television screens in the press section the images reappeared, but from another angle: Tom Brokaw and Mary Alice Williams again, broadcasting not just above us but also to us, the circle closed.

At the end of prime time, when the skyboxes went dark, the action moved across the skywalks and into the levels, into the lobbies, into one or another Hyatt or Marriott or Hilton or Westin. In the portage from lobby to lobby, level to level, the same people kept materializing, in slightly altered roles. On a level of the Hyatt in Atlanta I saw Ann Lewis in her role as a Jackson adviser. On a level of the Hyatt in New Orleans I saw Ann Lewis in her role as a correspondent for *Ms.* Some pictures were vivid: "I've been around this process awhile, and one thing I've noticed, it's the people who write the checks who get treated as if they have a certain amount of power," I recall Nadine Hack, the chairman of Dukakis's New York Finance Council, saying in a suite at the Hyatt in Atlanta: here

75

was a willowy woman with long blond hair standing barefoot on a table and trying to explain how to buy into the action. "The great thing about those evenings was you could even see Michael Harrington there," I recall Richard Viguerie saying to me at a party in New Orleans: here was the man who managed the action for the American right trying to explain the early 1960s, and evenings we had both spent on Washington Square.

There was in Atlanta in 1988, according to the Democratic National Committee, "twice the media presence" that there had been at the 1984 convention. There were in New Orleans "media workspaces" assigned not only to 117 newspapers and news services and to the American television and radio industry in full strength but to fifty-two foreign networks. On every corner one turned in New Orleans someone was doing a stand-up. There were telephone numbers to be called for quotes: "Republican State and Local Officials", or "Pat Robertson Campaign" or "Richard Wirthlin, Reagan's Pollster". Newspapers came with teams of thirty, forty, fifty. In every lobby there were stacks of fresh newspapers, the *Atlanta Constitution*, the *New Orleans Times-Picayune*, the *Washington Post*, the *Miami Herald*, the *Los Angeles Times*. In Atlanta these papers were collected in bins, and "recycled": made into thirty thousand posters, which were in turn distributed to the press in New Orleans.

This perfect recycling tended to present itself, in the narcosis of the event, as a model for the rest: like American political life itself, and like the printed and transmitted images on which that life depended, this was a world with no half-life. It was understood that what was said here would go on the wire and vanish. Garrison Keillor and his cute kids would vanish. Ann Richards and her peppery ripostes would vanish. Phyllis Schlafly and Olympia Snowe would vanish. All the opinions and all the rumors and all the house-maid Spanish spoken in both Atlanta and New Orleans would vanish, all the quotes would vanish, and all that would remain would be the huge arenas themselves, the arenas and the lobbies and the levels and the skywalks to which they connected, the incorporeal heart of the process itself, the agora, the symbolic marketplace in which the narrative was not only written but immediately, efficiently, entirely, consumed.

A certain time lag exists between this world of the arenas and the world as we know it. One evening in New York between the Democratic and Republican conventions I happened to go down to Lafayette Street, to the Public Theater, to look at clips from documentaries on which the English-born filmmaker Richard Leacock had worked during his fifty years in America. We saw folk singers in Virginia in 1941 and oil riggers in Louisiana in 1946 (this was *Louisiana Story*, which Leacock had shot for Robert Flaherty) and tent performers in the corn belt in 1954; we saw Eddy Sachs preparing for the Indianapolis 500 in 1960 and Piri Thomas in Spanish Harlem in 1961. We saw parades, we saw baton twirlers. We saw quints in South Dakota in 1963.

There on the screen at the Public Theater that evening were images and attitudes from an America that had largely vanished, and what was striking was this: these were the very images and attitudes on which "the campaign" was predicated. That "unknown territory" into which George Bush had pushed "with kids and a dog and a car" had existed in this vanished America, and long since been subdivided, cut up for those tract houses on which the people who were not part of the process had made down payments. Michael Dukakis's "snowblower", and both the amusing frugality and the admirable husbandry of resources it was meant to suggest, derived from some half-remembered idea of what citizens of this vanished America had laughed at and admired. "The Pledge" was an issue from that world. "A drug-free America" had perhaps seemed in that world an achievable ideal, as had "better schools". I recall listening in Atlanta to Dukakis's foreign policy expert, Madeleine Albright, as she conjured up, in the course of arguing against a "no first use" minority plank in the Democratic platform, a scenario in which "Soviet forces overrun Europe" and the United States has, by promising no first use of nuclear weapons, crippled its ability to act: she was talking about a world that had not turned since 1948. What was at work here seemed on the one hand a grave, although in many ways a comfortable, miscalculation of what people in America might have as their deepest concerns in 1988; it seemed on the other hand just another understanding, another of those agreements to overlook the observable.

4

It was into this sedative fantasy of a fixable imperial America that Jesse Jackson rode, on a Trailways bus. "You've never heard a sense of panic sweep the party as it has in the past few days," David Garth had told the *New York Times* during those perilous spring weeks in 1988 when there seemed a real possibility that a black candidate with no experience in elected office, a candidate believed to be so profoundly unelectable that he could take the entire Democratic party down with him, might go to Atlanta with more delegates than any other Democratic candidate. "The party is up against an extraordinary endgame," the pollster Paul Maslin had said. "I don't know where this leaves us," Robert S. Strauss had said. One uncommitted superdelegate, the *New York Times* had reported, "said the Dukakis campaign had changed its message since Mr. Dukakis lost the Illinois primary. Mr. Dukakis is no longer the candidate of 'inevitability' but the candidate of order, he said. 'They're not doing the train's leaving the station and you better be on it routine anymore,' this official said. 'They're now saying that the station's about to be blown up by terrorists and we're the only ones who can defuse the bomb.' "

The threat, or the possibility, presented by Jesse Jackson, the "historic" (as people liked to say after it became certain he would not have the numbers) part of his candidacy, derived from something other than the fact that he was black, a circumstance that had

79

before been and could again be compartmentalized. For example: "Next week, when we launch our black radio buys, when we start doing our black media stuff, Jesse Jackson needs to be on the air in the black community on our behalf," Donna Brazile of the Dukakis campaign said to the *New York Times* on September 8, 1988, by way of emphasizing how much the Dukakis campaign "sought to make peace" with Jackson.

"Black", in other words, could be useful, and even a moral force, a way for white Americans to attain more perfect attitudes: "His color is an enormous plus. . . . How moving it is, and how important, to see a black candidate meet and overcome the racism that lurks in virtually all of us white Americans," Anthony Lewis had noted in a March 1988 column explaining why the notion that Jesse Jackson could win was nonetheless "a romantic delusion" of the kind that had "repeatedly undermined" the Democratic party. "You look at what Jesse Jackson has done, you have to wonder what a Tom Bradley of Los Angeles could have done, what an Andy Young of Atlanta could have done," I heard someone say on one of the Sunday shows after the Jackson campaign had entered its "historic" (or, in the candidate's word, its "endless") phase.

"Black", then, by itself and in the right context—the "right context" being a reasonable constituency composed exclusively of blacks and supportive liberal whites—could be accommodated by the process. Something less traditional, and also less manageable, was at work in the 1988 Jackson candidacy. I recall having dinner, the weekend before the California primary, at the Pebble Beach house of the chairman of a large American corporation. There were sixteen people at the table, all white, all well-off, all well dressed, all well educated, all socially conservative. During the course of the evening it came to my attention that six of the sixteen, or every one of the registered Democrats present, intended to vote on Tuesday for Jesse Jackson. Their reasons were unspecific, but definite. "I heard him, he didn't sound like a politician," one said. "He's talking about right now," another said. "You get outside the gate here, take a look around, you have to know we've got some problems, and he's talking about them."

What made the 1988 Jackson candidacy a bomb that had to be defused, then, was not that blacks were supporting a black candidate, but that significant numbers of whites were supporting—not only supporting but in many cases overcoming deep emotional and economic conflicts of their own in order to support—a candidate who was attractive to them not because of but in spite of the fact that he was black, a candidate whose most potent attraction was that he "didn't sound like a politician". "Character" seemed not to be, among these voters, the point-of-sale issue the narrative made it out to be: a number of white Jackson supporters to whom I talked would quite serenely describe their candidate as a "con man", or even as, in George Bush's word, a "hustler".

"And yet . . . ," they would say. What "and yet" turned out to mean, almost without variation, was that they were willing to walk off the edge of the known political map for a candidate who was running against, as he repeatedly said, "politics as usual", against what he called "consensualist centrist politics"; against what had come to be the very premise of the process, the notion that the winning of and the maintaining of public office warranted the invention of a public narrative based at no point on observable reality.

In other words they were not idealists, these white Jackson voters, but empiricists. By the time Jesse Jackson got to California, where he would eventually get 25 percent of the entire white vote and 49 percent of the total vote from voters between the demographically key ages of thirty to forty-four, the idealists had rallied behind the sole surviving alternative, who was, accordingly, just then being declared "presidential". In Los Angeles, during May and early June of 1988, those Democrats who had not fallen in line behind Dukakis were described as "self-indulgent", or as "immature"; they were even described, in a dispiriting phrase that prefigured the tenor of the campaign to come, as "issues wimps". I recall talking to a rich and politically well-connected Californian who had been, through the primary campaign there, virtually the only prominent Democrat on the famously liberal west side of Los Angeles who was backing Jackson. He said that he could afford "the luxury of being more interested in issues than in process," but that he would pay for it: "When I want something, I'll have a hard time getting people to pick up the phone. I recognize that. I made the choice."

On the June night in 1988 when Michael Dukakis was declared the winner of the California Democratic primary, and the bomb officially defused, there took place in the Crystal Room of the Biltmore Hotel in Los Angeles a "victory party" that was less a celebration than a ratification by the professionals, a ritual convergence of those California Democrats for whom the phones would continue to get picked up. Charles Manatt was there. John Emerson and Charles Palmer were there. John Van de Kamp was there. Leo McCarthy was there. Robert Shrum was there. All the custom-made suits and monogrammed shirts in Los Angeles that night were there, met in the wide corridors of the Biltmore in order to murmur assurances to one another. The ballroom in fact had been cordoned as if to repel late invaders, roped off in such a way that once the Secret Service, the traveling press, the local press, the visiting national press, the staff, and the candidate had assembled, there would be room for only a controllable handful of celebrants, over whom the cameras would dutifully pan.

In fact the actual "celebrants" that evening were not at the Biltmore at all, but a few blocks away at the Los Angeles Hilton, dancing under the mirrored ceiling of the ballroom in which the Jackson campaign had gathered, its energy level in defeat notably higher than that of other campaigns in victory. Jackson parties tended to spill out of ballrooms onto several levels of whatever hotel they were in, and to last until three or four in the morning: anyone who wanted to be at a Jackson party was welcome at a Jackson party, which was unusual among the campaigns, and tended to reinforce the populist spirit that had given this one its extraordinary animation.

Of that evening at the Los Angeles Hilton I recall a pretty woman in a gold lamé dress, dancing with a baby in her arms. I recall empty beer bottles, Corona and Excalibur and Budweiser, sitting among the loops of television cable. I recall the candidate himself, dancing on the stage, and, on this June evening when the long shot had not come in, this evening when the campaign was effectively over, giving the women in the traveling press the little parody wave they liked to give him, "the press chicks' wave", the stiff-armed palm movement they called "the Nancy Reagan wave"; then taking off his tie and throwing it into the crowd, like a rock star. This was of course a narrative of its own, but a relatively current one, and one that had, because it seemed at some point grounded in the recognizable, a powerful glamour for those estranged from the purposeful nostalgia of the traditional narrative.

In the end the predictable decision was made to go with the process, with predictable, if equivocal, results. On the last afternoon of the 1988 Republican convention in New Orleans I walked from the hotel in the Quarter where I was staying over to Camp Street. I wanted to see 544 Camp, a local point of interest not noted on the points-of-interest maps distributed at the convention but one that figures large in the literature of American conspiracy. "544 Camp Street" was the address stamped on the leaflets Lee Harvey Oswald was distributing around New Orleans between May and September of 1963, the "Fair Play for Cuba Committee" leaflets that, in the years after Lee Harvey Oswald assassinated John F. Kennedy, suggested to some that he had been acting for Fidel Castro and to others that he had been set up to appear to have been acting for Fidel Castro. Guy Banister had his detective agency at 544 Camp. David Ferrie and Jack Martin frequented the coffee shop on the ground floor at 544 Camp. The Cuban Revolutionary Council rented an office at 544 Camp. People had taken the American political narrative seriously at 544 Camp. They had argued about it, fallen out over it, had hit each other over the head with pistol butts over it.

In fact I never found 544 Camp, because there was no more such address: the small building had been bought and torn down in order to construct a new federal courthouse. Across the street in Lafayette Square that afternoon there had been a loudspeaker, and a young man on a makeshift platform talking about abortion, and unwanted babies being put down the Disposall and "clogging the main sewer drains of New Orleans", but no one except me had been there to listen. "Satan—you're the liar," the young woman with him on the platform had sung, lip-syncing a tape originally made, she told me, by a woman who sang with an Alabama traveling ministry, the Ministry of the Happy Hunters. "There's one thing you can't deny . . . you're the father of every lie . . ." The young woman had been wearing a black cape, and was made up to portray Satan, or Death, I was unclear which and it had not seemed a distinction worth pursuing.

Still, there were clouds off the Gulf that day and the air was wet and there was about the melancholy of Camp Street a certain sense of abandoned historic moment, heightened, quite soon, by something unusual: the New Orleans police began lining Camp Street, blocking every intersection from Canal Street west. I noticed a man in uniform on a roof. Before long there were Secret Service agents, with wires in their ears. The candidates, it seemed, would be traveling east on Camp Street on their way from the Republican National Committee Finance Committee Gala (Invitation Only) at the Convention Center to the Ohio Caucus Rally (Media Invited) at the Hilton. I stood for a while on Camp Street, on this corner that might be construed as one of those occasional accidental intersections where the remote narrative had collided with the actual life of the country, and waited until the motorcade itself, entirely and perfectly insulated, a mechanism dedicated like the process for which it stood only to the maintenance of itself, had passed, and then I walked to the Superdome. "I hear he did OK with Brinkley," they said that night in the Superdome, and, then, as the confetti fell, "Quayle, zip."

—1988

Shooters Inc.

IN AUGUST of 1986, George Bush, traveling in his role as vice president of the United States and accompanied by his staff, the Secret Service, the traveling press, and a personal camera crew wearing baseball caps reading "Shooters, Inc." and working on a $10,000 retainer paid by a Bush PAC called the Fund for America's Future, spent several days in Israel and Jordan. The schedule in Israel included, according to reports in the *Los Angeles Times* and the *New York Times*, shoots at the Western Wall, at the Holocaust memorial, at David Ben-Gurion's tomb, and at thirty-two other locations chosen to produce campaign footage illustrating that George Bush was, as Marlin Fitzwater, at that time the vice-presidential press secretary, put it, "familiar with the issues". The Shooters, Inc. crew did not go on to Jordan (there was, an official explained to the *Los Angeles Times*, "nothing to be gained from showing him schmoozing with Arabs"), but the Bush advance team had nonetheless directed, in Amman, considerable attention toward improved visuals for the traveling press. The advance team had requested, for example, that the

Jordanian army marching band change its uniforms from white to red; that the Jordanians, who did not have enough helicopters to transport the press, borrow some from the Israeli air force; that, in order to provide the color of live military action behind the vice president, the Jordanians stage maneuvers at a sensitive location overlooking Israel and the Golan Heights; that the Jordanians raise the American flag over their base there; that Bush be photographed looking through binoculars studying "enemy territory", a shot ultimately vetoed by the State Department since the "enemy territory" at hand was Israel; and, possibly the most arresting detail, that camels be present at every stop on the itinerary.

Some months later I happened to be in Amman, and mentioned reading about this Bush trip to several officials at the American embassy there. They could have, it was agreed, "cordially killed" the reporters in question, particularly Charles P. Wallace from the *Los Angeles Times*, but the reports themselves had been accurate. "You didn't hear this, but they didn't write half of it," one said.

This is in fact the kind of story we expect to hear about our elected officials. We not only expect them to use other nations as changeable scrims in the theater of domestic politics but encourage them to do so. After the April failure of the Bay of Pigs in 1961, John Kennedy's job approval rating was four points higher than it had been in March. After the 1965 intervention in the Dominican Republic, Lyndon Johnson's job approval rating rose six points. After the 1983 invasion of Grenada, Ronald Reagan's job approval rating rose four points, and what was that winter referred to in Washington as "Lebanon"—the sending of American Marines into Beirut, the killing of the 241, and the subsequent pullout—was, in the afterglow of this certified success in the Caribbean, largely forgotten. "Gemayel could fall tonight and it would be a two-day story," I recall David Gergen saying a few months later. In May of 1984, Francis X. Clines of the *New York Times* described the view taken by James Baker, who was routinely described during his years in the Reagan White House as "the ultimate pragmatist", a manager of almost supernatural executive ability: "In attempting action in Lebanon, Baker argues, President Reagan avoided another 'impotent' episode, such as the taking of American hostages in Iran, and in withdrawing the Marines, the President avoided another 'Vietnam' . . . 'Pulling the Marines out put the lie to the argument that the President's trigger-happy,' he [Baker] said." The "issue", in other words, was one of preserving faith in President Reagan at home, a task that, after the ultimate pragmatist left the White House, fell into the hands of the less adroit.

History is context. At a moment when the nation had seen control of its economy pass to its creditors and when the administration-elect had for political reasons severely limited its ability to regain that control, this extreme reliance on the efficacy of faith over works meant something different from what it might have meant in 1984 or 1980. On the night in New Orleans in August of 1988 when George Bush accepted the Republican nomination and spoke of his intention to "speak for freedom, stand for freedom, and be a patient friend to anyone, east or west, who will fight for freedom", the word "patient" was construed by some in the Louisiana Superdome as an abandonment of the Reagan Doctrine, a suggestion that a Bush administration would play a passive rather than an active role in any dreams of rollback. This overlooked the real nature of the Reagan Doctrine, the usefulness of which to the Reagan administration was exclusively political.

Administrations with little room to maneuver at home have historically looked for sideshows abroad, for the creation of what the pollsters call "a dramatic event", an external crisis, preferably one so remote that it remains an abstraction. On the evening of the November 1988 election and on several evenings that followed, I happened to sit at dinner next to men with considerable experience in the financial community. They were agreed that the foreign markets would allow the new Bush administration, which was seen to have limited its options by promising for political reasons not to raise taxes, only a limited time before calling in the markers; they disagreed only as to the length of that time and to the nature of the downturn. One thought perhaps two years, another six months. Some saw a "blowout" ("blowout" was a word used a good deal), others saw a gradual tightening, a transition to the era of limited expectations of which Jerry

Brown had spoken when he was governor of California.

These men were, among themselves, uniformly pessimistic. They saw a situation in which the space available for domestic maneuvering had been reduced to zero. In this light it did not seem encouraging that George Bush, on the Thursday he left for his post-election Florida vacation, found time to meet not with those investors around the world who were sending him a message that week (the dollar was again dropping against the yen, against the mark, and against the pound; the Dow was dropping 78.47 points), not with the Germans, not with the Japanese, not even with anyone from the American financial community, but with representatives of the Afghan resistance. "Once in a while I think about those things, but not much," the president-elect told a CBS News crew which asked him, a few days later in Florida, about the falling market.

—1988

CALIFORNIA

Girl
of the Golden West

THE DOMESTIC details spring to memory. Early on the evening of February 4, 1974, in her duplex apartment at 2603 Benvenue in Berkeley, Patricia Campbell Hearst, age nineteen, a student of art history at the University of California at Berkeley and a granddaughter of the late William Randolph Hearst, put on a blue terry-cloth bathrobe, heated a can of chicken-noodle soup and made tuna fish sandwiches for herself and her fiancé, Steven Weed; watched "Mission Impossible" and "The Magician" on television; cleaned up the dishes; sat down to study just as the doorbell rang; was abducted at gunpoint and held blindfolded, by three men and five women who called themselves the Symbionese Liberation Army, for the next fifty-seven days.

From the fifty-eighth day, on which she agreed to join her captors and was photographed in front of the SLA's cobra flag carrying a sawed-off M-1 carbine, until September 18, 1975, when she was arrested in San Francisco, Patricia Campbell Hearst participated actively in the robberies of the Hibernia Bank in San Francisco and the Crocker National Bank outside Sacramento; sprayed Crenshaw Boulevard in Los Angeles with a submachine gun to cover a comrade apprehended for shoplifting; and was party or witness to a number of less publicized thefts and several bombings, to which she would later refer as "actions", or "operations".

On trial in San Francisco for the Hibernia Bank operation she appeared in court wearing frosted-white nail polish, and demonstrated for the jury the bolt action necessary to chamber an M-1. On a psychiatric test administered while she was in custody she completed the sentence "Most men . . ." with the words ". . . are assholes". Seven years later she was living with the bodyguard she had married, their infant daughter, and two German shepherds "behind locked doors in a Spanish-style house equipped with the best electronic security system available", describing herself as "older and wiser", and dedicating her account of these events, *Every Secret Thing*, to "Mom and Dad".

It was a special kind of sentimental education, a public coming-of-age with an insistently literary cast to it, and it seemed at the time to offer a parable for the period. Certain of its images entered the national memory. We had Patricia Campbell Hearst in her first-communion dress, smiling, and we had Patricia Campbell Hearst in the Hibernia Bank surveillance stills, not smiling. We again had her smiling in the engagement picture, an unremarkably pretty girl in a simple dress on a sunny lawn, and we again had her not smiling in the "Tania" snapshot, the famous Polaroid with the M-1. We had her with her father and her sister Anne in a photograph taken at the Burlingame Country Club some months before the kidnapping: all three Hearsts smiling there, not only smiling but wearing leis, the father in maile and orchid leis, the daughters in pikake, that rarest and most expensive kind of lei, strand after strand of tiny Arabian jasmine buds strung like ivory beads.

We had the bank of microphones in front of the Hillsborough house whenever Randolph and Catherine Hearst ("Dad" and "Mom" in the first spectral messages from the absent daughter, "pig Hearsts" as the spring progressed) met the press, the potted flowers on the steps changing with the seasons, domestic upkeep intact in the face of crisis: azaleas, fuchsias, then cymbidium orchids massed for Easter. We had, early on, the ugly images of looting and smashed cameras and frozen turkey legs hurled through windows in West Oakland, the violent result of the Hearsts' first attempt to meet the SLA ransom demand, and we had, on television the same night, the news that William Knowland, the former United States senator from California and the most prominent member of the family that had run Oakland for half a century, had taken the pistol he was said to carry as protection against terrorists, positioned himself on a bank of the Russian River, and blown off the top of his head.

All of these pictures told a story, taught a dramatic lesson, carrying as they did the *frisson* of one another, the invitation to compare and contrast. The image of Patricia Campbell Hearst on the FBI "wanted" fliers was for example cropped from the image of the unremarkably pretty girl in the simple dress on the sunny lawn, schematic evidence that even a golden girl could be pinned in the beam of history. There was no actual connection between turkey legs thrown through windows in West Oakland and William Knowland lying facedown in the Russian River, but the paradigm was manifest, one California busy being born and another busy dying. Those cymbidiums on the Hearsts' doorstep in Hillsborough dissolved before our eyes into the image of a flaming palm tree in south-central Los Angeles (the model again was two Californias), the palm tree above the stucco bungalow in which Patricia Campbell Hearst was believed for a time to be burning to death on live television. (Actually Patricia Campbell Hearst was in yet a third California, a motel room at Disneyland, watching the palm tree burn as we all were, on television, and it was Donald De-Freeze, Nancy Ling Perry, Angela Atwood, Patricia Soltysik, Camilla Hall, and William Wolfe, one black escaped convict and five children of the white middle class, who were dying in the stucco bungalow.)

Not only the images but the voice told a story, the voice on the tapes, the depressed voice with the California inflection, the voice that trailed off, now almost inaudible, then a hint of whine, a schoolgirl's sarcasm, a voice every parent recognized: *Mom, Dad. I'm OK. I had a few scrapes and stuff, but they washed them up. . . . I just hope you'll do what they say, Dad. . . . If you can get*

*the food thing organized before the nineteenth then that's OK.
. . . Whatever you come up with is basically OK, it was
never intended that you feed the whole state. . . . I am here
because I am a member of a ruling-class family and I think
you can begin to see the analogy. . . . People should stop
acting like I'm dead, Mom should get out of her black dress,
that doesn't help at all. . . . Mom, Dad . . . I don't believe
you're doing all you can . . . Mom, Dad . . . I'm starting
to think that no one is concerned about me anymore. . . .*
And then: *Greetings to the people. This is Tania.*

Patricia Campbell Hearst's great-grandfather had
arrived in California by foot in 1850, unschooled, unmarried, thirty years old with few graces and no prospects, a Missouri farmer's son who would spend his
thirties scratching around El Dorado and Nevada and
Sacramento counties looking for a stake. In 1859 he
found one, and at his death in 1891 George Hearst
could leave the schoolteacher he had married in 1862
a fortune taken from the ground, the continuing proceeds from the most productive mines of the period,
the Ophir in Nevada, the Homestake in South Dakota, the Ontario in Utah, the Anaconda in Montana,
the San Luis in Mexico. The widow, Phoebe Apper-
son Hearst, a tiny, strong-minded woman then only
forty-eight years old, took this apparently artesian income and financed her only child in the publishing
empire he wanted, underwrote a surprising amount of
the campus where her great-granddaughter would be
enrolled at the time she was kidnapped, and built for

99

herself, on sixty-seven thousand acres on the Mc-Cloud River in Siskiyou County, the original Wyntoon, a quarried-lava castle of which its architect, Bernard Maybeck, said simply: "Here you can reach all that is within you."

The extent to which certain places dominate the California imagination is apprehended, even by Californians, only dimly. Deriving not only from the landscape but from the claiming of it, from the romance of emigration, the radical abandonment of established attachments, this imagination remains obdurately symbolic, tending to locate lessons in what the rest of the country perceives only as scenery. Yosemite, for example, remains what Kevin Starr has called "one of the primary California symbols, a fixed factor of identity for all those who sought a primarily Californian aesthetic". Both the community of and the coastline at Carmel have a symbolic meaning lost to the contemporary visitor, a lingering allusion to art as freedom, freedom as craft, the "bohemian" pantheism of the early twentieth century. The Golden Gate Bridge, referring as it does to both the infinite and technology, suggests, to the Californian, a quite complex representation of land's end, and also of its beginning.

Patricia Campbell Hearst told us in *Every Secret Thing* that the place the Hearsts called Wyntoon was "a mystical land", "fantastic, otherworldly", "even more than San Simeon", which was in turn "so emotionally moving that it is still beyond my powers of description". That first Maybeck castle on the Mc-

Cloud River was seen by most Californians only in photographs, and yet, before it burned in 1933, to be replaced by a compound of rather more playful Julia Morgan chalets ("Cinderella House", "Angel House", "Brown Bear House"), Phoebe Hearst's gothic Wyntoon and her son's baroque San Simeon seemed between them to embody certain opposing impulses in the local consciousness: northern and southern, wilderness sanctified and wilderness banished, the aggrandizement of nature and the aggrandizement of self. Wyntoon had mists, and allusions to the infinite, great trunks of trees left to rot where they fell, a wild river, barbaric fireplaces. San Simeon, swimming in sunlight and the here and now, had two swimming pools, and a zoo.

It was a family in which the romantic impulse would seem to have dimmed. Patricia Campbell Hearst told us that she "grew up in an atmosphere of clear blue skies, bright sunshine, rambling open spaces, long green lawns, large comfortable houses, country clubs with swimming pools and tennis courts and riding horses". At the Convent of the Sacred Heart in Menlo Park she told a nun to "go to hell", and thought herself "quite courageous, although very stupid". At Santa Catalina in Monterey she and Patricia Tobin, whose family founded one of the banks the SLA would later rob, skipped Benediction, and received "a load of demerits". Her father taught her to shoot, duck hunting. Her mother did not allow her to wear jeans into San Francisco. These were inheritors who tended to keep their names out of the paper, to exhibit not much interest in the world at large ("Who the hell is this guy again?" Randolph Hearst asked Steven Weed when the latter suggested trying to approach the SLA through Regis Debray, and then, when told, said, "We need a goddamn South American revolutionary mixed up in this thing like a hole in the head"), and to regard most forms of distinction with the reflexive distrust of the country club.

Yet if the Hearsts were no longer a particularly arresting California family, they remained embedded in the symbolic content of the place, and for a Hearst to be kidnapped from Berkeley, the very citadel of Phoebe Hearst's aspiration, was California as opera. "My thoughts at this time were focused on the single issue of survival," the heiress to Wyntoon and San Simeon told us about the fifty-seven days she spent in the closet. "Concerns over love and marriage, family life, friends, human relationships, my whole previous life, had really become, in SLA terms, bourgeois luxuries."

This abrupt sloughing of the past has, to the California ear, a distant echo, and the echo is of emigrant diaries. "Don't let this letter dishearten anybody, never take no cutoffs and hurry along as fast as you can," one of the surviving children of the Donner Party concluded her account of that crossing. "Don't worry about it," the author of *Every Secret Thing* reported having told herself in the closet after her first sexual encounter with a member of the SLA. "Don't examine your feelings. Never examine your feelings —they're no help at all." At the time Patricia Campbell Hearst was on trial in San Francisco, a number of psychiatrists were brought in to try to plumb what seemed to some an unsoundable depth in the narrative, that moment at which the victim binds over her fate to her captors. "She experienced what I call the death anxiety and the breaking point," Robert Jay Lifton, who was one of these psychiatrists, said. "Her external points of reference for maintenance of her personality had disappeared," Louis Jolyon West, another of the psychiatrists, said. Those were two ways of looking at it, and another was that Patricia Campbell Hearst had cut her losses and headed west, as her great-grandfather had before her.

The story she told in 1982 in *Every Secret Thing* was received, in the main, querulously, just as it had been when she told it during *The United States of America v. Patricia Campbell Hearst*, the 1976 proceeding during which she was tried for and convicted of the armed robbery of the Hibernia Bank (one count) and (the second count), the use of a weapon during the commission of a felony. Laconic, slightly ironic, resistant not only to the prosecution but to her own defense, Patricia Hearst was not, on trial in San Francisco, a conventionally ingratiating personality. "I don't know," I recall her saying over and over again during the few days I attended the trial. "I don't remember." "I suppose so." Had there not been, the prosecutor

asked one day, telephones in the motels in which she
had stayed when she drove across the country with
Jack Scott? I recall Patricia Hearst looking at him as if
she thought him deranged. I recall Randolph Hearst
looking at the floor. I recall Catherine Hearst arrang-
ing a Galanos jacket over the back of her seat.

"Yes, I'm sure," their daughter said.

Where, the prosecutor asked, were these motels?

"One was . . . I think . . ." Patricia Hearst paused,
and then: "Cheyenne? Wyoming?" She pronounced
the names as if they were foreign, exotic, information
registered and jettisoned. One of these motels had
been in Nevada, the place from which the Hearst
money originally came: the heiress pronounced the
name *Nevahda*, like a foreigner.

In *Every Secret Thing* as at her trial, she seemed to
project an emotional distance, a peculiar combination
of passivity and pragmatic recklessness ("I had crossed
over. And I would have to make the best of it . . . to
live from day to day, to do whatever they said, to play
my part, and to pray that I would survive") that many
people found inexplicable and irritating. In 1982 as in
1976, she spoke only abstractly about *why*, but quite
specifically about *how*. "I could not believe that I had
actually fired that submachine gun," she said of the
incident in which she shot up Crenshaw Boulevard,
but here was how she did it: "I kept my finger pressed
on the trigger until the entire clip of thirty shots had
been fired. . . . I then reached for my own weapon,
the semiautomatic carbine. I got off three more
shots . . ."

And, after her book as after her trial, the questions raised were not exactly about her veracity but about her authenticity, her general intention, about whether she was, as the assistant prosecutor put it during the trial, "for real". This was necessarily a vain line of inquiry (whether or not she "loved" William Wolfe was the actual point on which the trial came to turn), and one that encouraged a curious rhetorical regression among the inquisitors. "Why did she choose to write this book?" Mark Starr asked about *Every Secret Thing* in *Newsweek*, and then answered himself: "Possibly she has inherited her family's journalistic sense of what will sell." "The rich get richer," Jane Alpert concluded in *New York* magazine. "Patty," Ted Morgan observed in the *New York Times Book Review*, "is now, thanks to the proceeds of her book, reverting to a more traditional family pursuit, capital formation."

These were dreamy notions of what a Hearst might do to turn a dollar, but they reflected a larger dissatisfaction, a conviction that the Hearst in question was telling less than the whole story, "leaving something out", although what the something might have been, given the doggedly detailed account offered in *Every Secret Thing*, would be hard to define. If "questions still linger", as they did for *Newsweek*, those questions were not about how to lace a bullet with cyanide: the way the SLA did it was to drill into the lead tip to a point just short of the gunpowder, dip the tiny hole in a mound of cyanide crystals, and seal it with paraffin. If *Every Secret Thing* "creates more puzzles than it solves", as it did for Jane Alpert, those questions

105

were not about how to make a pipe bomb: the trick here was to pack enough gunpowder into the pipe for a big bang and still leave sufficient oxygen for ignition, a problem, as Patricia Hearst saw it, of "devising the proper proportions of gunpowder, length of pipe and toaster wire, minus Teko's precious toilet paper". "Teko", or Bill Harris, insisted on packing his bombs with toilet paper, and, when one of them failed to explode under a police car in the Mission District, reacted with "one of his worst temper tantrums". Many reporters later found Bill and Emily Harris the appealing defendants that Patricia Hearst never was, but *Every Secret Thing* presented a convincing case for their being, as the author put it, not only "unattractive" but, her most pejorative adjective, "incompetent".

As notes from the underground go, Patricia Hearst's were eccentric in detail. She told us that Bill Harris's favorite television program was "S.W.A.T." (one could, he said, "learn a lot about the pigs' tactics by watching these programs"); that Donald DeFreeze, or "Cinque", drank plum wine from half-gallon jugs and listened to the radio for allusions to the revolution in song lyrics; and that Nancy Ling Perry, who was usually cast by the press in the rather glamorous role of "former cheerleader and Goldwater Girl", was four feet eleven inches tall, and affected a black accent. Emily Harris trained herself to "live with deprivation" by chewing only half sticks of gum. Bill Harris bought a yarmulke, under the impression that this was the way, during the sojourn in the Catskills after the Los Angeles shoot-out, to visit Grossinger's unnoticed.

Life with these people had the distorted logic of dreams, and Patricia Hearst seems to have accepted it with the wary acquiescence of the dreamer. Any face could turn against her. Any move could prove lethal. "My sisters and I had been brought up to believe that we were responsible for what we did and could not blame our transgressions on something being wrong inside our heads. I had joined the SLA because if I didn't they would have killed me. And I remained with them because I truly believed that the FBI would kill me if they could, and if not, the SLA would." She had, as she put it, crossed over. She would, as she put it, make the best of it, and not "reach back to family or friends".

This was the point on which most people foundered, doubted her, found her least explicable, and it was also the point at which she was most specifically the child of a certain culture. Here is the single personal note in an emigrant diary kept by a relative of mine, William Kilgore, the journal of an overland crossing to Sacramento in 1850: "This is one of the trying mornings for me, as I now have to leave my family, or back out. Suffice it to say, we started." Suffice it to say. Don't examine your feelings, they're no help at all. Never take no cutoffs and hurry along as fast as you can. We need a goddamn South American revolutionary mixed up in this thing like a hole in the head. This was a California girl, and she was raised on a history that placed not much emphasis on *why*.

She was never an idealist, and this pleased no one. She was tainted by survival. She came back from the other side with a story no one wanted to hear, a dispiriting account of a situation in which delusion and incompetence were pitted against delusion and incompetence of another kind, and in the febrile rhythms of San Francisco in the midseventies it seemed a story devoid of high notes. The week her trial ended in 1976, the *San Francisco Bay Guardian* published an interview in which members of a collective called New Dawn expressed regret at her defection. "It's a question of your self-respect or your ass," one of them said. "If you choose your ass, you live with nothing." This idea that the SLA represented an idea worth defending (if only on the grounds that any idea must be better than none) was common enough at the time, although most people granted that the idea had gone awry. By March of 1977 another writer in the *Bay Guardian* was making a distinction between the "unbridled adventurism" of the SLA and the "discipline and skill" of the New World Liberation Front, whose "fifty-odd bombings without a casualty" made them a "definitely preferable alternative" to the SLA.

As it happened I had kept this issue of the *Bay Guardian*, dated March 31, 1977 (the *Bay Guardian* was not at the time a notably radical paper, by the way, but one that provided a fair guide to local tofu cookery and the mood of the community), and when I got it out to look at the piece on the SLA I noticed for the first time another piece: a long and favorable report on a San Francisco minister whose practice it was to "confront people and challenge their basic assumptions . . . as if he can't let the evil of the world pass him by, a characteristic he shares with other moral leaders." The minister, who was compared at one point to Cesar Chavez, was responsible, according to the writer, for a "mind-boggling" range of social service programs—food distribution, legal aid, drug rehabilitation, nursing homes, free Pap smears—as well as for a "twenty-seven-thousand-acre agricultural station". The agricultural station was in Guyana, and the minister of course was the Reverend Jim Jones, who eventually chose self-respect over his own and nine hundred other asses. This was another local opera, and one never spoiled by a protagonist who insisted on telling it her way.

—1982

Pacific Distances

1

A GOOD PART of any day in Los Angeles is spent driving, alone, through streets devoid of meaning to the driver, which is one reason the place exhilarates some people, and floods others with an amorphous unease. There is about these hours spent in transit a seductive unconnectedness. Conventional information is missing. Context clues are missing. In Culver City as in Echo Park as in East Los Angeles, there are the same pastel bungalows. There are the same leggy poinsettia and the same trees of pink and yellow hibiscus. There are the same laundromats, body shops, strip shopping malls, the same travel agencies offering bargain fares on LACSA and TACA. *San Salvador*, the signs promise, on Beverly Boulevard as on Pico as on Alvarado and Soto. *¡No más barata!* There is the same sound, that of the car radio, tuned in my case to KRLA, an AM station that identifies itself as "the heart and soul of rock and roll" and is given to dislocating programming concepts, for example doing the top hits ("Baby, It's You", "Break

It to Me Gently", "The Lion Sleeps Tonight") of 1962. Another day, another KRLA concept: "The Day the Music Died", an exact radio recreation of the day in 1959, including news breaks (Detroit may market compacts), when the plane carrying Buddy Holly, Ritchie Valens, and the Big Bopper crashed near Clear Lake, Iowa. A few days later, KRLA reports a solid response on "The Day the Music Died", including "a call from Ritchie Valens's aunt".

Such tranced hours are, for many people who live in Los Angeles, the dead center of being there, but there is nothing in them to encourage the normal impulse toward "recognition", or narrative connection. Those glosses on the human comedy (the widow's heartbreak, the bad cop, the mother-and-child reunion) that lend dramatic structure to more traditional forms of urban life are hard to come by here. There are, in the pages of the Los Angeles newspapers, no Crack Queens, no Coma Moms or Terror Tots. Events may be lurid, but are rarely personalized. "Mother Apologizes to Her Child, Drives Both Off Cliff," a headline read in the *Los Angeles Times* one morning in December 1988. (Stories like this are relegated in the *Times* either to the Metro Section or to page three, which used to be referred to as "the freak-death page", not its least freaky aspect being that quite arresting accounts of death by Clorox or by rattlesnake or by Dumpster tended to appear and then vanish, with no follow-up.) Here was the story, which had to do with a young woman who had lived with her daughter, Brooke, in a Redondo Beach condomin-

111

ium and was said by a neighbor to have "looked like she was a little down":

> A Redondo Beach woman apologized to her 7-year-old daughter, then apparently tried to take both their lives by driving over a cliff in the Malibu area Tuesday morning, authorities said. The mother, identified by the county coroner's office as Susan Sinclair, 29, was killed, but the child survived without serious injury. "I'm sorry I have to do this," the woman was quoted as telling the child just before she suddenly swerved off Malibu Canyon Road about 2½ miles north of Pacific Coast Highway.

"I'm sorry I have to do this." This was the last we heard of Susan and Brooke Sinclair. When I first moved to Los Angeles from New York, in 1964, I found this absence of narrative a deprivation. At the end of two years I realized (quite suddenly, alone one morning in the car) that I had come to find narrative sentimental. This remains a radical difference between the two cities, and also between the ways in which the residents of those cities view each other.

2

OUR CHILDREN remind us of how random our lives have been. I had occasion in 1979 to speak at my daughter's school in Los Angeles, and I stood there, apparently a grown woman, certainly a woman who had stood up any number of times and spoken to students around the country, and tried to confront a question that suddenly seemed to me almost impenetrable: How had I become a writer, how and why had I made the particular choices I had made in my life? I could see my daughter's friends in the back of the room, Claudia, Julie, Anna. I could see my daughter herself, flushed with embarrassment, afraid, she told me later, that her presence would make me forget what I meant to say.

I could tell them only that I had no more idea of how I had become a writer than I had had, at their age, of how I would become a writer. I could tell them only about the fall of 1954, when I was nineteen and a junior at Berkeley and one of perhaps a dozen students admitted to the late Mark Schorer's English 106A, a kind of "fiction workshop" that met for discussion three hours a week and required that each student produce, over the course of the semester, at least five short stories. No auditors were allowed. Voices were kept low. English 106A was widely regarded in the fall of 1954 as a kind of sacramental experience, an initiation into the grave world of real writers, and I remember each meeting of this class as an occasion of acute excitement and dread. I remember each other member of this class as older and wiser than I had hope of ever being (it had not yet struck me in any visceral way that being nineteen was not a long-term proposition, just as it had not yet struck

Claudia and Julie and Anna and my daughter that they would recover from being thirteen), not only older and wiser but more experienced, more independent, more interesting, more possessed of an exotic past: marriages and the breaking up of marriages, money and the lack of it, sex and politics and the Adriatic seen at dawn: not only the stuff of grown-up life itself but, more poignantly to me at the time, the very stuff that might be transubstantiated into five short stories. I recall a Trotskyist, then in his forties. I recall a young woman who lived, with a barefoot man and a large white dog, in an attic lit only by candles. I recall classroom discussions that ranged over meetings with Paul and Jane Bowles, incidents involving Djuna Barnes, years spent in Paris, in Beverly Hills, in the Yucatán, on the Lower East Side of New York and on Repulse Bay and even on morphine. I had spent seventeen of my nineteen years more or less in Sacramento, and the other two in the Tri Delt house on Warring Street in Berkeley. I had never read Paul or Jane Bowles, let alone met them, and when, some fifteen years later at a friend's house in Santa Monica Canyon, I did meet Paul Bowles, I was immediately rendered as dumb and awestruck as I had been at nineteen in English 106A.

I suppose that what I really wanted to say that day at my daughter's school is that we never reach a point at which our lives lie before us as a clearly marked open road, never have and never should expect a map to the years ahead, never do close those circles that seem, at thirteen and fourteen and nineteen, so urgently in need of closing. I wanted to tell my daughter and her friends, but did not, about going back to the English department at Berkeley in the spring of 1975 as a Regents' Lecturer, a reversal of positions that should have been satisfying but proved unsettling, moved me profoundly, answered no questions but raised the same old ones. In Los Angeles in 1975 I had given every appearance of being well settled, grown-up, a woman in definite charge of her own work and of a certain kind of bourgeois household that made working possible. In Berkeley in 1975 I had unpacked my clothes and papers in a single room at the Faculty Club, walked once across campus, and regressed, immediately and helplessly, into the ghetto life of the student I had been twenty years before. I hoarded nuts and bits of chocolate in my desk drawer. I ate tacos for dinner (combination plates, *con arroz y fri-joles*), wrapped myself in my bedspread and read until two A.M., smoked too many cigarettes and regretted, like a student, only their cost. I found myself making daily notes, as carefully as I had when I was an undergraduate, of expenses, and my room at the Faculty Club was littered with little scraps of envelopes:

> *$1.15, papers, etc.*
> *$2.85, taco plate*
> *$ .50, tips*
> *$ .15, coffee*

I fell not only into the habits but into the moods of the student day. Every morning I was hopeful, deter-

115

mined, energized by the campanile bells and by the smell of eucalyptus and by the day's projected accomplishments. On the way to breakfast I would walk briskly, breathe deeply, review my "plans" for the day: I would write five pages, return all calls, lunch on raisins and answer ten letters. I would at last read E. H. Gombrich. I would once and for all get the meaning of the word "structuralist". And yet every afternoon by four o'clock, the hour when I met my single class, I was once again dulled, glazed, sunk in an excess of carbohydrates and in my own mediocrity, in my failure—still, after twenty years!—to "live up to" the day's possibilities.

In certain ways nothing at all had changed in those twenty years. The clean light and fogs were exactly as I had remembered. The creek still ran clear among the shadows, the rhododendron still bloomed in the spring. On the bulletin boards in the English department there were still notices inviting the reader to apply to Mrs. Diggory Venn for information on the Radcliffe Publishing Procedures course. The less securely tenured members of the department still yearned for dramatic moves to Johns Hopkins. Anything specific was rendered immediately into a general principle. Anything concrete was rendered abstract. That the spring of 1975 was, outside Berkeley, a season of remarkably specific and operatically concrete events seemed, on the campus, another abstract, another illustration of a general tendency, an instance tending only to confirm or not confirm one or another idea of the world. The wire photos from Phnom Penh and Saigon seemed as deliberately composed as symbolist paintings. The question of whether one spoke of Saigon "falling" or of Saigon's "liberation" reduced the fact to a political attitude, a semantic question, another idea.

Days passed. I adopted a shapeless blazer and no makeup. I remember spending considerable time, that spring of 1975, trying to break the code that Telegraph Avenue seemed to present. There, just a block or two off the campus, the campus with its five thousand courses, its four million books, its five million manuscripts, the campus with its cool glades and clear creeks and lucid views, lay this mean wasteland of small venture capital, this unweeded garden in which everything cost more than it was worth. Coffee on Telegraph Avenue was served neither hot nor cold. Food was slopped lukewarm onto chipped plates. Pita bread was stale, curries were rank. Tatty "Indian" stores offered faded posters and shoddy silks. Bookstores featured sections on the occult. Drug buys were in progress up and down the street. The place was an illustration of some tropism toward disorder, and I seemed to understand it no better in 1975 than I had as an undergraduate.

I remember trying to discuss Telegraph Avenue with some people from the English department, but they were discussing a paper we had heard on the plotting of *Vanity Fair*, *Middlemarch*, and *Bleak House*. I remember trying to discuss Telegraph Avenue with an old friend who had asked me to dinner, at a place far enough off campus to get a drink, but he was

discussing Jane Alpert, Eldridge Cleaver, Daniel Ells-
berg, Shana Alexander, a Modesto rancher of his acquaintance, Jules Feiffer, Herbert Gold, Herb Caen,
Ed Janss, and the movement for independence in Mi-
cronesia. I remember thinking that I was still, after
twenty years, out of step at Berkeley, the victim of a
different drummer. I remember sitting in my office in
Wheeler Hall one afternoon when someone, not a student, walked in off the street. He said that he was a
writer, and I asked what he had written. "Nothing
you'll ever dare to read," he said. He admired only
Céline and Djuna Barnes. With the exception of
Djuna Barnes, women could not write. It was possible
that I could write but he did not know, he had not
read me. "In any case," he added, sitting on the edge
of my desk, "your time's gone, your fever's over." It
had probably been a couple of decades, English 106A,
since I last heard about Céline and Djuna Barnes and
how women could not write, since I last encountered
this particular brand of extraliterary machismo, and
after my caller had left the office I locked the door and
sat there a long time in the afternoon light. At nineteen I had wanted to write. At forty I still wanted to
write, and nothing that had happened in the years
between made me any more certain that I could.

3

ETCHEVERRY HALL, half a block uphill from
the north gate of the University of California at Berke-

ley, is one of those postwar classroom and office buildings that resemble parking structures and seem designed to suggest that nothing extraordinary has been or will be going on inside. On Etcheverry's east terrace, which is paved with pebbled concrete and bricks, a few students usually sit studying or sunbathing. There are benches, there is grass. There are shrubs and a small tree. There is a net for volleyball, and, on the day in late 1979 when I visited Etcheverry, someone had taken a piece of chalk and printed the word RADIATION on the concrete beneath the net, breaking the letters in a way that looked stenciled and official and scary. In fact it was here, directly below the volleyball court on Etcheverry's east terrace, that the Department of Nuclear Engineering's TRIGA Mark III nuclear reactor, light-water cooled and reflected, went critical, or achieved a sustained nuclear reaction, on August 10, 1966, and had been in continuous operation since. People who wanted to see the reactor dismantled said that it was dangerous, that it could emit deadly radiation and that it was perilously situated just forty yards west of the Hayward Fault. People who ran the reactor said that it was not dangerous, that any emission of measurable radioactivity was extremely unlikely and that "forty yards west of" the Hayward Fault was a descriptive phrase without intrinsic seismological significance. (This was an assessment with which seismologists agreed.) These differences of opinion represented a difference not only in the meaning of words but in cultures, a difference in images and probably in expectations.

Above the steel door to the reactor room in the basement of Etcheverry Hall was a sign that glowed either green or Roman violet, depending on whether what it said was SAFE ENTRY, which meant that the air lock between the reactor room and the corridor was closed and the radiation levels were normal and the level of pool water was normal, or UNSAFE ENTRY, which meant that at least one of these conditions, usually the first, had not been met. The sign on the steel door itself read only ROOM 1140 / EXCLUSION AREA / ENTRY LIST A, B, or C / CHECK WITH RECEPTIONIST. On the day I visited Etcheverry I was issued a dosimeter to keep in my pocket, then shown the reactor by Tek Lim, at that time the reactor manager, and Lawrence Grossman, a professor of nuclear engineering. They explained that the Etcheverry TRIGA was a modification of the original TRIGA, which is an acronym for Training/Research/Isotopes/General Atomic, and was designed in 1956 by a team, including Edward Teller and Theodore Taylor and Freeman Dyson, that had set for itself the task of making a reactor so safe, in Freeman Dyson's words, "that it could be given to a bunch of high school children to play with, without any fear that they would get hurt".

They explained that the TRIGA operated at a much lower heat level than a power reactor, and was used primarily for "making things radioactive". Nutritionists, for example, used it to measure trace elements in diet. Archaeologists used it for dating. NASA used it for high-altitude pollution studies, and for a study on how weightlessness affects human calcium metabolism. Stanford was using it to study lithium in the brain. Physicists from the Lawrence Berkeley Laboratory, up the hill, had been coming down to use it for experiments in the development of a fusion, or "clean", reactor. A researcher from Ghana used it for a year, testing samples from African waterholes for the arsenic that could kill the animals.

The reactor was operating at one megawatt as we talked. All levels were normal. We were standing, with Harry Braun, the chief reactor operator, on the metal platform around the reactor pool, and I had trouble keeping my eyes from the core, the Cerenkov radiation around the fuel rods, the blue shimmer under twenty feet of clear water. There was a skimmer on the side of the pool, and a bath mat thrown over the railing. There was a fishing pole, and a rubber duck. Harry Braun uses the fishing rod to extract samples from the specimen rack around the core, and the rubber duck to monitor the water movement. "Or when the little children come on school tours," he added. "Sometimes they don't pay any attention until we put the duck in the pool."

I was ten years old when "the atomic age", as we called it then, came forcibly to the world's attention. At the time the verbs favored for use with "the atomic age" were "dawned" or "ushered in", both of which implied an upward trend to events. I recall being told that the device which ended World War II was "the size of a lemon" (this was not true) and that the University of California had helped build it (this was true). I recall listening all one Sunday afternoon to a special radio report called "The Quick and the Dead", three or four hours during which the people who had built and witnessed the bomb talked about the bomb's and (by extension) their own eerie and apparently unprecedented power, their abrupt elevation to that place from whence they had come to judge the quick and the dead, and I also recall, when summer was over and school started again, being taught to cover my eyes and my brain stem and crouch beneath my desk during atomic-bomb drills.

So unequivocal were these impressions that it never occurred to me that I would not sooner or later—most probably sooner, certainly before I ever grew up or got married or went to college—endure the moment of its happening: first the blinding white light, which appeared in my imagination as a negative photographic image, then the waves of heat, the sound, and, finally, death, instant or prolonged, depending inflexibly on where one was caught in the scale of concentric circles we all imagined pulsing out from ground zero. Some years later, when I was an undergraduate at Berkeley and had an apartment in an old shingled house a few doors from where Etcheverry now stands, I could look up the hill at night and see the lights at the Lawrence Berkeley Laboratory, at what was then called "the rad lab", at the cyclotron and the Bevatron, and I still expected to wake up one night and see those lights in negative, still expected the blinding white light, the heat wave, the logical conclusion.

After I graduated I moved to New York, and after some months or a year I realized that I was no longer anticipating the blinding flash, and that the expectation had probably been one of those ways in which children deal with mortality, learn to juggle the idea that life will end as surely as it began, to perform in the face of definite annihilation. And yet I know that for me, and I suspect for many of us, this single image —this blinding white light that meant death, this seductive reversal of the usual associations around "light" and "white" and "radiance"—became a metaphor that to some extent determined what I later thought and did. In my Modern Library copy of *The Education of Henry Adams*, a book I first read and scored at Berkeley in 1954, I see this passage, about the 1900 Paris Great Exposition, underlined:

> . . . to Adams the dynamo became a symbol of infinity. As he grew accustomed to the great gallery of machines, he began to feel the forty-foot dynamos as a moral force, much as the early Christians felt the Cross.

It had been, at the time I saw the TRIGA Mark III reactor in the basement of Etcheverry Hall, seventy-nine years since Henry Adams went to Paris to study Science as he had studied Mont-Saint-Michel and Chartres. It had been thirty-four years since Robert Oppenheimer saw the white light at Alamogordo. The "nuclear issue", as we called it, suggesting that the course of the world since the Industrial Revolution was provisional, open to revision, up for a vote, had been under discussion all those years, and yet something about the fact of the reactor still resisted interpretation: the intense blue in the pool water, the Cerenkov radiation around the fuel rods, the blue past all blue, the blue like light itself, the blue that is actually a shock wave in the water and is the exact blue of the glass at Chartres.

4

AT THE UNIVERSITY of California's Lawrence Livermore Laboratory, a compound of heavily guarded structures in the rolling cattle and orchard country southeast of Oakland, badges had to be displayed not only at the gate but again and again, at various points within the compound, to television cameras mounted between two locked doors. These cameras registered not only the presence but the color of the badge. A red badge meant "No Clearance U.S. Citizen" and might or might not be issued with the white covering badge that meant "Visitor Must Be Escorted". A yellow badge meant "No Higher Than Confidential Access". A green badge banded in yellow indicated that access was to be considered top level but not exactly unlimited: "Does Need to Know Exist?" was, according to a sign in the Badge Office, LLL Building 310, the question to ask as the bearer moved from station to station among the mysteries of the compound.

The symbolic as well as the literal message of a badge at Livermore—or at Los Alamos, or at Sandia, or at any of the other major labs around the country —was that the government had an interest here, that big money was being spent, Big Physics done. Badges were the totems of the tribe, the family. This was the family that used to keep all the plutonium in the world in a cigar box outside Glenn Seaborg's office in Berkeley, the family that used to try different ways of turning on the early twenty-seven-and-one-half-inch Berkeley cyclotron so as not to blow out large sections of the East Bay power grid. "Very gently" was said to work best. I have a copy of a photograph that suggests the day-to-day life of this family with considerable poignance, a snapshot taken during the fifties, when Livermore was testing its atmospheric nuclear weapons in the Pacific. The snapshot shows a very young Livermore scientist, with a flattop haircut and an engaging smile, standing on the beach of an unidentified atoll on an unspecified day just preceding or just following (no clue in the caption) a test shot. He is holding a fishing rod, and, in the other hand, a queen triggerfish, according to the caption "just a few ounces short of a world record". He is wearing only swimming trunks, and his badge.

On the day in February 1980 when I drove down to Livermore from Berkeley the coast ranges were green from the winter rains. The acacia was out along the highway, a haze of chrome yellow in the window. Inside the compound itself, narcissus and daffodil shoots pressed through the asphalt walkways. I had driven down because I wanted to see Shiva, Livermore's twenty-beam laser, the $35 million tool that was then Livermore's main marker in the biggest Big

Physics game then going, the attempt to create a controlled fusion reaction. An uncontrolled fusion reaction was easy, and was called a hydrogen bomb. A controlled fusion reaction was harder, so much harder that it was usually characterized as "the most difficult technological feat ever undertaken", but the eventual payoff could be virtually limitless nuclear power produced at a fraction the hazard of the fission plants then operating. The difficulty in a controlled fusion reaction was that it involved achieving a thermonuclear burn of 100 million degrees centigrade, or more than six times the heat of the interior of the sun, without exploding the container. That no one had ever done this was, for the family, the point.

Ideas about how to do it were intensely competitive. Some laboratories had concentrated on what was called the "magnetic bottle" approach, involving the magnetic confinement of plasma; others, on lasers, and the theoretical ability of laser beams to trigger controlled fusion by simultaneously heating and compressing tiny pellets of fuel. Livermore had at that time a magnetic-bottle project but was gambling most heavily on its lasers, on Shiva and on Shiva's then unfinished successor, Nova. This was a high-stakes game: the prizes would end up at those laboratories where the money was, and the money would go to those laboratories where the prizes seemed most likely. It was no accident that Livermore was visited by so many members of Congress, by officials of the Department of Defense and of the Department of Energy, and by not too many other people: friends in high places were essential to the family. The biogra-

phy of Ernest O. Lawrence, the first of the Berkeley
Nobel laureates and the man after whom the Lawrence Berkeley and the Lawrence Livermore laboratories were named, is instructive on this point: there
were meetings at the Pacific Union Club, sojourns at
Bohemian Grove and San Simeon, even "a short trip
to Acapulco with Randy and Catherine Hearst". The
Eniwetok tests during the fifties were typically preceded for Lawrence by stops in Honolulu, where, for
example,

> . . . he was a guest of Admiral John E. Ging-
> rich, a fine host. He reciprocated with a din-
> ner for the admiral and several others at
> the Royal Hawaiian Hotel the night before
> departure for Eniwetok, a ten-hour flight
> from Honolulu. Eniwetok had much the at-
> mosphere of a South Seas resort. A fine of-
> ficers' club on the beach provided relaxation
> for congressmen and visitors. The tropical
> sea invited swimmers and scuba divers.
> There were no phones to interrupt conver-
> sations with interesting and important men
> . . . chairs had been placed on the beach
> when observers assembled at the club near
> dawn [to witness the shot]. Coffee and sand-
> wiches were served, and dark glasses distrib-
> uted . . .

On the day I visited Livermore the staff was still
cleaning up after a January earthquake, a Richter 5.5
on the Mount Diablo–Greenville Fault. Acoustical

127

tiles had fallen from the ceilings of the office buildings. Overhead light fixtures had plummeted onto
desks, and wiring and insulation and air-conditioning
ducts still hung wrenched from the ceilings. "You get
damage in the office buildings because the office buildings are only built to local code," I was told by John
Emmett, the physicist then in charge of the Livermore
laser program. When the ceilings started falling that
particular January, John Emmett had been talking to
a visitor in his office. He had shown the visitor out,
run back inside to see if anyone was trapped under
the toppled bookshelves and cabinets, and then run
over to the building that houses Shiva. The laser had
been affected so slightly that all twenty beams were
found, by the sixty-three microcomputers that constantly aligned and realigned the Shiva beams, to be
within one-sixteenth of an inch of their original align-
ment. "We didn't anticipate any real damage and we
didn't get any," John Emmett said. "That's the way
the gadget is designed."

What John Emmett called "the gadget" was framed
in an immaculate white steel scaffolding several stories
high and roughly the size of a football field. This
frame was astonishingly beautiful, a piece of pure theater, a kind of abstract set on which the actors wore
white coats, green goggles, and hard hats. "You wear
the goggles because even when we're not firing we've
got some little beams bouncing around," John Emmett
said. "The hard hat is because somebody's always
dropping something." Within the frame, a single infrared laser beam was split into twenty beams, each

of which was amplified and reamplified until, at the instant two or three times a day when all twenty beams hit target, they were carrying sixty times as much power as was produced in the entire (exclusive of this room) United States. The target under bombardment was a glass bead a fraction the size of a grain of salt. The entire shoot took one-half billionth of a second. John Emmett and the Livermore laser team had then achieved with Shiva controlled temperatures of 85 million degrees centigrade, or roughly five times the heat at the center of the sun, but not 100 million. They were gambling on Nova for 100 million, the prize.

I recall, that afternoon at Livermore, asking John Emmett what would happen if I looked at the invisible infrared beam without goggles. "It'll blow a hole in your retina," he said matter-of-factly. It seemed that he had burned out the retina of one of his own eyes with a laser when he was a graduate student at Stanford. I asked if the sight had come back. "All but one little spot," he said. *Give me a mind that is not bored, that does not whimper, whine or sigh / Don't let me worry overmuch about the fussy thing called I:* these are two lines from a popular "prayer", a late-twenties precursor to the "Desiderata" that Ernest O. Lawrence kept framed on his desk until his death. The one little spot was not of interest to John Emmett. Making the laser work was.

5

WINTERTIME and springtime, Honolulu: in the winter there was the garbage strike, forty-two days during which the city lapsed into a profound and seductive tropicality. Trash drifted in the vines off the Lunalilo Freeway. The airport looked Central American, between governments. Green plastic bags of garbage mounded up on the streets, and orange peels and Tab cans thrown in the canals washed down to the sea and up to the tide line in front of our rented house on Kahala Avenue. A day goes this way: in the morning I rearrange our own green plastic mounds, pick up the orange peels and Tab cans from the tide line, and sit down to work at the wet bar in the living room, a U-shaped counter temporarily equipped with an IBM Selectric typewriter. I turn on the radio for news of a break in the garbage strike: I get a sig-alert for the Lunalilo, roadwork between the Wilder Avenue off-ramp and the Punahou overpass. I get the weather: mostly clear. Actually water is dropping in great glassy sheets on the windward side of the island, fifteen minutes across the Pali, but on leeward Oahu the sky is quicksilver, chiaroscuro, light and dark and sudden falls of rain and rainbow, mostly clear. Some time ago I stopped trying to explain to acquaintances on the mainland the ways in which the simplest routines of a day in Honolulu can please and interest me, but on these winter mornings I am reminded that they do. I keep an appointment with a dermatologist at Kapiolani-Children's Medical Center, and am pleased by the drive down Beretania Street in the rain. I stop for groceries at the Star Market in the Kahala Mall, and am pleased by the sprays of vanda orchids and the foot-long watercress and the little Manoa lettuces in the produce department. Some mornings I am even pleased by the garbage strike.

The undertone of every day in Honolulu, the one fact that colors every other, is the place's absolute remove from the rest of the world. Many American cities began remote, but only Honolulu is fated to remain so, and only in Honolulu do the attitudes and institutions born of extreme isolation continue to set the tone of daily life. The edge of the available world is sharply defined: one turns a corner or glances out an office window and there it is, blue sea. There is no cheap freedom to be gained by getting in a car and driving as far as one can go, since as far as one can go on the island of Oahu takes about an hour and fifteen minutes. "Getting away" involves actual travel, scheduled carriers, involves reservations and reconfirmations and the ambiguous experience of being strapped passive in a darkened cabin and exposed to unwanted images on a flickering screen; involves submission to other people's schedules and involves, most significantly, money.

I have rarely spent an evening at anyone's house in Honolulu when someone in the room was not just off or about to catch an airplane, and the extent to which ten-hour flights figure in the local imagination tends to reinforce the distinction between those who can afford them and those who cannot. More people probably travel in Honolulu than can actually afford to: one study showed recent trips to the mainland in almost 25 percent of Oahu households and recent trips to countries outside the United States in almost 10 percent. Very few of those trips are to Europe, very few to the east coast of the United States. Not only does it take longer to fly from Honolulu to New York than from Honolulu to Hong Kong (the actual air time is about the same, ten or eleven hours either way, but no carrier now flies nonstop from Honolulu to New York), but Hong Kong seems closer in spirit, as do Manila, Tokyo, Sydney. A druggist suggests that I stock up on a prescription over the counter the next time I am in Hong Kong. The daughter of a friend gets a reward for good grades, a sweet-sixteen weekend on the Great Barrier Reef. The far Pacific is home, or near home in mood and appearance (there are parts of Oahu that bear more resemblance to Southeast Asia than to anywhere in the mainland United States), and the truly foreign lies in the other direction: airline posters feature the New England foliage, the Statue of Liberty, exotic attractions from a distant culture, a culture in which most people in Honolulu have no roots at all and only a fitful interest. This leaning toward Asia makes Honolulu's relation to the rest of America oblique, and divergent at unexpected points, which is part of the place's great but often hidden eccentricity.

To buy a house anywhere on the island of Oahu in the spring of 1980 cost approximately what a similar

property would have cost in Los Angeles. Three bedrooms and a bath-and-a-half in the tracts near Pearl
Harbor were running over $100,000 ("$138,000" was
a figure I kept noticing in advertisements, once under
the headline "This Is Your Lucky Day"), although the
occasional bungalow with one bath was offered in the
nineties. At the top end of the scale (where "life is
somehow bigger and disappointment blunted", as one
advertisement put it), not quite two-thirds of an acre
with a main house, guesthouse, gatehouse, and salt-
water pool on the beach at Diamond Head was offered
—"fee simple", which was how a piece of property
available for actual sale was described in Honolulu—
at $3,750,000.

"Fee simple" was a magical phrase in Honolulu,
since one of the peculiarities of the local arrangement
had been that not much property actually changed
hands. The island of Oahu was, at its longest and
widest points, forty-five miles long and thirty miles
wide, a total land mass—much of it vertical, unbuild-
able, the sheer volcanic precipices of the Koolau and
Waianae ranges—of 380,000 acres. Almost 15 percent
of this land was owned by the federal government and
an equal amount by the State of Hawaii. Of the remaining privately owned land, more than 70 percent
was owned by major landholders, by holders of more
than five thousand acres, most notably, on Oahu, by
the Campbell Estate, the Damon Estate, Castle and
Cooke, and, in the most densely populated areas of
Honolulu, the Bishop Estate. The Bishop Estate
owned a good part of Waikiki, and the Kahala and
Waialae districts, and, farther out, Hawaii Kai, which

was a Kaiser development but a Bishop holding. The purchaser of a house on Bishop land bought not title to the property itself but a "leasehold", a land lease, transferred from buyer to buyer, that might be within a few years of expiration or might be (the preferred situation) recently renegotiated, fixed for a long term. An advertisement in the spring of 1980 for a three-bedroom, two-bath, $230,000 house in Hawaii Kai emphasized its "long, low lease", as did an advertisement for a similar house in the Kahala district offered at $489,000. One Sunday that spring, the Dolman office, a big residential realtor in Honolulu, ran an advertisement in the *Star-Bulletin & Advertiser* featuring forty-seven listings, of which thirty-nine were leasehold. The Earl Thacker office, the same day, featured eighteen listings, ten of which were leasehold, including an oceanfront lease for a house on Kahala Avenue at $1,250,000.

This situation, in which a few owners held most of the land, was relatively unique in the developed world (under 30 percent of the private land in California was held by owners of more than five thousand acres, compared to the more than 70 percent of Oahu) and lent a rather feudal and capricious uncertainty, a note of cosmic transience, to what was in other places a straightforward transaction, a direct assertion of territory, the purchase of a place to live. In some areas the Bishop Estate had offered "conversions", or the opportunity to convert leasehold to fee-simple property at prices then averaging $5.62 a square foot. This was regarded as a kind of land reform, but it worked adversely on the householder who had already invested all he or she could afford in the leasehold. Someone I know whose Bishop lease came up recently was forced to sell the house in which she had lived for some years because she could afford neither the price of the conversion nor the raised payments of what would have been her new lease. I went with another friend in 1980 to look at a house on the "other", or non-oceanfront, side of Kahala Avenue, listed at $695,000. The Bishop lease was fixed for thirty years and graduated: $490 a month until 1989, $735 until 1999, and $979 until 2009. The woman showing the house suggested that a conversion might be obtained. No one could promise it, of course, nor could anyone say what price might be set, if indeed a price were set at all. It was true that nothing on Kahala Avenue itself had at that time been converted. It was also true that the Bishop Estate was talking about Kahala Avenue as a logical place for hotel development. Still, the woman and my friend seemed to agree, it was a pretty house, and a problematic stretch to 2009.

When I first began visiting Honolulu, in 1966, I read in a tourist guidebook that the conventional points of the compass—north, south, east, west—were never employed locally, that one gave directions by saying that a place was either *makai*, toward the sea, or *mauka*, toward the mountains, and, in the city, usually either "diamond head" or "ewa", depending on whether the place in question lay, from where one

135

stood, toward Diamond Head or Ewa Plantation. The Royal Hawaiian Hotel, for example, was diamond head of Ewa, but ewa of Diamond Head. The Kahala Hilton Hotel, since it was situated between Diamond Head and Koko Head, was said to be koko head of Diamond Head, and diamond head of Koko Head. There was about this a resolute colorfulness that did not seem entirely plausible to me at the time, particularly since the federally funded signs on the Lunalilo Freeway read EAST and WEST, but as time passed I came to see not only the chimerical compass but the attitude it seemed to reflect as intrinsic to the local accommodation, a way of maintaining fluidity in the rigid structure and isolation of an island society.

This system of bearings is entirely relative (nothing is absolutely ewa, for instance; the Waianae coast is makaha of Ewa, or toward Makaha, and beyond Makaha the known world metamorphoses again), is used at all levels of Honolulu life, and is common even in courtrooms. I recall spending several days at a murder trial during which the HPD evidence specialist, a quite beautiful young woman who looked as if she had walked off "Hawaii Five-O", spoke of "picking up latents ewa of the sink". The police sergeant with whom she had fingerprinted the site said that he had "dusted the koko head bedroom and the koko head bathroom, also the ewa bedroom and the kitchen floor". The defendant was said to have placed his briefcase, during a visit to the victim's apartment, "toward the ewa-makai corner of the couch". This was a trial, incidentally, during which one of the witnesses, a young woman who had worked a number of call dates with the victim (the victim was a call girl who had been strangled with her own telephone cord in her apartment near Ala Moana), gave her occupation as "full-time student at the University of Hawaii, carrying sixteen units". Another witness, also a call girl, said, when asked her occupation, that she was engaged in "part-time construction".

The way to get to Ewa was to go beyond Pearl Harbor and down Fort Weaver Road, past the weathered frame building that was once the hospital for Ewa Plantation and past the Japanese graveyard, and turn right. (Going straight instead of turning right would take the driver directly to Ewa Beach, a different proposition. I remember being advised when I first visited Honolulu that if I left the keys in a car in Waikiki I could look for it stripped down in Ewa Beach.) There was no particular reason to go to Ewa, no shops, no businesses, no famous views, no place to eat or even walk far (walk, and you walked right into the cane and the KAPU, or KEEP OUT, signs of the Oahu Sugar Company); there was only the fact that the place was there, intact, operational, a plantation town from another period. There was a school, a post office, a grocery. There were cane tools for sale in the grocery, and the pint bottles of liquor were kept in the office, a kind of wire-mesh cage with a counter. There was the Immaculate Conception Roman Catholic Church, there was the Ewa Hongwanji Mission. On

137

the telephone poles there were torn and rain-stained posters for some revolution past or future, some May Day, a rally, a caucus, a "Mao Tse-tung Memorial Meeting".

Ewa was a company town, and its identical frame houses were arranged down a single street, the street that led to the sugar mill. Just one house on this street stood out: a house built of the same frame as the others but not exactly a bungalow, a house transliterated from the New England style, a *haole* house, a manager's house, a house larger than any other house for miles around. A Honolulu psychiatrist once told me, when I asked if he saw any characteristic island syndrome, that, yes, among the children of the planter families, children raised among the memories of the island's colonial past, he did. These patients shared the conviction that they were being watched, being observed, and not living up to what was expected of them. In Ewa one understood how that conviction might take hold. In Ewa one watched the larger house.

On my desk I used to keep a clock on Honolulu time, and around five o'clock by that clock I would sometimes think of Ewa. I would imagine driving through Ewa at that time of day, when the mill and the frame bungalows swim in the softened light like amber, and I would imagine driving on down through Ewa Beach and onto the tract of military housing at Iroquois Point, a place as rigidly structured and culturally isolated in one way as Ewa was in another. From the shoreline at Iroquois Point one looks across the curve of the coast at Waikiki, a circumstance so poignant, suggesting as it does each of the tensions in Honolulu life, that it stops discussion.

6

ON THE DECEMBER morning in 1979 when I visited Kai Tak East, the Caritas transit camp for Vietnamese refugees near Kai Tak airport, Kowloon, Hong Kong, a woman of indeterminate age was crouched on the pavement near the washing pumps bleeding out a live chicken. She worked at the chicken's neck with a small paring knife, opening and re-opening the cut and massaging the blood into a tin cup, and periodically she would let the bird run free. The chicken did not exactly run but stumbled, staggered, and finally lurched toward one of the trickles of milky waste water that drained the compound. A flock of small children with bright scarlet rashes on their cheeks giggled and staggered, mimicking the chicken. The woman retrieved the dying chicken and, with what began to seem an almost narcoleptic languor, resumed working the blood from the cut, stroking rhythmically along the matted and stained feathers of the chicken's neck. The chicken had been limp a long time before she finally laid it on the dusty pavement. The children, bored, drifted away. The woman still crouched beside her chicken in the thin December sunlight.

When I think of Hong Kong I remember a particular smell in close places, a smell I construed as jasmine and excrement and sesame oil in varying proportions, and at Kai Tak East, where there were too many people and too few places for them to sleep and cook and eat and wash, this smell pervaded even the wide and dusty exercise yard that was the center of the camp. The smell was in fact what I noticed first, the smell and the dustiness and a certain immediate sense of physical dislocation, a sense of people who had come empty-handed and been assigned odd articles of cast-off clothing, which they wore uneasily: a grave little girl in a faded but still garish metallic bolero, an old man in a Wellesley sweatshirt, a wizened woman in a preteen sweater embroidered with dancing cats. In December in Hong Kong the sun lacked real warmth, and the children in the yard seemed bundled in the unfamiliar fragments of other people's habits. Men talking rubbed their hands as if to generate heat. Women cooking warmed their hands over the electric woks. In the corrugated-metal barracks, each with tiers of 144 metal and plywood bunks on which whole families spread their clothes and eating utensils and straw sleeping mats, mothers and children sat huddled in thin blankets. Outside one barrack a little boy about four years old pressed me to take a taste from his rice bowl. Another urinated against the side of the building.

After a few hours at Kai Tak East the intrinsic inertia and tedium of the camp day became vivid. Conversations in one part of the yard gave way only to conversations in another part of the yard. Preparations for one meal melted into preparations for the next. At the time I was in Hong Kong there were some three hundred thousand Vietnamese refugees, the largest number of whom were "ethnic Chinese", or Vietnamese of Chinese ancestry, waiting to be processed in improvised camps in the various countries around the South China Sea, in Hong Kong and Thailand and Malaysia and Macao and Indonesia and the Philippines. More than nine thousand of these were at Kai Tak East, and another fifteen thousand at Kai Tak North, the adjoining Red Cross camp. The details of any given passage from Vietnam to Hong Kong differed, but, in the case of the ethnic Chinese, the journey seemed typically to have begun with the payment of gold and the covert collusion of Vietnamese officials and Chinese syndicates outside Vietnam. The question was shadowy. Refugees were a business in this part of the world. Once in Hong Kong, any refugee who claimed to be Vietnamese underwent, before assignment to Kai Tak East or Kai Tak North or one of the other transit camps in the colony, an initial processing and screening by the Hong Kong police, mostly to establish that he or she was not an illegal immigrant from China looking to be relocated instead of repatriated, or, as they said in Hong Kong, "sent north". Only after this initial screening did refugees receive the yellow photographic identification cards that let them pass freely through the transit camp gates. The Vietnamese at Kai Tak East came and went all day, going out to work and out to market and out just to get out, but the perimeter of the camp was

141

marked by high chain-link fencing, and in some places by concertina wire. The gates were manned by private security officers. The yellow cards were scrutinized closely. "This way we know," a camp administrator told me, "that what we have here is a genuine case of refugee."

They were all waiting, these genuine cases of refugee, for the consular interview that might eventually mean a visa out, and the inert tension of life at Kai Tak East derived mainly from this aspect of waiting, of limbo, of suspended hopes and plans and relationships. Of the 11,573 Vietnamese who had passed through Kai Tak East since the camp opened, in June 1979, only some 2,000 had been, by December, relocated, the largest number of them to the United States and Canada. The rest waited, filled out forms, pretended fluency in languages they had barely heard spoken, and looked in vain for their names on the day's list of interviews. Every week or so a few more would be chosen to go, cut loose from the group and put on the truck and taken to the airport for a flight to a country they had never seen.

Six Vietnamese happened to be leaving Kai Tak East the day I was there, two sisters and their younger brother for Australia, and a father and his two sons for France. The three going to Australia were the oldest children of a family that had lost its home and business in the Cholon district of Saigon and been ordered to a "new economic zone", one of the supervised wastelands in the Vietnamese countryside where large numbers of ethnic Chinese were sent to live off the land and correct their thinking. The parents had paid gold, the equivalent of six ounces, to get these three children out of Saigon via Haiphong, and now the children hoped to earn enough money in Australia to get out their parents and younger siblings. The sisters, who were twenty-three and twenty-four, had no idea how long this would take or if it would be possible. They knew only that they were leaving Hong Kong with their brother on the evening Qantas. They were uncertain in what Australian city the evening Qantas landed, nor did it seem to matter.

I talked to the two girls for a while, and then to the man who was taking his sons to France. This man had paid the equivalent of twelve or thirteen ounces of gold to buy his family out of Hanoi. Because his wife and daughters had left Hanoi on a different day, and been assigned to a different Hong Kong camp, the family was to be, on this day, reunited for the first time in months. The wife and daughters would already be on the truck when it reached Kai Tak East. The truck would take them all to the airport and they would fly together to Nice, *"toute la famille"*. Toward noon, when the truck pulled up to the gate, the man rushed past the guards and leapt up to embrace a pretty woman. *"Ma femme!"* he cried out again and again to those of us watching from the yard. He pointed wildly, and maneuvered the woman and little girls into better view. *"Ma femme, mes filles!"*

I stood in the sun and waved until the truck left, then turned back to the yard. In many ways refugees had become an entrenched fact of Hong Kong life.

"They've got to go, there's no room for them here," a young Frenchwoman, Saigon born, had said to me at dinner the night before. Beside me in the yard a man sat motionless while a young woman patiently picked the nits from his hair. Across the yard a group of men and women watched without expression as the administrator posted the names of those selected for the next day's consular interviews. A few days later the *South China Morning Post* carried reports from intelligence sources that hundreds of boats were being assembled in Vietnamese ports to carry out more ethnic Chinese. The headline read, "HK Alert to New Invasion." It was believed that weather would not be favorable for passage to Hong Kong until the advent of the summer monsoon. Almost a dozen years later, the British government, which had agreed to relinquish Hong Kong to the Chinese in 1997, reached an accord with the government of Vietnam providing for the forcible repatriation of Hong Kong's remaining Vietnamese refugees. The flights back to Vietnam began in the fall of 1991. Some Vietnamese were photographed crying and resisting as they were taken to the Hong Kong airport. Hong Kong authorities stressed that the guards escorting the refugees were unarmed.

—1979–1991

Los Angeles Days

1

DURING ONE of the summer weeks I spent in
Los Angeles in 1988 there was a cluster of small earth-
quakes, the most noticeable of which, on the Garlock
Fault, a major lateral-slip fracture that intersects the
San Andreas in the Tehachapi range north of Los
Angeles, occurred at six minutes after four on a Friday
afternoon when I happened to be driving in Wilshire
Boulevard from the beach. People brought up to believe that the phrase "terra firma" has real meaning
often find it hard to understand the apparent equanimity with which earthquakes are accommodated in
California, and tend to write it off as regional spaci-
ness. In fact it is less equanimity than protective detachment, the useful adjustment commonly made in
circumstances so unthinkable that psychic survival
precludes preparation. I know very few people in California who actually set aside, as instructed, a week's
supply of water and food. I know fewer still who
could actually lay hands on the wrench required to
turn off, as instructed, the main gas valve; the scenario

145

in which this wrench will be needed is a catastrophe, and something in the human spirit rejects planning on a daily basis for catastrophe. I once interviewed, in the late sixties, someone who did prepare: a Pentecostal minister who had received a kind of heavenly earthquake advisory, and on its quite specific instructions was moving his congregation from Port Hueneme, north of Los Angeles, to Murfreesboro, Tennessee. A few months later, when a small earthquake was felt not in Port Hueneme but in Murfreesboro, an event so novel that it was reported nationally, I was, I recall, mildly gratified.

A certain fatalism comes into play. When the ground starts moving all bets are off. Quantification, which in this case takes the form of guessing where the movement at hand will rank on the Richter scale, remains a favored way of regaining the illusion of personal control, and people still crouched in the nearest doorjamb will reach for a telephone and try to call Caltech, in Pasadena, for a Richter reading. "Rock and roll," the D.J. said on my car radio that Friday afternoon at six minutes past four. "This console is definitely shaking . . . no word from Pasadena yet, is there?"

"I would say this is a three," the D.J.'s colleague said.

"Definitely a three, maybe I would say a little higher than a three."

"Say an eight . . . just joking."

"It felt like a six where I was."

What it turned out to be was a five-two, followed

by a dozen smaller aftershocks, and it had knocked out four of the six circuit breakers at the A. D. Edmonston pumping plant on the California Aqueduct, temporarily shutting down the flow of Northern California water over the Tehachapi range and cutting off half of Southern California's water supply for the weekend. This was all within the range not only of the predictable but of the normal. No one had been killed or seriously injured. There was plenty of water for the weekend in the system's four southern reservoirs, Pyramid, Castaic, Silverwood, and Perris lakes. A five-two earthquake is not, in California, where the movements people remember tend to have Richter numbers well over six, a major event, and the probability of earthquakes like this one had in fact been built into the Aqueduct: the decision to pump the water nineteen hundred feet over the Tehachapi was made precisely because the Aqueduct's engineers rejected the idea of tunneling through an area so geologically complex, periodically wrenched by opposing displacements along the San Andreas and the Garlock, that it has been called California's structural knot.

Still, this particular five-two, coming as it did when what Californians call "the Big One" was pretty much overdue (the Big One is the eight, the Big One is the seven in the wrong place or at the wrong time, the Big One could even be the six-five centered near downtown Los Angeles at nine on a weekday morning), made people a little uneasy. There was some concern through the weekend that this was not merely an ordinary five-two but a "foreshock", an earthquake pre-figuring a larger event (the chances of this, according to Caltech seismologists, run about one in twenty), and by Sunday there was what seemed to many people a sinister amount of activity on other faults: a three-four just east of Ontario at twenty-two minutes past two in the afternoon, a three-six twenty-two minutes later at Lake Berryessa, and, four hours and one minute later, northeast of San Jose, a five-five on the Calaveras Fault. On Monday, there was a two-three in Playa del Rey and a three in Santa Barbara.

Had it not been for the five-two on Friday, very few people would have registered these little quakes (the Caltech seismological monitors in Southern California normally record from twenty to thirty earth-quakes a day with magnitudes below three), and in the end nothing came of them, but this time people did register them, and they lent a certain moral gravity to the way the city happened to look that weekend, a temporal dimension to the hard white edges and empty golden light. At odd moments during the next few days people would suddenly clutch at tables, or walls. "Is it going," they would say, or "I think it's moving." They almost always said "it", and what they meant by "it" was not just the ground but the world as they knew it. I have lived all my life with the promise of the Big One, but when it starts going now even I get the jitters.

2

WHAT IS STRIKING about Los Angeles after a period away is how well it works. The famous freeways work, the supermarkets work (a visit, say, to the Pacific Palisades Gelson's, where the aisles are wide and the shelves full and checkout is fast and free of attitude, remains the zazen of grocery shopping), the beaches work. The 1984 Olympics were not supposed to work, but they did (daily warnings of gridlock and urban misery gave way, during the first week, to a county-wide block party, with pink and aquamarine flags fluttering over empty streets and parking spaces for once available even in Westwood); not only worked but turned a profit, of almost $223 million, about which there was no scandal. Even the way houses are bought and sold seems to work more efficiently than it does in New York (for all practical purposes there are no exclusive listings in Los Angeles, and the various contingencies on which closing the deal depends are arbitrated not by lawyers but by an escrow company), something that came to my attention when my husband and I arranged to have our Los Angeles house shown for the first time to brokers at eleven o'clock one Saturday morning, went out to do a few errands, and came back at one to find that we had three offers, one of them for appreciably more than the asking price.

Selling a house in two hours was not, in 1988 in Los Angeles, an entirely unusual experience. Around February of 1988, midway through what most people call the winter but Californians call the spring ("winter" in California is widely construed as beginning and ending with the Christmas season, reflecting a local preference for the upside), at a time when residential real estate prices in New York were already plunging in response to the October 1987 stock market crash, there had in fact developed on the west side of Los Angeles a heightened enthusiasm for committing large sums of money to marginal improvements in one's domestic situation: to moving, say, from what was called in the listings a "convertible 3" in Santa Monica (three bedrooms, one of which might be converted into a study) to a self-explanatory "4 + lib" in Brentwood Park, or to acquiring what was described in the listings as an "H/F pool", meaning heated and filtered, or a "N/S tennis court", meaning the preferred placement on the lot, the north-south orientation believed to keep sun from the players' eyes.

By June of 1988 a kind of panic had set in, of a kind that occurs periodically in Southern California but had last occurred in 1979. Multiple offers were commonplace, and deals stalled because bank appraisers could not assess sales fast enough to keep up with the rising market. Residential real estate offices were routinely reporting "record months". People were buying one- and two-million-dollar houses as investments, to give their adolescent children what brokers referred to as "a base in the market", which was one reason why small houses on modest lots priced at a million-four were getting, the day they were listed, thirty and forty offers.

All this seemed to assume an infinitely upward trend, and to be one of those instances in which the preoccupations and apprehensions of people in Los Angeles, a city in many ways predicated on the ability to deal with the future at a rather existential remove, did not exactly coincide with those of the country at large. October 19, 1987, which had so immediately affected the New York market that asking prices on some apartments had in the next three or four months dropped as much as a million dollars, seemed, in Los Angeles, not to have happened. Those California brokers to whom I talked, if they mentioned the crash at all, tended to see it as a catalyst for good times, an event that had emphasized the "real" in real estate.

The *Los Angeles Times* had taken to running, every Sunday, a chat column devoted mainly to the buying and selling of houses: Ruth Ryon's "Hot Property", from which one could learn that the highest price paid for a house in Los Angeles to that date was $20.25 million (by Marvin Davis, to Kenny Rogers, for The Knoll in Beverly Hills); that the $2.5 million paid in 1986 for 668 St. Cloud Road in Bel Air (by Earle Jorgenson and Holmes Tuttle and some eighteen other friends of President and Mrs. Reagan, for whom the house was bought and who rent it with an option to buy) was strikingly under value, since even an un-built acre in the right part of Bel Air (the house bought by the Reagans' friends is definitely in the right part of Bel Air) will sell for $3 million; and that two houses in the Reagans' new neighborhood sold recently for

151

$13.5 million and $14.75 million respectively. A typical "Hot Property" item ran this way:

> Newlyweds Tracey E. Bregman Recht, star of the daytime soap "The Young and the Restless", and her husband Ron Recht, a commercial real estate developer, just bought their first home, on 2.5 acres in a nifty neighborhood. They're just up the street from Merv Griffin's house (which I've heard is about to be listed at some astronomical price) and they're just down the street from Pickfair, now owned by Pia Zadora and her husband. The Rechts bought a house that was built in 1957 on San Ysidro Drive in Beverly Hills for an undisclosed price, believed to be several million dollars, and now they're fixing it up . . .

I spent some time, before this 1988 bull market broke, with two West Side brokers, Betty Budlong and Romelle Dunas of the Jon Douglas office, both of whom spoke about the going price of "anything at all" as a million dollars, and of "something decent" as two million dollars. "Right now I've got two clients in the price range of five to six hundred thousand dollars," Romelle Dunas said. "I sat all morning trying to think what I could show them today."

"I'd cancel the appointment," Betty Budlong said.

"I just sold their condo for four. I'm sick. The houses for five-fifty are smaller than their condo."

"I think you could still find something in Ocean Park," Betty Budlong said. "Ocean Park, Sunset Park, somewhere like that. Brentwood Glen, you know, over here, the Rattery tract . . . of course that's inching towards six."

"Inching toward six and you're living in the right lane of the San Diego Freeway," Romelle Dunas said.

"In seventeen hundred square feet," Betty Budlong said.

"If you're lucky. I saw one that was fifteen hundred square feet. I have a feeling when these people go out today they're not going to close on their condo."

Betty Budlong thought about this. "I think you should make a good friend of Sonny Fox," she said at last.

Sonny Fox was a Jon Douglas agent in Sherman Oaks, in the San Fernando Valley, only a twenty-minute drive from Beverly Hills on the San Diego Freeway but a twenty-minute drive toward which someone living on the West Side—even someone who would drive forty minutes to Malibu—was apt to display considerable sales resistance.

"In the Valley," Romelle Dunas said after a pause.

Betty Budlong shrugged. "In the Valley."

"People are afraid to get out of this market," Romelle Dunas said.

"They can't afford to get out," Betty Budlong said. "I know two people who in any other market would have sold their houses. One of them has accepted a job in Chicago, the other is in Washington for at least two years. They're both leasing their houses. Because until they're sure they're not coming back, they don't want to get out."

The notion that land will be worth more tomorrow

153

than it is worth today has been a real part of the California experience, and remains deeply embedded in the California mentality, but this seemed extreme, and it occurred to me that the buying and selling of houses was perhaps one more area in which the local capacity for protective detachment had come into play, that people capable of compartmentalizing the Big One might be less inclined than others to worry about getting their money out of a 4 + lib, H/F pool. I asked if foreign buyers could be pushing up the market.

Betty Budlong thought not. "These are people who are moving, say, from a seven-fifty house to a million-dollar house."

I asked if the market could be affected by a defense cutback.

Betty Budlong thought not. "Most of the people who buy on the West Side are professionals, or in the entertainment industry. People who work at Hughes and Douglas, say, don't live in Brentwood or Santa Monica or Beverly Hills."

I asked Betty Budlong if she saw anything at all that could affect the market.

"Tight money could affect this market," Betty Budlong said. "For a while."

"Then it always goes higher," Romelle Dunas said.

"Which is why people can't afford to get out," Betty Budlong said.

"They couldn't get back in," Romelle Dunas said.

3

THIS ENTIRE QUESTION of houses and what they were worth (and what they should be worth, and what it meant when the roof over someone's head was also his or her major asset) was, during the spring and summer of 1988, understandably more on the local mind than it perhaps should have been, which was one reason why a certain house then under construction just west of the Los Angeles Country Club became the focus of considerable attention, and of emotions usually left dormant on the west side of Los Angeles. The house was that being built by the television producer ("Dynasty", "Loveboat", "Fantasy Island") Aaron Spelling and his wife Candy at the corner of Mapleton and Club View in Holmby Hills, on six acres the Spellings had bought in 1983, for $10,250,000, from Patrick Frawley, the chairman of Schick.

At the time of the purchase there was already a fairly impressive house on the property, a house once lived in by Bing Crosby, but the Spellings, who had become known for expansive domestic gestures (crossing the country in private railroad cars, for example, and importing snow to Beverly Hills for their children's Christmas parties), had decided that the Crosby/Frawley house was what is known locally as a teardown. The progress of the replacement, which was rising from the only residential site I have ever seen with a two-story contractor's office and a sign reading CONSTRUCTION AREA: HARD HATS REQUIRED, became over the next several months not just a form of popular entertainment but, among inhabitants of a city without much common experience, a unifying, even a political, idea.

At first the project was identified, on the kind of site sign usually reserved for office towers in progress, as "THE MANOR"; later "THE MANOR" was modified to what seemed, given the resemblance of the structure to a resort Hyatt, the slightly nutty discretion of "594 SOUTH MAPLETON DRIVE". It was said that the structure ("house" seemed not entirely to cover it) would have 56,500 square feet. It was said that the interior plan would include a bowling alley, and 560 square feet of extra closet space, balconied between the second and the attic floors. It was said, by the owner, that such was the mass of the steel frame construction that to break up the foundation alone would take a demolition crew six months, and cost from four to five million dollars.

Within a few months the site itself had become an established attraction, and evening drive-bys were enlivened by a skittish defensiveness on the part of the guards, who would switch on the perimeter floods and light up the steel girders and mounded earth like a prison yard. The *Los Angeles Times* and *Herald Examiner* published periodic reports on and rumors about the job ("Callers came out of the woodwork yesterday in the wake of our little tale about Candy Spelling having the foundation of her $45-million mansion-in-progress lowered because she didn't want to see the Robinson's department store sign from where her bed-to-be was to sit"), followed by curiously provocative corrections, or "denials", from Aaron Spelling. "The only time Candy sees the Robinson's sign is when she's shopping" was one correction that got everyone's attention, but in many ways the most compelling was this: "They say we have an Olympic-sized swimming pool. Not true. There's no gazebo, no guesthouse. . . . When people go out to dinner, unless they talk about their movies, they have nothing else to talk about, so they single out Candy."

In that single clause, "unless they talk about their movies", there was hidden a great local truth, and the inchoate heart of the matter: this house was, in the end, that of a television producer, and people who make movies did not, on the average evening, have dinner with people who make television. People who make television had most of the money, but people who make movies still had most of the status, and believed themselves the keepers of the community's unspoken code, of the rules, say, about what constituted excess on the housing front. This was a distinction usually left tacit, but the fact of the Spelling house was making people say things out loud. "There are people in this town worth hundreds of millions of dollars," Richard Zanuck, one of the most successful motion picture producers in the business, once said to my husband, "and they can't get a table at Chasen's." This was a man whose father had run a studio and who had himself run a studio, and his bewilderment was that of someone who had uncovered an anomaly in the wheeling of the stars.

4

WHEN PEOPLE in Los Angeles talk about "this town", they do not mean Los Angeles, nor do they exactly mean what many of them call "the community". "The community" is more narrowly defined, and generally confined to those inhabitants of this town who can be relied upon to sit at one another's tables on approved evenings (benefiting the American Film Institute, say) and to get one another's daughters into approved schools, say Westlake, in Holmby Hills, not far from the Spellings' house but on eleven acres rather than six. People in the community meet one another for lunch at Hillcrest, but do not, in the main, attend Friars' Club Roasts. People in the community sojourn with their children in Paris, and Aspen, and at the Kahala Hilton in Honolulu, but visit Las Vegas only on business. "The community" is made up of people who can, in other words, get a table at Chasen's.

"This town" is broader, and means just "the industry", which is the way people who make television and motion pictures refer, tellingly, to the environment in which they work. The extent to which the industry in question resembles conventional industries is often obscured by its unconventional product, which requires that its "workers" perform in unconventional ways, for which they are paid unconventional sums of money: some people do make big money writing and directing and producing and acting in television, and some people also make big money, although considerably less big, writing and directing and producing and acting in motion pictures.

Still, as in other entrepreneurial enterprises, it is not those who work on the line in this industry but those who manage it who make the biggest money of all, and who tend to have things their way, which is what the five-month 1988 Writers Guild of America strike, which had become by the time of its settlement in early August 1988 perhaps the most acrimonious union strike in recent industry history, was initially and finally about. It was not about what were inflexibly referred to by both union and management as "the so-called creative issues", nor was it exclusively about the complicated formulas and residuals that were the tokens on the board. It was about respect, and about whether the people who made the biggest money were or were not going to give a little to the people who made the less big money.

In other words, it was a class issue, which was hard for people outside the industry—who in the first place did not understand the essentially adversarial nature of the business (a good contract, it is understood in Hollywood, is one that ensures the other party's breach) and in the second place believed everybody involved to be overpaid—to entirely understand. "Whose side does one take in such a war—that of the writers with their scads of money, or that of the producers with their tons of money?" the *Washington Post*'s television reporter, Tom Shales, demanded (as it turned out, rhetorically) in a June 29, 1988, piece

159

arguing that the writers were "more interested in strutting and swaggering than in reaching a settlement", that "a handful of hotheads" who failed to realize that "the salad days are over" were bringing down an industry beset by "dwindling" profits, and that the only effect of the strike was to crush "those in the lowest-paying jobs", for example a waitress, laid off when Universal shut down its commissary, who Tom Shales perceived to be "not too thrilled with the writers and their grievances" when he saw her interviewed on a television newscast. (This was an example of what became known locally during the strike as "the little people argument", and referred to the traditional practice among struck companies of firing their nonunion hostages. When hard times come to Hollywood, the typing pool goes first, and is understood to symbolize the need of the studio to "cut back", or "slash costs".) "Just because the producers are richer doesn't mean the writers are right. Or righteous," Tom Shales concluded. "These guys haven't just seen too many Rambo movies, they've written too many Rambo movies."

This piece, which reflected with rather impressive fidelity the arguments then being made by the Alliance of Motion Picture and Television Producers, the negotiating body for management, was typical of most coverage of the strike, and also of what had become, by early summer of 1988, the prevailing mood around town. Writers have never been much admired in Hollywood. In an industry predicated on social fluidity, on the daily calibration and reassessment of status and power, screenwriters, who perform a function that remains only dimly understood even by the people who hire them, occupy a notably static place: even the most successful of them have no real power, and therefore no real status. "I can always get a writer," Ray Stark once told my husband, who had expressed a disinclination to join the team on a Stark picture for which he had been, Ray Stark had told him a few weeks before, "the only possible writer".

Writers (even the only possible writers), it is universally believed, can always be replaced, which is why they are so frequently referred to in the plural. Writers, it is believed by many, are even best replaced, hired serially, since they bring, in this view, only a limited amount of talent and energy to bear on what directors often call their "vision". A number of directors prefer to hire fresh writers—usually writers with whom they have previously worked—just before shooting: Sydney Pollack, no matter who wrote the picture he is directing, has the habit of hiring for the period just before and during production David Rayfiel or Elaine May or Kurt Luedtke. "I want it in the contract when David Rayfiel comes in," a writer I know once said when he and Pollack were talking about doing a picture together; this was a practical but unappreciated approach.

The previous writer on a picture is typically described as "exhausted", or "worn-out on this". What is meant by "this" is the task at hand, which is seen as narrow and technical, one color in the larger vision, a matter of taking notes from a producer or an actor or

161

a director, and adding dialogue—something, it is understood, that the producer or actor or director could do without a writer, if only he or she had the time, if only he or she were not required to keep that larger vision in focus. "I've got the ideas," one frequently hears in the industry. "All I need is a writer."

Such "ideas", when explored, typically tend toward the general ("relationships between men and women", say, or "rebel without a cause in the west Valley"), and the necessity for paying a writer to render such ideas specific remains a source of considerable resentment. Writers are generally seen as balky, obstacles to the forward flow of the project. They take time. They want money. They are typically the first element on a picture, the people whose job it is to invent a world sufficiently compelling to interest actors and directors, and, as the first element, they are often unwilling to recognize the necessity for keeping the front money down, for cutting their fees in order to get a project going. "Everyone", they are told, is taking a cut ("everyone" in this instance generally means every one of the writers), yet they insist on "irresponsible" fees. A director who gets several million dollars a picture will often complain, quite bitterly, about being "held up" by the demands of his writers. "You're haggling over pennies," a director once complained to me.

This resentment surfaces most openly in contract negotiations ("We don't give points to writers," studio business-affairs lawyers will say in a negotiation, or, despite the fact that a writer has often delivered one or two drafts on the basis of a deal memo alone, "Our policy is no payment without a fully executed contract"), but in fact suffuses every aspect of life in the community. Writers do not get gross from dollar one, nor do they get the Thalberg Award, nor do they even determine when and where a meeting will take place: these are facts of local life known even to children. Writers who work regularly live comfortably, but not in the houses with the better N/S courts. Writers sometimes get to Paris on business, but rarely on the Concorde. Writers occasionally have lunch at Hillcrest, but only when their agents take them. Writers have at best a provisional relationship with the community in which they live, which is precisely what has made them, over the years, such convenient pariahs. "Fuck 'em, they're weaklings," as one director I know said about the Guild.

As the strike wore on, then, a certain natural irritation, even a bellicosity, was bound to surface when the subject of the writers (or, as some put it, "the writers and their so-called demands") came up, as was an impatience with the whole idea of collective bargaining. "If you're good enough, you can negotiate your own contract," I recall being told by one director. It was frequently suggested that the strike was supported only by those members of the Guild who were not full-time working writers. "A lot of them aren't writers," an Alliance spokesman told the *Los Angeles Times*. "They pay their one-hundred-dollar-a-year dues and get invitations to screenings." A television producer suggested to me that perhaps the answer was "another guild," one that would function, although he did not say this, as a sweetheart union. "A guild for working writers," he said. "That's a guild we could negotiate with."

I heard repeatedly during the strike that I, as a member of the Guild "but an intelligent person", had surely failed to understand what "the leadership" of the Guild was doing to me; when I said that I did understand it, that I had lost three pictures during the course of the strike and would continue to vote against a settlement until certain money issues had been resolved, I was advised that such intransigence would lead nowhere, because "the producers won't budge", because "they're united on this", because "they're going to just write off the Guild", and because, an antic note, "they're going to start hiring college kids —they're even going to start hiring journalists".

In this mounting enthusiasm to punish the industry's own writers by replacing them "even" with journalists ("Why not air traffic controllers?" said a writer to whom I mentioned this threat), certain facts about the strike receded early into the mists of claim and counterclaim. Many people preferred to believe that, as Tom Shales summarized it, the producers had "offered increases", and that the writers had "said they were not enough". In fact the producers had offered, on the key points in the negotiation, rollbacks on a residual payment structure established in 1985, when the WGA contract had been last negotiated. Many people preferred to believe, as Tom Shales seemed to believe, that it was the writers, not the producers, who were refusing to negotiate. In fact the strike had been, from the Alliance's "last and final offer" on March 6, 1988, until a federal mediator called both sides to meet on May 23, 1988, less a strike than a lockout, with the producers agreeing to attend only a single meeting, on April 8, which lasted twenty minutes before the Alliance negotiators walked out. "It looks like the writers are shooting the whole industry in the foot—and they're doing it willfully and stupidly," Grant Tinker, the television producer and former chairman of NBC, told the *Los Angeles Times* after the Guild rejected, by a vote of 2,789 to 933, the June version of the Alliance's series of "last and final" offers. "It's just pigheaded and stupid for the writers to have so badly misread what's going on here."

What was going on here was interesting. This had not been an industry unaccustomed to labor disputes, nor had it been one, plans to hire "journalists" notwithstanding, historically hospitable to outsiders. ("We don't go for strangers in Hollywood," Cecilia Brady said in *The Last Tycoon;* this remains the most succinct description I know of the picture business.) For reasons deep in the structure of the industry, writers' strikes have been a fixed feature of local life, and gains earned by the writers have traditionally been passed on to the other unions—who themselves strike only rarely—in a fairly inflexible ratio: for every dollar in residuals the Writers Guild gets, another dollar goes to the Directors Guild, three dollars go to the Screen Actors Guild, and eight or nine dollars go to IATSE, the principal craft union, which needs the

165

higher take because its pension and health benefits, unlike those of the other unions, are funded entirely from residuals. "So when the WGA negotiates for a dollar increase in residuals, say, the studios don't think just a dollar, they think twelve or thirteen," a former Guild president told me. "The industry is a kind of family, and its members are interdependent."

Something new was at work, and it had to do with a changed attitude among the top executives. I recall being told, quite early in this strike, by someone who had been a studio head of production and had bargained for management in previous strikes, that this strike would be different, and in many ways unpredictable. The problem, he said, was the absence at the bargaining table of "a Lew Wasserman, an Arthur Krim". Lew Wasserman, the chairman of MCA-Universal, it is said in the industry, was always looking for the solution; as he grew less active, Arthur Krim, at United Artists, and to a lesser extent Ted Ashley, at Warner Brothers, fulfilled this function, which was essentially that of the *consigliere*. "The guys who are running the studios now, they don't deal," he said. "Sid Sheinberg bargaining for Universal, Barry Diller for Fox, that's ridiculous. They won't even talk. As far as the Disney guys go, Eisner, Katzenberg, they play hardball, that's the way they run their operation."

Roger Fisher, the Williston Professor of Law at Harvard Law School and director of the Harvard Negotiation Project, suggested, in an analysis of the strike published in the *Los Angeles Times*, that what had been needed between management and labor in this case was "understanding, two-way communication, reliability, and acceptance", the very qualities that natural selection in the motion picture industry had tended to eliminate. It was in fact June of 1988, three months into the strike, before the people running the studios actually entered the negotiating sessions, which they referred to, significantly, as "downtime". "I talked to Diller, Mancuso, Daly," I was told by one of the two or three most powerful agents in the industry. He meant Barry Diller at Twentieth Century-Fox and Frank Mancuso at Paramount and Robert Daly at Warner Brothers. "I said look, you guys, you want this thing settled, you better indicate you're taking it seriously enough to put in the downtime yourselves. Sheinberg [Sidney Sheinberg of MCA-Universal] and Mancuso have kind of emerged as the point players for management, but you've got to remember, these guys are all prima donnas, they hate each other, so it was a big problem presenting a sufficiently united front to put somebody out there speaking for all of them."

In the context of an industry traditionally organized, like a mob family, around principles of discretion and unity, this notion of the executive as prima donna was a new phenomenon, and not one tending toward an appreciation of the "interdependence" of unions and management. It did not work toward the settlement of this strike that the main players on one side of the negotiations were themselves regarded as stars, the subjects of fan profiles, pieces often written by people who admired and wanted to work in the industry. Michael Eisner of Disney had been on the cover of *Time*. Sidney Sheinberg of Universal had been on the cover of *Manhattan, inc*. Executive foibles had been detailed (Jeffrey Katzenberg of Disney "guzzled" Diet Coke, and "sold his Porsche after he almost killed himself trying to shift gears and dial at the same time"), as had, and this presented a problem, company profits and executive compensation. Nineteen eighty-seven net profit for Warner Communications was up 76.6 percent over 1986. Nineteen eighty-seven net profit for Paramount was up 130 percent over 1986. CBS was up 21 percent, ABC 53 percent. The chairman and CEO of Columbia, Victor Kaufman, received in 1987 $826,154 in salary and an additional $1,506,142 in stock options and bonuses. Michael Eisner was said to have received, including options and bonuses, a figure that ranged from $23 million (this was Disney's own figure) to more than $80 million (this was what the number of shares involved in the stock options seemed to suggest), but was most often given as $63 million.

During a season when management was issuing white papers explaining the "new, colder realities facing the entertainment industry", this last figure in particular had an energizing effect on the local consciousness, and was frequently mentioned in relation to another figure, that for the combined total received in residual payments by all nine thousand members of the Writers Guild. This figure was $58 million, which, against Michael Eisner's $63, made it

hard for many people to accept the notion that residual rollbacks were entirely imperative. Trust seemed
lacking, as did a certain mutuality of interest. "We
used to sit across the table from people we had personally worked with on movies," I was told by a writer
who had sat in on negotiating sessions during this and
past strikes. "These people aren't movie people. They
think like their own business-affairs lawyers. You take
somebody like Jeff Katzenberg, he has a very ideological position. He said the other night, 'I'm speaking as
a dedicated capitalist. I own this screenplay. So why
should I hand anybody else the right to have any say
about it?' "

In June of 1988, three months into the strike, it was
said around Los Angeles that the strike was essentially
over, because the producers said it was over, and that
the only problem remaining was to find a way for the
Guild negotiators to save face—"a bone", as Jeffrey
Katzenberg was said to be calling it, to throw the
writers. "This has largely come down to a question of
how Brian will look," I was told that month by someone close to management. He was talking about Brian
Walton, the Guild's executive director and chief negotiator. "It's a presentation problem, a question of
giving him something he can present to the membership, after fifteen weeks, as something approaching
win-win." It was generally conceded that the producers, despite disavowals, were determined to break the
union; even the disavowals, focusing as they did on

169

the useful clerical work done by the Guild ("If the Guild didn't exist we'd have to invent it," Sidney Sheinberg said at one point), suggested that what the producers had in mind was less a union than a trade association. It was taken for granted that it was not the producers but the writers who, once the situation was correctly "presented", would give in. "Let's get this town back to work," people were saying, and "This strike has to end."

Still, this strike did not end. By late July, it was said around Los Angeles that the negotiations once again in progress were not really negotiations at all; that "they" were meeting only because a federal mediator had ordered them to meet, and that the time spent at the table was just that, time spent at a table, downtime. Twenty-one writers had announced their intention of working in spite of the strike, describing this decision as evidence of "the highest form of loyalty" to the Guild. "What's it for?" people were saying, and "This is lose-lose."

"Writers are children," Monroe Stahr had said almost half a century before, in *The Last Tycoon*, by way of explaining why his own negotiations with the Writers Guild had reached, after a year, a dead end. "They are not equipped for authority. There is no substitute for will. Sometimes you have to fake will when you don't feel it at all. . . . So I've had to take an attitude in this Guild matter." In the end, the attitude once again was taken and once again prevailed. "This strike has run out of gas," people began to say, and "This is ridiculous, this is enough," as if the writers were not

only children but bad children, who had been hu-
mored too long. "We've gotten to the end of the road
and hit a brick wall," the negotiator for the Alliance
of Motion Picture and Television Producers, J. Nich-
olas Counter III, said on the Sunday afternoon of July
31, 1988, at a press conference called by the Alliance
to announce that negotiations with the Writers Guild
were at an end, "hopelessly" deadlocked. "I suggest
it's time for Mr. Walton to look to himself for the
answer as to why his guild is still on strike," Jeffrey
Katzenberg said that afternoon to Aljean Harmetz of
the *New York Times*. That evening, Jeffrey Katzenberg
and the other executives of the major studios met with
Kenneth Ziffren, a prominent local lawyer who represented several Guild members who, because they
had television production companies, had a particular
interest in ending the strike; the marginally different
formulas suggested by Kenneth Ziffren seemed to
many the bone they had been looking for: a way of
solving "the presentation problem", of making the
strike look, now that the writers understood that it
had run out of gas, "like something approaching win-
win". On the following Sunday, August 7, 1988, the
Guild membership voted to end the strike, on essentially the same terms it had turned down in June.

During the five months of the dispute many people
outside the industry had asked me what the strike was
about, and I had heard myself talk about ancillary
markets and about the history of pattern bargaining,

171

about the "issues", but the dynamic of the strike, the particular momentum that kept several thousand people with not much in common voting for at least a while against what appeared to be their own best interests, had remained hard to explain. The amounts of money to be gained or lost had seemed, against the money lost during the course of the strike, insignificant. The "creative" issues, the provisions that touched on the right of the writer to have some say in the production, would have been, if won, unenforceable.

Yet I had been for the strike, and felt toward that handful of writers who had declared their intention to desert it, and by so doing encouraged the terms on which it would end, a coolness bordering on distaste, as if we had gone back forty years, and they had named names. "You need to have worked in the industry," I would say by way of explanation, or "You have to live there." Not until July of 1988, at the Democratic National Convention in Atlanta, did the emotional core of the strike come clear to me. I had gone to Atlanta in an extra-industry role, that of "reporter" (or, as we say in Hollywood, "journalist"), with credentials that gave me a seat in the Omni but access to only a rotating pass to go on the floor. I was waiting for this rotating pass one evening when I ran into a director I knew, Paul Mazursky. We talked for a moment, and I noticed that he, like all the other industry people I saw in Atlanta, had a top pass, one of the several all-access passes. In this case it was a floor pass, and, since I was working and he seemed not about to go on the floor, I asked if I might borrow it for half an hour.

He considered this.

He would, he said, "really like" to do this for me, but thought not. He seemed surprised that I had asked, and uncomfortable that I had breached the natural order of the community as we both knew it: directors and actors and producers, I should have understood, have floor passes. Writers do not, which is why they strike.

—1988

Down at City Hall

JUST INSIDE the main lobby of City Hall in Los Angeles there was for some time a curious shrine to Tom Bradley, the seventy-one-year-old black former police officer who was in April of 1989 elected to his fifth four-year term as mayor of Los Angeles. There was an Olympic flag, suspended behind glass and lit reverentially, its five interlocking rings worked in bright satin. There were, displayed in a kind of architectural niche, various other mementos of the 1984 Los Angeles Olympics, the event that remained the symbolic centerpiece not only of Tom Bradley's sixteen-year administration (arriving passengers at LAX, for example, were for some years after 1984 confronted on the down escalators by large pictures of Mayor Bradley and the somewhat unsettling legend "Welcome to Los Angeles XXIII Olympiad", as if the plane had touched down in a time warp), but of what Bradley's people liked to present as the city's ascension, under his guidance, to American capital of the Pacific rim.

And there was, behind a crimson silk rope, a sheet of glass on which a three-dimensional holographic image of Tom Bradley, telephone to ear, appeared and disappeared. If the viewer moved to the right, the mayor could be seen to smile; if the viewer moved to the left, the mayor turned grave, and lowered his head to study a paper. From certain angles the mayor vanished altogether, leaving only an eerie blue. It was this disappearing effect, mirroring as it did what many saw as a certain elusiveness about the mayor himself, that most often arrested the passing citizen. "That's the shot on the Jackson endorsement," I recall a television cameraman saying as we passed this dematerializing Tom Bradley one afternoon in June of 1988, a few days before the California presidential primary, on our way from a press conference during which the actual Tom Bradley had successfully, and quite characteristically, managed to appear with Jesse Jackson without in the least recommending him.

In fact it seemed the shot on the entire Bradley administration, the enduring electability of which was something many people in Los Angeles found hard to define, or even to talk about. "I don't think Tom Bradley is beatable," I was told not long before the 1989 mayoralty election by Zev Yaroslavsky, a Los Angeles City Council member who ran an abortive campaign against Bradley in 1985 and aborted a second campaign against him in January of 1989. "At least not by me. His personal popularity transcends the fact that he has been presiding over a city that in some aspects has been experiencing serious difficulties during his term in office. Most people agree that we've got this traffic, that air quality stinks, that they see a hundred

175

and one things wrong with the quality of life. But nobody blames him for it."

In part because of this perceived ability to float free of his own administration and in part because of his presumed attractiveness to black voters, Tom Bradley was over the years repeatedly mentioned, usually in the same clause with Andrew Young, as a potential national figure, even a vice-presidential possibility. This persistent white fantasy to one side, Tom Bradley was never a charismatic, or even a particularly comfortable, candidate. His margin in the April 1989 election, for which a large majority of Los Angeles voters did not bother even to turn out, was surprisingly low. His votes never traveled outside Los Angeles. He twice tried, in 1982 and in 1986, to become governor of California, and was twice defeated by George Deukmejian, not himself noted for much sparkle as a candidate.

Bradley's strength in Los Angeles did not derive exclusively or even principally from the black community, which, in a city where the fastest-growing ethnic groups were Asian and Hispanic, constituted a decreasing percentage of the population and in any case had come to vote for Bradley, who was the first black ever elected to the Los Angeles City Council, grudgingly at best. One city official to whom I spoke during the 1989 campaign pointed out that when Bradley last ran for governor, there was a falling off in even those low-income black precincts in south-central Los Angeles that had previously been, however unenthusiastically, his territory. "He assumed south-central would be there for him," she said. "And so he didn't work it. And having been taken for granted, it wasn't there."

"He is probably less liked in south-central than other elected officials who represent south-central," another city official conceded. "I mean they view him as somebody who is maybe more interested in wining and dining Prince Andrew and Princess Sarah or whatever her name is than in dealing with the crumbling floor in the Nickerson Gardens gymnasium."

Nickerson Gardens was a housing project in Watts, where people may vote but tended not to bid on city contracts, tended not to exhibit interest in the precise location of proposed freeway exits, tended not to have projects that could be made "important" to the mayor because they were "important" to them; tended not, in other words, to require the kind of access that generates contributions to a campaign. Tom Bradley was an access politician in the traditional mold. "We would be rather disappointed if, having supported him, he were inaccessible to us," Eli Broad, a longtime Bradley supporter and the chairman of Kaufman & Broad, told the *Los Angeles Times* during the summer of 1988. "It's not really a quid pro quo. [But] there's no question that . . . if someone . . . wants money for the campaign, and if you want to talk to them six months later and don't hear from them, you just don't give any more."

Kaufman & Broad was at that time the largest builder of single-family houses in California, the developer and builder of such subdivisions as Cali-

177

fornia Dawn ("From $108,990, 2, 3, and 4 Bedroom Homes"), California Esprit ("From the low $130,000s, 3 and 4 Bedroom Homes"), and California Gallery ("From $150,000, 3 and 4 Bedroom Homes"). California Dawn, California Esprit, and California Gallery were all in Palmdale, on the Mojave desert, an hour and a half northeast of Los Angeles. According to the final report of the Los Angeles 2000 Committee, a group appointed by Mayor Bradley to recommend a development strategy for the city, the Los Angeles Department of Airports was reviving a languishing plan to build an international airport on 17,750 acres the city happened to own six miles from the center of Palmdale.

The notion of building a Palmdale airport, first proposed in 1968 and more or less dormant since the midseventies, had met, over the years, considerable resistance, not the least of which derived from an almost total disinclination on the part of both carriers and passengers to go to Palmdale. But the possibilities were clear at the outset. There would be first of all the acquisition of the 17,750 acres (which would ultimately cost the city about $100 million to buy and to maintain), and the speculative boom that would accompany any such large-scale public acquisition. There would be the need for a highway project, estimated early on at another $100 million, to link Palmdale with the population. There could even be the eventual possibility of a $1.5 billion mountain tunnel, cutting the distance roughly in half. The construction of a monorail could be investigated. The creation of a foreign-trade zone could be studied. There would be the demand not only for housing (as in California Dawn, California Esprit, and California Gallery) but for schools, shopping centers, aircraft-related industry.

This hypothetical Palmdale International Airport, then, had survived as that ideal civic project, the one that just hangs in there, sometimes a threat, sometimes a promise, in either case a money machine. Here was the way the machine worked: with the encouragement of interested investors and an interested city government, the city would eventually reach Palmdale, and the Palmdale International Airport would reach critical mass, at which point many possibilities would be realized and many opportunities generated, both for development and for the access required to facilitate that development. This has been the history of Los Angeles.

Tom Bradley turned up in June of 1988 at a dinner dance honoring Eli Broad. He turned up in September of 1988 as a speaker at a party celebrating Kaufman & Broad's thirtieth anniversary. Bradley's most useful tool as a campaigner may well have been this practice of turning up wherever a supporter or potential supporter asked him to turn up, an impassive and slightly baffling stranger at bar mitzvahs and anniversary cocktail parties and backyard barbecues. "It is just something that I do because I enjoy it," Bradley told the *Los Angeles Times* in the summer of 1988 about another such event, a neighborhood barbecue at the South El Monte home of one of his planning commissioners. "I showed up and I tell you, you've never seen a happier couple in your life than that man and his wife. And the whole family was there. . . . As we were out in the front yard chatting or taking pictures, everybody who drove by was honking and waving. It was important to him. He enjoyed that. And I enjoyed his enjoyment. I get a pleasure out of that."

This fairly impenetrable style was often referred to locally as "low-keyed", or "conciliatory", which seemed in context to be code words for staying out of the way, not making waves, raising the money and granting the access the money is meant to secure. Tom Bradley was generally regarded as a pro-business, pro-development mayor, a supporter of the kinds of redevelopment and public works projects that tend, however problematical their ultimate public benefit, to suggest considerable opportunity to the kinds of people who are apt to support one or another political campaign. He was often credited with having built the downtown skyline, which translated roughly into having encouraged developers to think of downtown Los Angeles, which was until his tenure a rather somnolent financial district enlivened by the fact that it was also *el centro*, the commercial core of the Mexican and Central American communities, as bulldozable, a raw canvas to be rendered indistinguishable from Atlanta or Houston.

Bradley was redeveloping Watts. He was redeveloping Hollywood. He was redeveloping, in all, more than seven thousand acres around town. He was building—in a city so decentralized as to render conventional mass transit virtually useless and at a time when big transit projects had been largely discredited (one transportation economist had demonstrated that San Francisco's BART system must operate for 535 years before the energy presumably saved by its use catches up with the energy expended on its construction)—one of the world's most expensive mass-transit projects: $3.5 billion for the projected twenty miles of track, from downtown through Hollywood and over Cahuenga Pass to the San Fernando Valley, that would constitute the system's "first phase" and "second phase". This route was one that, according to the project's opponents, could serve at maximum use only 1.5 percent of the work force; most of that 1.5 percent, however, either lived or worked in the heart of the Hollywood Redevelopment. "You go out to where the houses stop and buy land," Bob Hope is supposed to have said when he was asked how he made so much money. This is, in Los Angeles, one way to make money, and the second is to buy land on which the houses have already been built, and get the city to redevelop it.

Metrorail and the Hollywood Redevelopment were of course big projects, major ways of creating opportunity. The true Bradley style was perhaps most apparent when the opportunities were small, for example in the proposal during the spring of 1989 to sell a thirty-five-year-old public housing project, Jordan Downs, to a private developer. Jordan Downs was in Watts, south-central. The price asked for Jordan Downs was reported to be around $10 million. The deal was to include a pledge by the prospective buyer to spend an additional $14 million renovating the project.

Now. When we talk about Jordan Downs we are talking about seven hundred rental units in a virtual war zone, an area where the median family income was $11,427 and even children carried AK-47s. Presented with a developer who wants to spend $24 million to take on the very kind of property that owners all over the country are trying, if not to torch, at least to abandon, the average urban citizen looks for subtext. The subtext in this instance was not hard to find: Jordan Downs was a forty-acre piece of property, only 15 percent of which was developed. This largely undeveloped property bordered both the Century Freeway, which was soon to be completed, and the Watts Redevelopment. In other words the property would very soon, if all went as planned, vastly increase in value, and 85 percent of it would be in hand, available either for resale or for development.

Nor was the developed 15 percent of the property, Jordan Downs itself, the problem it might have seemed at first glance. The project, it turned out, would have to be maintained as low-income rental housing for an estimated period of at most fifteen years, during which time the developer stood in any case to receive, from the federal Department of Housing and Urban Development and the city housing authority, a guaranteed subsidy of $420,000 a month plus federal tax credits estimated at $1.6 million a year. This was the kind of small perfect deal—nobody is actually hurt by it, unless the nobody happens to be a tenant at Jordan Downs, and unable to pay the rent required to make the property break even—that has traditionally been the mother's milk of urban politics. But many people believed Los Angeles to be different, and in one significant aspect it was: the difference in Los Angeles was that very few of its citizens seemed to notice the small perfect deals, or, if they did notice, to much care.

It was believed for a while during 1988 in Los Angeles that Zev Yaroslavsky, who represented the largely west-side and affluent Fifth District in the Los Angeles City Council (the Fifth includes, in the basin, Beverly-Fairfax, Century City, Bel Air, Westwood, and part of West Los Angeles, and, in the San Fernando Valley, parts of Sherman Oaks, Van Nuys, and North Hollywood), could beat Bradley. It was, people said, "Zev's year". It was said to be "time for Zev". It was to be, Zev Yaroslavsky himself frequently said, "an election about who runs Los Angeles", meaning do a handful of developers run it or do the rest of the citizens run it. He had raised almost $2 million. He had gained the support of a number of local players who had previously backed Bradley, including Marc Nathanson, the chairman of Falcon Cable TV, and Barry Diller, the chairman of Twentieth Century-Fox. He had flat-out won what many saw as an exhibition game for the mayoralty race: a showdown, in November of 1988, between Armand Hammer's Occidental Petroleum Corporation, which had wanted since 1966 to begin drilling for oil on two acres it was holding across the Pacific Coast Highway from Will Rogers State Beach, and the many people who did not want—and had so far, through a series of legal maneuvers, managed to prevent—this drilling.

The showdown took the form of placing opposing propositions, one co-sponsored by Zev Yaroslavsky and the other by an Occidental front calling itself the Los Angeles Public and Coastal Protection Committee, before the voters on the November 8, 1988, ballot. The Los Angeles Public and Coastal Protection Committee had some notable talent prepared to labor on its behalf. It had the support of Mayor Bradley. It would have, by the eve of the election, the endorsement of the *Los Angeles Times*. It had not only Armand Hammer's own attorney, Arthur Groman, but also, and perhaps most importantly, Mickey Kantor, of Manatt, Phelps, Rothenberg, and Phillips, a law firm so deeply connected to Democratic power in California that most people believed Bradley to be backing the Occidental proposition not for Armand Hammer but for Manatt. It had Robert Shrum, of Doak & Shrum, who used to write speeches for Ted Kennedy but was now running campaigns in California. It had, above all, $7.3 million, $7.1 million of it provided directly by Occidental.

There was considerable opacity about this entire

endeavor. In the first place, the wording of the Los Angeles Public and Coastal Protection Committee (or Occidental) proposition tended to equate a vote for drilling with a vote for more efficient crime fighting, for more intensive drug-busting, for better schools, and for the cleanup of toxic wastes, all of which were floated as part of Occidental's dedication to public and coastal protection. In the second place, the players themselves had kept changing sides. On the side of the antidrilling proposition there was of course its co-author, Zev Yaroslavsky, but Zev Yaroslavsky had backed Occidental when the drilling question came before the City Council in 1978. On the side of the Occidental proposition there was of course Tom Bradley, but Tom Bradley had first been elected mayor, in 1973, on an anti-Occidental platform, and in 1978 he had vetoed drilling on the Pacific Coast Highway site after the City Council approved it.

During the summer and fall of 1988, when the drilling and the antidrilling propositions were placed fairly insistently before the voters, there were seventeen operating oil fields around town, with tens of thousands of wells. There were more wells along the highways leading north and south. Oil was being pumped from the Beverly Hills High School campus. Oil was being pumped from the golf course at the Hillcrest Country Club. Oil was being pumped from the Twentieth Century-Fox lot. Off Carpinteria, south of Santa Barbara, oil was being pumped offshore, and even people who had expensive beach houses at Rincon del Mar had come to think of the rigs as not entirely unattractive features of the view—something a little mysterious out there in the mist, something a little Japanese on the horizon. In other words the drilling for and pumping of crude oil in Southern California had not historically carried much true political resonance, which made this battle of the propositions a largely symbolic, or "political", confrontation, not entirely about oil drilling. That Zev Yaroslavsky won it—and won it spending only $2.8 million, some $4 million less than Occidental spent—seemed to many to suggest a certain discontent with the way things were going, a certain desire for change: the very desire for change on which Zev Yaroslavsky was planning, in the course of his campaign for the mayor's office, to run.

There was, early on, considerable interest in this promised mayoralty race between Tom Bradley and Zev Yaroslavsky. Some saw the contest, and this was the way the Bradley people liked to present it, as a long-awaited confrontation between the rest of the city (Bradley) and the West Side (Yaroslavsky), which was well-off, heavily Jewish, and the only part of the city that visitors to Los Angeles normally saw. This scenario had in fact been laid out in the drilling battle, during which Occidental, by way of Mickey Kantor and Robert Shrum, introduced the notion that a vote for Occidental was a vote against "a few selfish people who don't want their beach view obstructed", against "elitists", against, in other words, the West Side. "The

euphemism they kept using here was that it was another ploy by the 'rich Westsiders' against the poor
minorities and the blacks," I was told by a deputy to
Councilman Marvin Braude, who had co-authored the
antidrilling proposition with Zev Yaroslavsky and in
whose district Occidental's Pacific Coast Highway
property lay. "You always heard about 'rich Westsiders' in connection with anything we were doing. It
was the euphemism for the Jews."

Others saw the race, and this was increasingly the
way the Yaroslavsky people liked to frame it, as a
confrontation between the forces of unrestricted
growth (developers, the oil business, Bradley) and the
proponents of controlled, or "slow", growth (environmentalists, the No Oil lobby, the West Side, Yaroslavsky). Neither version was long on nuance, and
both tended to overlook facts that did not support the
favored angles (Bradley had for years been the West
Side's own candidate, for example, and Yaroslavsky
had himself broken bread with a developer or two),
but the two scenarios, Yaroslavsky's *Greed v. Slow
Growth* and Bradley's *The People v. the West Side*, continued to provide, for that handful of people in Los
Angeles who actually followed city politics, a kind of
narrative line. The election would fall, as these people
saw it, to whoever told his story best, to whoever had
the best tellers, the best fixers.

Only a few people in Los Angeles were believed to
be able to fix things, whether the things to be fixed,

or arranged, or managed, were labor problems or city permits or elections. There was the master of them all, Paul Ziffren, whose practice as a lawyer had often been indistinguishable from the practice of politics, but he was by the time of this race less active than he had once been. There was his son Kenneth Ziffren, who settled the Writers Guild of America strike in the summer of 1988. There was, operating in a slightly different arena, Sidney Korshak, who settled the Delano grape strike against Schenley in 1966. There was almost anybody at the Manatt office. There was Joseph Cerrell, a political consultant about whom it had been said, "You want to get elected to the judicial, you call him, a campaign can run you fifty thousand dollars." There was Robert Shrum, who worked Alan Cranston's last campaign for the Senate and Representative Richard Gephardt's campaign in the 1988 presidential primaries. There were Michael Berman and Carl D'Agostino, of BAD Campaigns, Inc., who were considered direct mail (most of it negative) geniuses and were central to what was locally called "the Waxman-Berman machine", the Democratic and quite specifically Jewish political organization built by Michael Berman; his brother, Representative Howard Berman; Representative Henry Waxman; and Representative Mel Levine, who was positioning himself to run for Alan Cranston's Senate seat in 1992. It was Michael Berman who figured out how to send Howard Berman and Henry Waxman and Mel Levine to Congress in the first place. It was Michael Berman and Carl D'Agostino who continued to figure out how to elect Waxman-Berman candidates on the state and local levels.

These figures were not without a certain local glamour, and a considerable amount of the interest in this mayoralty race derived from the fact that Doak & Shrum—which, remember, had been part of Mickey Kantor's team on the Occidental proposition—was working for Bradley, while Berman and D'Agostino, who had been hired by Yaroslavsky and Braude to run their antidrilling proposition, were backing Yaroslavsky. A mayoralty contest between Shrum and the Berman-D'Agostino firm, Bill Boyarsky wrote in the *Los Angeles Times*, could be "one of the great matchups of low-down campaigning"; in other words a chance, as I recall being told in June of 1988 by someone else, "for Berman and D'Agostino to knock off Doak & Shrum".

Then something happened, nobody was saying quite how. One Friday in August of 1988, a reporter at the *Los Angeles Times*, Kenneth Reich, got a phone call from a woman who refused to identify herself but said that she was sending him certain material prepared by BAD Campaigns, Inc. The material—delivered the following Monday with a typewritten and unsigned note reading, "You should be interested to see this. Government is bad enough without BAD"—consisted of three strategy memos addressed to Zev Yaroslavsky. One was dated March 29, 1988, another was dated May 4, 1988, and the third, headed "Things to Do", was undated.

Berman and D'Agostino acknowledged that the two

dated documents were early drafts of memos prepared by their office, but denied having written the undated memo, which, accordingly, was never printed by the *Times*. The memos that were printed, which Yaroslavsky charged had been stolen from a three-ring binder belonging to one of his aides, had, however, an immediately electrifying effect, not because they said anything that most interested people in Los Angeles did not know or believe but because they violated the local social contract by saying it out loud, and in the vernacular. The memos printed in the *Times* read, in part:

> The reason why BAD thinks you [Yaroslavsky] can beat Bradley is: you've got fifty IQ-points on him (and that's no compliment). . . . Just because you are more slow-growth than Bradley does not mean you can take anti-growth voters for granted . . . many are racially tolerant people who are strongly pulled to Bradley because of his height, skin color, and calm demeanor. They like voting for him—they feel less guilty about how little they used to pay their household help. . . .
>
> Yaroslavsky's vision [should be that] there is no reason on this earth why some flitty restaurateur should be allowed to build a hotel at the corner of Beverly and La Cienega. . . . The Yaroslavsky vision says "there is no reason on earth why anyone should be building more places to shop in

West L.A." . . . There is no reason for guilt-
ridden liberals to vote out of office that fine,
dignified "person of color" except that your
Vision is total, unwavering and convincing.
You want to hug every tree, stop every new
building, end the traffic jams and clean up
the Bay. . . .

To beat Bradley, you must be intensely,
thoroughly and totally committed to your
vision of L.A. . . . It is the way you overcome the racial tug many Jews and non-
Jewish liberals feel toward Bradley. It is
also the way you overcome the possible
Republican preference for the conservative
black over the Jewish kid friendly with the
Waxman-Berman machine. . . .

Bradley can and will excite black voters to
outvote the white electorate especially if
there is a runoff where his mayoral office is
seen as jeopardized by a perfidious Jew. . . .

What we do know is that Jewish wealth in
Los Angeles is endless. That almost every
Jewish person who meets you will like you
and that asking for $2,000 is not an unrea-
sonable request to people who are both
wealthy and like you. . . .

The Yaroslavsky campaign becomes the
United Jewish appeal. . . .

This was not, on the face of it, remarkable stuff.
The language in the memos was widely described as
"cynical", but of course it was not: it was just the
working shorthand of people who might even be said,

on the evidence of what they wrote down, to have an idealized view of the system, people who noticed the small perfect deals and did not approve of them, or at any rate assumed that there was an electorate out there that did not approve of them. This may have been an erroneous assumption, a strategic miscalculation, but the idea that some of Yaroslavsky's people might have miscalculated the electorate was not, for some people who had supported him and were now beginning to back away, the problem.

"Make a complete list of mainstream Jewish charities," the March 29 memo had advised. "Find a person in each charity to slip us a list with name, address and phone numbers of $1,000-and-above contributors. . . . Zev begins dialing for dollars. . . . Make a list of 50 contributors to Zev who have not participated to their ability and who belong to every Jewish country club in the L.A. area. . . . Make a list of every studio, Hollywood PR firm and 100 top show business personalities in Jewish Los Angeles. . . . You cannot let Bradley become the chichi, in, campaign against the pushy Jew. . . ."

It was this acknowledgment, even this insistence, that there were in Los Angeles not only Jewish voters but specifically Jewish interests, and Jewish money, that troubled many people, most particularly those very members of the West Side Jewish community on whose support the Yaroslavsky people were counting. What happened next was largely a matter of "perceptions", of a very few people talking among themselves, as they were used to talking whenever there was something to be decided, some candidate or cause to be backed or not backed. The word "divisive" started coming up again and again. It would be, people were saying, a "divisive" campaign, even a "disastrous" campaign, a campaign that would "pit the blacks against the Jews". There was, it was said, "already enough trouble", trouble that had been simmering, as these people saw it, since at least 1985, when Tom Bradley's Jewish supporters on the West Side had insisted that he denounce the Reverend Louis Farrakhan, and some black leaders had protested that Bradley should not be taking orders from the West Side. This issue of race, most people hastened to say, would never be raised by the candidates themselves. The problem would be, as Neil Sandberg of the American Jewish Committee put it to Bill Boyarsky of the *Los Angeles Times*, "undisciplined elements in both communities". The problem would be, in other words, the candidates' "people".

Discussions were held. Many telephone calls were made. In December of 1988, a letter was drafted and signed by some of the most politically active people on the West Side. This letter called on Zev Yaroslavsky to back off, not to run, not to proceed on a course that the signers construed as an invitation, if not to open ethnic conflict, at least to a breaking apart of the coalition between the black and Jewish communities that had given the West Side its recent power over the old-line Los Angeles establishment—the downtown and San Marino money base, which was what people in Los Angeles meant when they referred to the Cali-

---

fornia Club. On the sixth of January, citing a private poll that showed Bradley to be running far ahead, Zev Yaroslavsky announced that he would not run. The BAD memos, he said, had "played absolutely no role" in his decision to withdraw. The "fear of a divisive campaign", he said, had "played no role on my part".

This "fear of a divisive campaign", and the attendant specter of the membership of the California Club invading City Hall, seemed on the face of it incorporeal, one of those received fears that sometimes overtake a community and redirect the course of its affairs. Still, the convergence of the BAD memos and the polarization implicit in the Occidental campaign had generated a considerable amount of what could only be described as class conflict. "Most of us have known for a long time that the environmentalists are . . . white, middle-class groups who have not really shown a lot of concern about the black community or black issues," Maxine Waters, who represented part of south-central in the California State Assembly and was probably the most effective and visible black politician in Southern California, told Bill Boyarsky when he talked to her, after the publication of the BAD memos, about the drilling issue. "Yet we have continued to give support. . . . I want to tell you I may very well support the oil drilling. I feel such a need to assert independence from this kind of crap, and I feel such a need for the black community not to be led on by someone else's agenda and not even knowing what the agenda was."

194

One afternoon in February of 1989 when I happened to be in City Hall seeing Zev Yaroslavsky and Marvin Braude, I asked what they made of the "divisive campaign" question. The apprehension, Yaroslavsky said, had been confined to "a very small group of people", whose concern, as he saw it, had been "fueled by my neighbors here in the mayor's office, who were trying to say we could have another Chicago, another Ed Koch".

"Some of it started before your candidacy," Marvin Braude said to him. "With the Farrakhan incident. That set the tone of it."

"Let me tell you," Zev Yaroslavsky said. "If there's any reason why I would have run, it would have been to disprove that notion. Because nothing so offends me—politically and personally—as the notion that I, simply because I'm white or Jewish, don't have the right to run against a fourth-term incumbent just because he happens to be black."

Zev Yaroslavsky, at that point, was mounting a campaign to save his own council seat. He had put the mayoral campaign behind him. Still, it rankled. "Nothing I was talking about had remotely to do with race," he said. "It never would have been an issue, unless Bradley brought it up. But I must say they made every effort to put everything we did into a racial context. They tried to make the Oxy oil initiative racial. They tried to make Proposition U—which was our first slow-growth initiative—racial. They pitted rich against poor, white against black, West Side against South Side—"

"It wasn't only Bradley," Marvin Braude said, interrupting. "It was the people who were using this for their own selfish purposes. It was the developers. It was Occidental."

"I think if the election had gone on . . ." Zev Yaroslavsky paused. "It doesn't matter. At this point it's speculative. But I think the mayor and his people, especially his people, were running a very risky strategy of trying to make race an issue. For their candidate's benefit."

During the week in February 1989 when I saw Zev Yaroslavsky and Marvin Braude, the *Los Angeles Times* Poll did a telephone sampling to determine local attitudes toward the city and its mayor. About 60 percent of those polled, the *Times* reported a few days later, under the headline "People Turn Pessimistic About Life in Los Angeles", believed that the "quality of life" in Los Angeles had deteriorated during the last fifteen years. About 50 percent said that within the past year they had considered leaving Los Angeles, mainly for San Diego. Sixty-seven percent of those polled, however, believed that Tom Bradley, who had been mayor during this period when the quality of life had so deteriorated that many of them were thinking of moving to San Diego, had done a good job.

This was not actually news. On the whole, life in Los Angeles, perhaps because it is a city so largely populated by people who are ready to drop everything and move to San Diego (just as they or their parents or their grandparents had dropped everything and moved to Los Angeles), seems not to encourage a conventional interest in its elected officials. "Nobody but the press corps and a few elites care anything about the day-to-day workings in city government" is the way this was put in one of the "cynical" BAD memos.

In fact there were maybe a hundred people in Los Angeles, aside from the handful of reporters assigned to the city desk, who followed City Hall. A significant number of the hundred were lawyers at Manatt. All of the hundred were people who understand access. Some of these people said that of course Zev Yaroslavsky would run again, in 1993, when he would be only forty-four and Tom Bradley would be seventy-five and presumably ready to step aside. Nineteen ninety-three, in this revised view, would be "Zev's year". Nineteen ninety-three would be "time for Zev". Others said that 1993 would be too late, that the entire question of whether or not Zev Yaroslavsky could hold together Tom Bradley's famous black-Jewish coalition would be, in a Los Angeles increasingly populated by Hispanics and Asians, irrelevant, history, moot. Nineteen ninety-three, these people said, would be the year for other people altogether, for more recent figures on the local political landscape, for people like Gloria Molina or Richard Alatorre, people like Mike Woo, people whose names would tell a different story, although not necessarily to a different hundred people.

—1989

L.A. *Noir*

AROUND DIVISION 47, Los Angeles Municipal Court, the downtown courtroom where, for eleven weeks during the spring and summer of 1989, a preliminary hearing was held to determine if the charges brought in the 1983 murder of a thirty-three-year-old road-show promoter named Roy Alexander Radin should be dismissed or if the defendants should be bound over to superior court for arraignment and trial, it was said that there were, "in the works", five movies, four books, and "countless" pieces about the case. Sometimes it was said that there were four movies and five books "in the works", or one movie and two books, or two movies and six books. There were, in any event, "big balls" in the air. "Everybody's working this one," a reporter covering the trial said one morning as we waited to get patted down at the entrance to the courtroom, a security measure prompted by a telephoned bomb threat and encouraged by the general wish of everyone involved to make this a noticeable case. "Major money."

This was curious. Murder cases are generally of interest to the extent that they suggest some anomaly or lesson in the world revealed, but there seemed neither anomalies nor lessons in the murder of Roy Radin, who was last seen alive getting into a limousine to go to dinner at a Beverly Hills restaurant, La Scala, and was next seen decomposed, in a canyon off Interstate 5. Among the defendants actually present for the preliminary hearing was Karen Delayne ("Lanie") Jacobs Greenberger, a fairly attractive hard case late of South Florida, where her husband was said to have been the number-two man in the cocaine operation run by Carlos Lehder, the only major Colombian drug figure to have been tried and convicted in the United States. (Lanie Greenberger herself was said to have done considerable business in this line, and to have had nearly a million dollars in cocaine and cash stolen from her Sherman Oaks house not long before Roy Radin disappeared.) The other defendants present were William Mentzer and Alex Marti, somewhat less attractive hard cases, late of Larry Flynt's security staff. (Larry Flynt is the publisher of *Hustler*, and one of the collateral artifacts that turned up in the Radin case was a million-dollar check Flynt had written in 1983 to the late Mitchell Livingston WerBell III, a former arms dealer who operated a counterterrorism school outside Atlanta and described himself as a retired lieutenant general in the Royal Free Afghan Army. The Los Angeles County Sheriff's Department said that Flynt had written the check to WerBell as payment on a contract to kill Frank Sinatra, Hugh Hefner, Bob Guccione, and Walter Annenberg. Larry Flynt's lawyer said that there had been no contract, and described the check, on which payment was stopped, as a dinner-party joke.) There was also an absent defendant, a third Flynt security man, fighting extradition from Maryland.

In other words this was a genre case, and the genre, L.A. *noir*, was familiar. There is a *noir* case every year or two in Los Angeles. There was for example the Wonderland case, which involved the 1981 bludgeoning to death of four people. The Wonderland case, so called because the bludgeoning took place in a house on Wonderland Avenue in Laurel Canyon, turned, like the Radin case, on a million-dollar cocaine theft, but featured even more deeply *noir* players, including a nightclub entrepreneur and convicted cocaine dealer named Adel Nasrallah, aka "Eddie Nash"; a pornographic-movie star, now dead of AIDS, named John C. Holmes, aka "Johnny Wadd"; and a young man named Scott Thorson, who was, at the time he first testified in the case, an inmate in the Los Angeles County Jail (Scott Thorson was, in the natural ecology of the criminal justice system, the star witness for the state in the Wonderland case), and who in 1982 sued Liberace on the grounds that he had been promised $100,000 a year for life in return for his services as Liberace's lover, driver, travel secretary, and animal trainer.

In this context there would have seemed nothing particularly novel about the Radin case. It was true that there were, floating around the edges of the story, several other unnatural deaths, for example that of Lanie Greenberger's husband, Larry Greenberger, aka "Vinnie De Angelo", who either shot himself or was shot in the head in September of 1988 on the front porch of his house in Okeechobee, Florida, but these deaths were essentially unsurprising. It was also true that the Radin case offered not bad sidebar details. I was interested for example in how much security Larry Flynt apparently had patrolling Doheny Estates, where his house was, and Century City, where the *Hustler* offices were. I was interested in Dean Kahn, who ran the limousine service that provided the stretch Cadillac with smoked windows in which Roy Radin took, in the language of this particular revealed world, his last ride. I was interested in how Roy Radin, before he came to Los Angeles and decided to go to dinner at La Scala, had endeavored to make his way in the world by touring high school auditoriums with Tiny Tim, Frank Fontaine, and a corps of tap-dancing dwarfs.

Still, promoters of tap-dancing dwarfs who get done in by hard cases have not been, historically, the stuff of which five movies, four books, and countless pieces are made. The almost febrile interest in this case derived not from the principals but from what was essentially a cameo role, played by Robert Evans. Robert Evans had been head of production at Paramount during the golden period of *The Godfather* and *Love Story* and *Rosemary's Baby*, had moved on to produce independently such successful motion pictures as *Chinatown* and *Marathon Man*, and was, during what was generally agreed to be a dry spell in his career (he had recently made a forty-five-minute videotape on the life of John Paul II, and had announced that he was writing an autobiography, to be called *The Kid Stays in the Picture*), a district attorney's dream: a quite possibly desperate, quite famously risk-oriented, high-visibility figure with low-life connections.

It was the contention of the Los Angeles County District Attorney's office that Lanie Greenberger had hired her codefendants to kill Roy Radin after he refused to cut her in on his share of the profits from Robert Evans's 1984 picture *The Cotton Club*. It was claimed that Lanie Greenberger had introduced Roy Radin, who wanted to get into the movie business, to Robert Evans. It was claimed that Roy Radin had offered to find, in return for 45 percent of the profits from either one Evans picture (*The Cotton Club*) or three Evans pictures (*The Cotton Club*, *The Sicilian*, and *The Two Jakes*), "Puerto Rican investors" willing to put up either thirty-five or fifty million dollars.

Certain objections leap to the nonprosecutorial mind here (the "Puerto Rican investors" turned out to be one Puerto Rican banker with "connections", the money never actually materialized, Roy Radin therefore had no share of the profits, there were no profits in any case), but seem not to have figured in the state's case. The District Attorney's office was also hinting, if not quite contending, that Robert Evans himself had been in on the payoff of Radin's killers, and the DA's office had a protected witness (still another Flynt security man, this one receiving $3,000 a month from the Los Angeles County Sheriff's Department) who had agreed to say in court that one of the defendants, William Mentzer, told him that Lanie Greenberger and Robert Evans had, in the witness's words, "paid for the contract". Given the state's own logic, it was hard to know what Robert Evans might have thought to gain by putting out a contract on the goose with the $50 million egg, but the deputy district attorney on the case seemed unwilling to let go of this possibility, and had in fact told reporters that Robert Evans was "one of the people who we have not eliminated as a suspect".

Neither, on the other hand, was Robert Evans one of the people they had arrested, a circumstance suggesting certain lacunae in the case from the major-money point of view, and also from the district attorney's. Among people outside the criminal justice system, it was widely if vaguely assumed that Robert Evans was somehow "on trial" during the summer of 1989. "Evans Linked for First Time in Court to Radin's Murder," the headlines were telling them, and, in the past-tense obituary mode, "Evans' Success Came Early: Career Epitomized Hollywood Dream."

"Bob always had a premonition that his career would peak before he was fifty and fade downhill," Peter Bart, who had worked under Evans at Paramount, told the *Los Angeles Times*, again in the obituary mode. "He lived by it. He was haunted by it. . . . To those of us who knew him and knew what a good-spirited person he was, it's a terrible sadness." Here was a case described by the *Times* as "focused on the dark side of Hollywood deal making", a case offering

203

"an unsparing look at the film capital's unsavory side", a case everyone was calling just Cotton Club, or even just Cotton, as in " 'Cotton': Big Movie Deal's Sequel Is Murder".

Inside the system, the fact that no charge had been brought against the single person on the horizon who had a demonstrable connection with *The Cotton Club* was rendering Cotton Club, *qua* Cotton Club, increasingly problematic. Not only was Robert Evans not "on trial" in Division 47, but what was going on there was not even a "trial", only a preliminary hearing, intended to determine whether the state had sufficient evidence and cause to prosecute those charged, none of whom was Evans. Since 1978, when a California Supreme Court ruling provided criminal defendants the right to a preliminary hearing even after indictment by a grand jury, preliminary hearings have virtually replaced grand juries as a way of indicting felony suspects in California, and are one of the reasons that criminal cases in Los Angeles now tend to go on for years. The preliminary hearing alone in the McMartin child-abuse case lasted eighteen months.

On the days I dropped by Division 47, the judge, a young black woman with a shock of gray in her hair, seemed fretful, inattentive. The lawyers seemed weary. The bailiffs discussed their domestic arrangements on the telephone. When Lanie Greenberger entered the courtroom, not exactly walking but undulating forward on the balls of her feet, in a little half-time prance, no one bothered to look up. The courtroom had been full on the day Robert Evans appeared as the first witness for the prosecution and took the Fifth, but in the absence of Evans there were only a few reporters and the usual two or three retirees in the courtroom, perhaps a dozen people in all, reduced to interviewing each other and discussing alternative names for the Night Stalker case, which involved a man named Richard Ramirez who had been accused of thirteen murders and thirty other felonies committed in Los Angeles County during 1984 and 1985. One reporter was calling the Ramirez case, which was then in its sixth month of trial after nine weeks of preliminary hearings and six months of jury selection, Valley Intruder. Another had settled on Serial Killer. "I still slug it Night Stalker," a third said, and she turned to me. "Let me ask you," she said. "This is how hard up I am. Is there a story in your being here?"

The preliminary hearing in the Radin case had originally been scheduled for three weeks, and lasted eleven. On July 12, 1989, in Division 47, Judge Patti Jo McKay ruled not only that there was sufficient evidence to bind over Lanie Greenberger, Alex Marti, and William Mentzer for trial but also that the Radin murder may have been committed for financial gain, which meant that the defendants could receive, if convicted, penalties of death. "Mr. Radin was an obstacle to further negotiation involving *The Cotton Club*," the prosecuting attorney had argued in closing. "The deal could not go through until specific issues such as percentages were worked out. It was at that time that Mrs. Greenberger had the motive to murder Mr. Radin."

I was struck by this as a final argument, because it

seemed to suggest an entire case based on the notion that an interest in an entirely hypothetical share of the entirely hypothetical profits from an entirely hypothetical motion picture (at the time Roy Radin was killed, *The Cotton Club* had an advertising poster but no shooting script and no money and no cast and no start date) was money in the bank. All that had stood between Lanie Greenberger and Fat City, as the prosecutor saw it, was boilerplate, a matter of seeing that "percentages were worked out".

The prosecution's certainty on this point puzzled me, and I asked an acquaintance in the picture business if he thought there had ever been money to be made from *The Cotton Club*. He seemed not to believe what I was asking. There had been "gross positions", he reminded me, participants with a piece of the gross rather than the net. There had been previous investors. There had been commitments already made on *The Cotton Club*, paper out all over town. There had been, above all, a $26 million budget going in (it eventually cost $47 million), and a production team not noted for thrift. "It had to make a hundred to a hundred forty million, depending on how much got stolen, before anybody saw gross," he said. "Net on this baby was dreamland. Which could have been figured out, with no loss of life, by a junior agent just out of the William Morris mailroom."

There was always in the Cotton Club case a certain dreamland aspect, a looniness that derived in part from the ardent if misplaced faith of everyone involved, from the belief in windfalls, in sudden changes of fortune (five movies and four books would change someone's fortune, a piece of *The Cotton Club* someone else's, a high-visibility case the district attorney's); in killings, both literal and figurative. In fact this kind of faith is not unusual in Los Angeles. In a city not only largely conceived as a series of real estate promotions but largely supported by a series of confidence games, a city even then afloat on motion pictures and junk bonds and the B-2 Stealth bomber, the conviction that something can be made of nothing may be one of the few narratives in which everyone participates. A belief in extreme possibilities colors daily life. Anyone might have woken up one morning and been discovered at Schwab's, or killed at Bob's Big Boy. "Luck is all around you," a silky voice says on the California State Lottery's Lotto commercials, against a background track of "Dream a Little Dream of Me". "Imagine winning millions . . . what would you do?"

During the summer of 1989 this shimmer of the possible still lay on Cotton Club, although there seemed, among those dreamers to whom I spoke in both the picture business and the criminal justice business, a certain impatience with the way the case was actually playing out. There was nobody in either business, including the detectives on the case, who could hear the words "Cotton Club" and not see a possible score, but the material was resistant. It still lacked a bankable element. There was a definite wish to move on, as they say in the picture business, to screenplay. The detectives were keeping in touch with motion picture producers, car phone to car phone, sketching in connecting lines not apparent in the courtroom. "This friend of mine in the sheriff's office laid it out for me three years ago," one producer told me. "The deal was, 'This is all about drugs, Bob Evans is involved, we're going to get him.' And so forth. He wanted me to have the story when and if the movie was done. He called me a week ago, from his car, wanted to know if I was going to move on it."

I heard a number of alternative scenarios. "The story is in this one cop who wouldn't let it go," I was told by a producer. "The story is in the peripheral characters," I was told by a detective I had reached by dialing his car phone. Another producer reported having run into Robert Evans's lawyer, Robert Shapiro, the evening before at Hillcrest Country Club, where the Thomas Hearns–Sugar Ray Leonard fight was being shown closed circuit from Caesars Palace in Las Vegas. "I asked how our boy was doing," he said, meaning Evans. "Shapiro says he's doing fine. Scot-free, he says. Here's the story. A soft guy from our world, just sitting up there in his sixteen-room house, keeps getting visits from these detectives. Big guys. Real hard guys. Apes. Waiting for him to crack."

Here we had the rough line for several quite different stories, but it would have been hard not to notice that each of them depended for its dramatic thrust on the presence of Robert Evans. I mentioned this one day to Marcia Morrissey, who—as co-counsel with the Miami trial lawyer Edward Shohat, who had de-fended Carlos Lehder—was representing Lanie Greenberger. "Naturally they all *want* him in," Marcia Morrissey said.

I asked if she thought the District Attorney's Office would manage to get him in.

Marcia Morrissey rolled her eyes. "That's what it's called, isn't it? I mean face it. It's called Cotton Club."

—1989

Fire Season

"I've seen fire and I've seen rain," I recall James Taylor singing over and over on the news radio station between updates on the 1978 Mandeville and Kanan fires, both of which started on October 23 of that year and could be seen burning toward each other, systematically wiping out large parts of Malibu and Pacific Palisades, from an upstairs window of my house in Brentwood. It was said that the Kanan fire was burning on a twenty-mile front and had already jumped the Pacific Coast Highway at Trancas Canyon. The stand in the Mandeville fire, it was said, would be made at Sunset Boulevard. I stood at the window and watched a house on a hill above Sunset implode, its oxygen sucked out by the force of the fire.

Some thirty-four thousand acres of Los Angeles County burned that week in 1978. More than eighty thousand acres had burned in 1968. Close to a hundred and thirty thousand acres had burned in 1970. Seventy-four-some thousand had burned in 1975, sixty-some thousand would burn in 1979. Forty-six thousand would burn in 1980, forty-five thousand in 1982. In the hills behind Malibu, where the moist air off the Pacific makes the brush grow fast, it takes about twelve years before a burn is ready to burn again. Inland, where the manzanita and sumac and chamise that make up the native brush in Southern California grow more slowly (the wild mustard that turns the hills a translucent yellow after rain is not native but exotic, introduced in the 1920s in an effort to reseed burns), regrowth takes from fifteen to twenty years. Since 1919, when the county began keeping records of its fires, some areas have burned eight times.

In other words there is nothing unusual about fires in Los Angeles, which is after all a desert city with only two distinct seasons, one beginning in January and lasting three or four months during which storms come in from the northern Pacific and it rains (often an inch every two or three hours, sometimes and in some places an inch a minute) and one lasting eight or nine months during which it burns, or gets ready to burn. Most years it is September or October before the Santa Ana winds start blowing down through the passes and the relative humidity drops to figures like 7 or 6 or 3 percent and the bougainvillea starts rattling in the driveway and people start watching the horizon for smoke and tuning in to another of those extreme local possibilities, in this case that of imminent devastation. What was unusual in 1989, after two years of drought and a third year of less than average rainfall, was that it was ready to burn while the June fogs still lay on the coastline. On the first of May that year, months earlier than ever before, the California Department of Forestry had declared the start of fire season and begun hiring extras crews. By the last week in June there had already been more than two thousand brush and forest fires in California. Three hundred and twenty of them were burning that week alone.

One morning early that summer I drove out the San Bernardino Freeway to the headquarters of the Los Angeles County Fire Department, which was responsible not only for coordinating fire fighting and reseeding operations throughout the county but for sending, under the California Master Mutual Aid agreement, both equipment and strike teams to fires around the state. Los Angeles County sent strike teams to fight the 116,000-acre Wheeler fire in Ventura County in 1985. (The logistics of these big fires are essentially military. Within twelve hours of the first reports on the Wheeler fire, which eventually burned for two weeks and involved three thousand fire fighters flown in from around the country, a camp had materialized, equipped with kitchen, sanitation, transportation and medical facilities, a communications network, a "situation trailer", a "what if" trailer for long-range contingency planning, and a "pool coordinator", to get off-duty crews to and from the houses of residents who had offered the use of their swimming pools. "We simply superimposed a city on top of the incident," a camp spokesman said at the time.) Los Angeles County sent strike teams to fight the 100,000-acre Las Pilitas fire in San Luis Obispo County the same year. It sent specially trained people to act as "overhead" on, or to run, the crews of military personnel brought in from all over the United States to fight the Yellowstone fires in 1988.

On the June morning in 1989 when I visited the headquarters building in East Los Angeles, it was already generally agreed that, as one of the men to whom I spoke put it, "we pretty much know we're going to see some fires this year", with no probable break until January or February. (There is usually some November rain in Los Angeles, often enough to allow crews to gain control of a fire already burning, but only rarely does November rain put enough moisture into the brush to offset the Santa Ana winds that blow until the end of December.) There had been unusually early Santa Ana conditions, a week of temperatures over one hundred. The measurable moisture in the brush, a measurement the Fire Department calls the "fuel stick", was in some areas already down to single digits. The daily "burn index", which rates the probability of fire on a scale running from 0 to 200, was that morning showing figures of 45 for the Los Angeles basin, 41 for what is called the "high country", 125 for the Antelope Valley, and, for the Santa Clarita Valley, 192.

Anyone who has spent fire season in Los Angeles knows some of its special language—knows, for example, the difference between a fire that has been "controlled" and a fire that has so far been merely "contained" (a "contained" fire has been surrounded, usually by a trench half as wide as the brush is high,

213

but is still burning out of control within this line and may well jump it), knows the difference between "full" and "partial" control ("partial" control means, if the wind changes, no control at all), knows about "backfiring" and about "making the stand" and about the difference between a Red Flag Alert (there will probably be a fire today) and a Red Flag Warning (there will probably be a Red Flag Alert within three days).

Still, "burn index" was new to me, and one of the headquarters foresters, Paul Rippens, tried that morning to explain it. "Let's take the Antelope Valley, up around Palmdale, Lancaster," he said. "For today, temperature's going to be ninety-six, humidity's going to be seventeen percent, wind speed's going to be fifteen miles per hour, and the fuel stick is six, which is getting pretty low."

"Six burns very well," another forester, John Haggenmiller, said. "If the fuel stick's up around twelve, it's pretty hard to get it to burn. That's the range that you have. Anything under six and it's ready to burn very well."

"So you correlate all that, you get an Antelope Valley burn index today of one twenty-five, the adjective for which is 'high'," Paul Rippens continued. "The adjectives we use are 'low', 'moderate', 'high', 'very high', and 'extreme'. One twenty-five is 'high'. High probability of fire. We had a hundred-plus-acre fire out there yesterday, about a four-hour fire. Divide the burn index by ten and you get the average flame length. So a burn index of one twenty-five is going to give you a twelve-and-a-half-foot flame length out there. If you've got a good fire burning, flame length has a lot to do with it."

"There's a possibility of a grass fire going through and not doing much damage at all," John Haggenmiller said. "Other cases, where the fuel has been allowed to build up—say you had a bug kill or a dieback, a lot of decadent fuel—you're going to get a flame length of thirty, forty feet. And it gets up into the crown of a tree and the whole thing goes down. That does a lot of damage."

Among the men to whom I spoke that morning there was a certain grudging admiration for what they called "the big hitters", the major fires, the ones people remember. "I'd say about ninety-five percent of our fires, we're able to hold down to under five acres," I was told by Captain Garry Oversby, who did community relations and education for the Fire Department. "It's the ones when we have extreme Santa Ana conditions, extreme weather—they get started, all we can do is try to hold the thing in check until the weather lays down a little bit for us. Times like that, we revert to what we call a defensive attack. Just basically go right along the edges of that fire until we can get a break. Reach a natural barrier. Or sometimes we make a stand several miles in advance of the fire—construct a line there, and then maybe set a backfire. Which will burn back toward the main fire and take out the vegetation, rob the main fire of its fuel."

They spoke of the way a true big hitter "moved",

215

of the way it "pushed", of the way it could "spot", or throw embers and firebrands, a mile ahead of itself, rendering any kind of conventional firebreak useless; of the way a big hitter, once it got moving, would "outrun anybody". "You get the right weather conditions in Malibu, it's almost impossible to stop it," Paul Rippens said. He was talking about the fires that typically start somewhere in the brush off the Ventura Freeway and then burn twenty miles to the sea, the fires that roar over a ridge in a matter of seconds and make national news because they tend to take out, just before they hit the beach along Malibu, houses that belong to well-known people. Taking out houses is what the men at headquarters mean when they talk about "the urban interface".

"We can dump all our resources out there," Paul Rippens said, and he shrugged.

"You can pick up the flanks and channel it," John Haggenmiller said, "but until the wind stops or you run out of fuel, you can't do much else."

"You get into Malibu," Paul Rippens said, "you're looking at what we call two-story brush."

"You know the wind," John Haggenmiller said. "You're not going to change that phenomenon."

"You can dump everything you've got on that fire," Paul Rippens said. "It's still going to go to what we call the big blue break."

It occurred to me then that it had been eleven years since the October night in 1978 when I listened to James Taylor singing "Fire and Rain" between reports on how the Kanan fire had jumped the Pacific Coast

216

Highway to go to the big blue break. On the twelve-year-average fire cycle that regulates life in Malibu, the Kanan burn, which happened to include a beach on which my husband and daughter and I had lived from 1971 until June of 1978, was coming due again. "Beautiful country burn again," I wrote in my notebook, a line from a Robinson Jeffers poem I remember at some point during every fire season, and I got up to leave.

A week or so later 3,700 acres burned in the hills west of the Antelope Valley. The flames reached sixty feet. The wind was gusting at forty miles an hour. There were 250 fire fighters on the ground, and they evacuated 1,500 residents, one of whom returned to find her house gone but managed to recover, according to the *Los Angeles Times*, "an undamaged American flag and a porcelain Nativity set handmade by her mother". A week after this Antelope Valley fire, 1,500 acres burned in the Puente Hills, above Whittier. The temperatures that day were in the high nineties, and the flames were as high as fifty feet. There were more than 970 fire fighters on the line. Two hundred and fifty families were evacuated. They took with them what people always take out of fires, mainly snapshots, mementos small enough to put in the car. "We won't have a stitch of clothing, but at least we'll have these," a woman about to leave the Puente Hills told the *Times* as she packed the snapshots into the trunk of her car.

People who live with fires think a great deal about what will happen "when", as the phrase goes in the instruction leaflets, "the fire comes". These leaflets, which are stuck up on refrigerator doors all over Los Angeles County, never say "if". When the fire comes there will be no water pressure. The roof one watered all the night before will go dry in seconds. Plastic trash cans must be filled with water and wet gunny-sacks kept at hand, for smothering the sparks that blow ahead of the fire. The garden hoses must be connected and left where they can be seen. The cars must be placed in the garage, headed out. Whatever one wants most to save must be placed in the cars. The lights must be left on, so that the house can be seen in the smoke. I remember my daughter's Malibu kindergarten sending home on the first day of the fall semester a detailed contingency plan, with alterna-tive sites where, depending on the direction of the wind when the fire came, the children would be taken to wait for their parents. The last-ditch site was the naval air station at Point Mugu, twenty miles up the coast.

"Dry winds and dust, hair full of knots," our Mal-ibu child wrote when asked, in the fourth grade, for an "autumn" poem. "Gardens are dead, animals not fed. . . . People mumble as leaves crumble, fire ashes tumble." The rhythm here is not one that many peo-ple outside Los Angeles seem to hear. In the *New York Times* this morning I read a piece in which the way people in Los Angeles "persist" in living with fire was described as "denial". "Denial" is a word from a dif-ferent lyric altogether. This will have been only the second fire season over twenty-five years during which I did not have a house somewhere in Los Angeles County, and the second during which I did not keep the snapshots in a box near the door, ready to go when the fire comes.

—1989

Times Mirror Square

HARRISON GRAY OTIS, the first successful editor and publisher of the *Los Angeles Times* and in many ways the prototypical Los Angeles citizen, would seem to have been one of those entrepreneurial drifters at once set loose and energized by the Civil War and the westward expansion. He was born in a log house in Ohio in 1837. He went to work as an apprentice printer at fourteen. He was a delegate at twenty-three to the Republican National Convention at which Abraham Lincoln was nominated for the presidency. He spent forty-nine months in the Ohio Infantry, was wounded at Antietam in 1862 and again in Virginia in 1864, and then parlayed his Army connections into government jobs, first as a journeyman printer at the Government Printing Office in Washington and then at the Patent Office. He made his first foray to Southern California in 1874, to investigate a goat-raising scheme that never materialized, and pronounced the place "the fattest land I was ever in". He drifted first to Santa Barbara, where he published a small daily without notable success (he and his wife and three children, he noted later, were reduced to living in the fattest land on "not enough to keep a rabbit alive"), and struck out then for Alaska, where he had lucked into a $10-a-day government sinecure as the special agent in charge of poaching and liquor control in the Seal Islands.

In 1882, already a forty-five-year-old man with a rather accidental past and unremarkable prospects, Harrison Gray Otis managed finally to seize the moment: he quit the government job, returned to Southern California, and put down $6,000, $5,000 of it borrowed, for a quarter interest in the four-page *Los Angeles Daily Times*, a failed paper started a few months before by a former editor of the *Sacramento Union* (the *Union*, for which Mark Twain was a correspondent, is the oldest California daily still publishing) and abandoned almost immediately to its creditors. "Small beginnings, but great oaks, etc.," Harrison Gray Otis later noted of his purchase. He seems to have known immediately what kind of Los Angeles he wanted, and what role a newspaper could play in getting it: "Los Angeles wants no dudes, loafers and paupers; people who have no means and trust to luck," the new citizen announced in an early editorial, already shedding his previous skin, his middle-aged skin, the skin of a person who had recently had no means and trusted to luck. Los Angeles, as he saw it, was all capital formation, no service. It needed, he said, no "cheap politicians, failures, bummers, scrubs, impecunious clerks, bookkeepers, lawyers, doctors. The market is overstaffed already. We need workers! Hustlers! Men of brains, brawn and guts! Men who have a little capital and a good deal of energy—first-class men!"

The extent to which Los Angeles was literally invented by the *Los Angeles Times* and by its owners, Harrison Gray Otis and his descendants in the Chandler family, remains hard for people in less recent parts of the country to fully apprehend. At the time Harrison Gray Otis bought his paper there were only some five thousand people living in Los Angeles. There was no navigable river. The Los Angeles River was capable of providing ditch water for a population of two or three hundred thousand, but there was little other ground water to speak of. Los Angeles has water today because Harrison Gray Otis and his son-in-law Harry Chandler wanted it, and fought a series of outright water wars to get it. "With this water problem out of the way, the growth of Los Angeles will leap forward as never before," the *Times* advised its readers in 1905, a few weeks before the initial vote to fund the aqueduct meant to bring water from the Owens River, 233 miles to the north. "Adjacent towns will soon be knocking on our doors for admission to secure the benefits to be derived from our never-failing supply of life-giving water, and Greater Los Angeles will become a magnificent reality." Any citizen voting against the aqueduct bonds, the *Times* warned on the day before the election, would be "placing himself in the attitude of an *enemy of the city*."

To oppose the Chandlers, in other words, was to oppose the perfection of Los Angeles, the expansion that was the city's imperial destiny. The false

222

droughts and artful title transactions that brought Northern California water south are familiar stories in Los Angeles, and were made so in other parts of the country by the motion picture *Chinatown*. Without Owens River water the San Fernando Valley could not have been developed. The San Fernando Valley was where Harrison Gray Otis and Harry Chandler, through two interlocking syndicates, the San Fernando Mission Land Company and the Los Angeles Suburban Homes Company, happened to have bought or optioned, before the completion of the aqueduct and in some cases before the aqueduct vote, almost sixty-five thousand acres, virtually the entire valley from what is now Burbank to what is now Tarzana, at strictly dry-land prices, between $31 and $53 an acre. "Have A Contract for A Lot in Your Pocket When the Big Bonds are Voted," the advertisements read in the *Times* during the days before the initial vote on the aqueduct bonds. "Pacoima Will Feel the First Benefits of the Owens River Water and Every Purchaser Investing Now Will Reap the Fruits of his Wisdom in Gratifying Profits."

A great deal of Los Angeles as it appears today derived from this impulse to improve Chandler property. The Los Angeles Civic Center and Union Station and the curiosity known as Olvera Street (Olvera Street is part of El Pueblo de Los Angeles State Historic Park, but it was actually conceived in 1926 as the first local theme mall, the theme being "Mexican marketplace") are where they are because Harry Chandler wanted to develop the north end of downtown, where

223

the *Times* building and many of his other downtown
holdings lay. California has an aerospace industry
today because Harry Chandler believed that the development of Los Angeles required that new industry
be encouraged, and, in 1920, called on his friends to
lend Donald Douglas $15,000 to build an experimen-
tal torpedo plane.

The same year, Harry Chandler called on his
friends to build Caltech, and the year after that to
build a facility (the Coliseum, near the University of
Southern California) large enough to attract the 1932
Olympics. The Hollywood Bowl exists because
Harry Chandler wanted it. The Los Angeles highway
system exists because Harry Chandler knew that people would not buy land in his outlying subdivisions
unless they could drive to them, and also because
Harry Chandler sat on the board of Goodyear Tire &
Rubber, which by then had Los Angeles plants.
Goodyear Tire & Rubber had Los Angeles plants in
the first place because Harry Chandler and his friends
made an investment of $7.5 million to build them.

It was this total identification of the Chandler family's destiny with that of Los Angeles that made the
Times so peculiar an institution, and also such a rich
one. Under their corporate umbrella, the Times Mirror Company, the Chandlers now own, for all practical purposes, not only the *Times*, which for a number
of years carried more full-run advertising linage than
any other newspaper in the United States, but *Newsday*, *New York Newsday*, the *Baltimore Sun*, the *Hartford
Courant*, the *National Journal*, nine specialized book-

and educational-publishing houses, seventeen specialized magazines, the CBS affiliates in Dallas and Austin, the ABC affiliate in St. Louis, the NBC affiliate in Birmingham, a cable-television business, and a company that exists exclusively to dispose of what had been Times Mirror's timber and ranchland (this company, since it is meant to self-destruct, is described by Times Mirror as "entropic"): an empire with operating revenues for 1989 of $3,517,493,000.

The climate in which the *Times* prospered was a special one. Los Angeles had been, through its entire brief history, a boom town. People who lived there had tended to believe, and were encouraged to do so by the increasingly fat newspaper dropped at their doors every morning, that the trend would be unfailingly up. It seemed logical that the people who made business work in California should begin to desert San Francisco, which had been since the gold rush the financial center of the West, and look instead to Los Angeles, where the money increasingly was. It seemed logical that shipping should decline in San Francisco, one of the world's great natural ports, even as it flourished in Los Angeles, where a port had to be dredged, and was, at the insistence of the *Times* and Harry Chandler. It seemed logical that the wish to dredge this port should involve, since Los Angeles was originally landlocked, the annexation first of a twenty-mile corridor to the sea and then the "consolidation" with Los Angeles ("annexation" of one incor-

225

porated city by another was prohibited by state law) of two entire other cities, San Pedro and Wilmington, both of which lay on the Pacific.

The logic here was based on the declared imperative of unlimited opportunity, which in turn dictated unlimited growth. What was construed by people in the rest of the country as accidental—the sprawl of the city, the apparent absence of a cohesive center—was in fact purposeful, the scheme itself: this would be a new kind of city, one that would seem to have no finite limits, a literal cloud on the land that would eventually touch the Tehachapi range to the north and the Mexican border to the south, the San Bernardino Mountains to the east and the Pacific to the west; not just a city finally but its own nation, The Southland. That the Chandlers had been sufficiently prescient to buy up hundreds of thousands of acres on the far reaches of the expanding cloud—300,000 acres spanning the Tehachapi, 860,000 acres in Baja California, which Harrison Gray Otis and Harry Chandler were at one point trying to get the Taft administration to annex from Mexico, thereby redefining even what might have seemed Southern California's one fixed border (the Pacific was seen locally as not a border but an opportunity, a bridge to Hawaii and on to Asia)—was only what might be expected of any provident citizen: "The best interests of Los Angeles are paramount to the *Times*," Harry Chandler wrote in 1934, and it had been, historically, the *Times* that defined what those best interests were.

The *Times* under Harrison Gray Otis was a paper

in which the owners' opponents were routinely described as "thieves", "scoundrels", "blackmailers", "venal", "cowardly", "mean", "un-American", "assassinlike", "petty", "despotic", and "anarchic scum". It was said of General Otis (he had been commissioned a brigadier general when he led an expeditionary force to the Philippines during the Spanish-American War, and he was General Otis forever after, just as his houses were The Bivouac and The Outpost, the *Times* building was The Fortress, and the *Times* staff The Phalanx) that he had a remarkably even temper, that of a hungry tiger. A libel suit or judgment against the paper was seen as neither a problem nor an embarrassment but a journalistic windfall, an opportunity to reprint the offending story, intact and often. In November of 1884, after the election of Grover Cleveland to the presidency, the *Times* continued to maintain for eleven days that the president-elect was James G. Blaine, Harrison Gray Otis's candidate.

Even under Harry Chandler's son Norman, who was publisher from 1944 until 1960, the *Times* continued to exhibit a fitful willfulness. The Los Angeles for which the *Times* was at that time published was still remote from the sources of national and international power, isolated not only geographically but developmentally, a deliberately adolescent city, intent on its own growth and not much interested in the world outside. In 1960, when Norman Chandler's son Otis was named publisher of the *Times*, the paper had only one foreign correspondent, based in Paris. The city itself was run by a handful of men who worked for the banks and the old-line law firms downtown and drove home at five o'clock to Hancock Park or Pasadena or San Marino. They had lunch at the California Club or the Los Angeles Athletic Club. They held their weddings and funerals in Protestant or Catholic churches and did not, on the whole, know people who lived on the West Side, in Beverly Hills and Bel Air and Brentwood and Pacific Palisades, many of the most prominent of whom were in the entertainment business and were Jewish. As William Severns, the original general manager of the Los Angeles Music Center's operating company, put it in a recent interview with Patt Morrison of the *Times*, there was at that time a "big schism in society" between these downtown people and what he called "the movie group". The movie group, he said, "didn't even know where downtown was, except when they came downtown for a divorce". (This was in itself a cultural crossed connection, since people on the West Side generally got divorced not downtown but in Santa Monica.)

It was Norman Chandler's wife, Dorothy Buffum Chandler, called Buff, who perceived that it was in the interests of the city, and therefore of the *Times*, to draw the West Side into the power structure, and she saw the Music Center, for which she was then raising money, as a natural way to initiate this process. I once watched Mrs. Chandler, at a dinner sometime in 1964, try to talk the late Jules Stein, the founder and at that time the chairman of MCA, into contributing $25,000 toward the construction of the Music Center.

Jules Stein said that he would be glad to donate any amount to Mrs. Chandler's Music Center, and would then expect Mrs. Chandler to make a matching contribution, for this was the way things got done on the West Side, to the eye clinic he was then building at the UCLA Medical Center. "I can't do that," Mrs. Chandler said, and then she leaned across the table, and demonstrated what the Chandlers had always seen as the true usefulness of owning a newspaper: "But I can give you twenty-five thousand dollars' worth of free publicity in the paper."

By the time Mrs. Chandler was through, the Music Center and one of its support groups, The Amazing Blue Ribbon, had become the common ground on which the West Side met downtown. This was not to say that all the top editors and managers at the *Times* were entirely comfortable on the West Side; many of them tended still to regard it as alien, a place where people exchanged too many social kisses and held novel, if not dangerous, ideas. "I always enjoy visiting the West Side," I recall being told by Tom Johnson, who had in 1980 become the publisher of the *Times*, when we happened to be seated next to each other at a party in Brentwood. He then took a notepad and a pen from his pocket. "I like to hear what people out here think." Nor was it to say that an occasional citizen of a more self-absorbed Los Angeles did not still surface, and even write querulous letters to the *Times*:

Regarding "The Party Pace Picks Up During September" (by Jeannine Stein, Aug.

31): the social season in Los Angeles starts the first Friday in October when the Autumn Cotillion is held. This event, started over fifty years ago, brings together the socially prominent folks of Los Angeles who wouldn't be seen in Michael's and haven't yet decided if the opera is here to stay. By the time Cotillion comes around families are back from vacation, dove hunting season is just over and deer hunting season hasn't begun so the gentlemen of the city find no excuse not to attend. Following that comes the annual Assembly Ball and the Chevaliers du Tastevin dinner followed by the Las Madrinas Debutante Ball. If you are invited to these events you are in socially. No *nouveau riche* or publicity seekers nor social climbers need apply.

The *Times* in which this letter appeared, on September 10, 1989, was one that maintained six bureaus in Europe, five in Latin America, five in Asia, three in the Middle East, and two in Africa. It was reaching an area inhabited by between 13 and 14 million people, more than half of whom, a recent Rand Corporation study suggests, had arrived in Los Angeles as adults, eighteen years old or over, citizens whose memories did not include the Las Madrinas Debutante Ball. In fact there is in Los Angeles no memory everyone shares, no monument everyone knows, no historical reference as meaningful as the long sweep of the ramps where the San Diego and Santa Monica freeways intersect, as the way the hard Santa Ana light strikes the palm trees against the white western wall of the Carnation Milk building on Wilshire Boulevard. Mention of "historic" sites tends usually to signal a hustle under way, for example transforming a commercial development into historic Olvera Street, or wrapping a twenty-story office tower and a four-hundred-room hotel around the historic Mann's Chinese Theater (the historic Mann's Chinese Theater was originally Grauman's Chinese, but a significant percentage of the population has no reason to remember this), a featured part of the Hollywood Redevelopment.

Californians until recently spoke of the United States beyond Colorado as "back east". If they went to New York, they went "back" to New York, a way of speaking that carried with it the suggestion of living on a distant frontier. Californians of my daughter's generation speak of going "out" to New York, a meaningful shift in the perception of one's place in the world. The Los Angeles that Norman and Buff Chandler's son Otis inherited in 1960—and, with his mother, proceeded over the next twenty years to reinvent—was, in other words, a new proposition, potentially one of the world's great cities but still unformed, outgrowing its old controlling idea, its tropistic confidence in growth, and not yet seized by a new one. It was Otis Chandler who decided that what Los Angeles needed if it was to be a world-class city was a world-class newspaper, and he set out to get one.

Partly in response to the question of what a daily

newspaper could do that television could not do better, and partly in response to geography—papers on
the West Coast have a three-hour advantage going to
press, and a three-hour disadvantage when they come
off the press—Otis Chandler, then thirty-two, decided that the *Times* should be what was sometimes
called a daily magazine, a newspaper that would cover
breaking news competitively, but remain willing to
commit enormous resources to providing a kind of
analysis and background no one else was providing.
He made it clear at the outset that the paper was no
longer his father's but his, antagonizing members of
his own family in 1961 by running a five-part report
on the John Birch Society, of which his aunt and uncle
Alberta and Philip Chandler were influential members. Otis Chandler followed up the John Birch series,
in case anyone had missed the point, by signing the
Chandler name to a front-page editorial opposing
Birch activities. "His legs bestrid the ocean, his reared
arm crested the world," as the brass letters read (for
no clear reason, since it is what Cleopatra says about
Antony as the asps are about to arrive in the fifth act
of *Antony and Cleopatra*) at the base of the turning
globe in the lobby of the *Times* building. "His voice
was propertied to all the tuned spheres." One reason
Otis Chandler could property the voice of the *Times* to
all the tuned spheres was that his *Times* continued to
make more money than his father's. "The paper was
published every day and they could see it," he later
said about his family. "They disagreed endlessly with
my editorial policies. But they never disagreed with
the financial results."

In fact an unusual kind of reporting developed at the *Times*, the editorial philosophy of which was frequently said to be "run it long and run it once". The *Times* became a paper on which reporters were allowed, even encouraged, to give the reader the kind of detail that was known to everyone on the scene but rarely got filed. On the night Son of Sam was arrested in New York, according to Charles T. Powers, then in the *Times'* New York bureau, Roone Arledge was walking around Police Headquarters, "dressed as if for a touch football game, a glass of scotch in one hand, a portable two-way radio in the other, directing his network's feed to the Coast", details that told the reader pretty much all there was to know about celebrity police work. In San Salvador in the early spring of 1982, when representatives from the centrist Christian Democrats, the militarist National Conciliation Party, and the rightist ARENA were all meeting under a pito tree on Francisco ("Chachi") Guerrero's patio, Laurie Becklund of the *Times* asked Guerrero, who has since been assassinated, how people so opposed to one another could possibly work together. "We all know each other—we've known each other for years," he said. "You underestimate our *política tropical*." A few days later, when Laurie Becklund asked an ARENA leader why ARENA, then trying to close out the Christian Democrats, did not fear losing American aid, the answer she got, and filed, summed up the entire relationship between the United States and the Salvadoran right: "We believe in gringos."

This kind of detail was sometimes dismissed by re-

porters at other papers as "L.A. color", but really it
was something different: the details gave the tone of
the situation, the subtext without which the text could
not be understood, and sharing this subtext with the
reader was the natural tendency of reporters who, because of the nature of both the paper on which they
worked and the city in which it was published, tended
not to think of themselves as insiders. "Jesse don't
wanna run nothing but his mouth," Mayor Marion
Barry of Washington, D.C., was quoted as having
said, about Jesse Jackson, early in 1990 in a piece by
Bella Stumbo in the *Los Angeles Times;* there was in
this piece, I was told in New York, after both the *New
York Times* and the *Washington Post* had been forced to
report the ensuing controversy, nothing that many
Post and *New York Times* reporters in Washington did
not already know. This was presumably true, but
only the *Los Angeles Times* had printed it.

Unconventional choices were made at the *Times*.
Otis Chandler had insisted that the best people in the
country be courted and hired, regardless of their politics. The political cartoonist Paul Conrad was lured
from the *Denver Post*, brought out for an interview,
and met at the airport, per his demand, by the editor
of the paper. Robert Scheer, who had a considerable
reputation as a political journalist at *Ramparts* and *New
Times* but no newspaper experience, was not only
hired but given whatever he wanted, including the use
of the executive dining room, the Picasso Room. "For
the money we're paying Scheer, I should hope he'd
be abrasive," William Thomas, the editor of the *Times*

from 1971 until 1989, said to a network executive who
called to complain that Scheer had been abrasive in an
interview. The *Times* had by then abandoned traditional ideas of what newspaper reporters and editors
should be paid, and was in some cases paying double
the going rate. "I don't think newspapers should take
a back seat to magazines, TV, or public relations,"
Otis Chandler had said early on. He had bought the
Times a high-visibility Washington bureau. He had
bought the *Times* a foreign staff.

By 1980, when Otis Chandler named Tom Johnson
the publisher of the *Times* and created for himself the
new title of editor in chief, the *Times* was carrying, in
the average week, more columns of news than either
the *New York Times* or the *Washington Post*. It was running long analytical background pieces from parts of
the country and of the world that other papers left to
the wires. Its Washington bureau, even Bob Wood-
ward of the *Washington Post* conceded recently, was
frequently beating the *Post*. Its foreign coverage, particularly from Central America and the Middle East,
was, day for day, stronger than that of the national
competition. "Otis was a little more specific than just
indicating he wanted the *Times* to be among the top
U.S. newspapers," Nick Williams, the editor of the
Times from 1958 until 1971, said later of Otis Chandler's ascension to publisher of the *Times*. "He said, 'I
want it to be the number one newspaper in the country.' " What began worrying people in Los Angeles
during the fall of 1989, starting on the morning in
October when the *Times* unveiled the first edition of

235

what it referred to on billboards and television advertisements and radio spots and bus shelters and bus
tails and rack cards and in-paper advertisements and
even in its own house newsletter as "the new, faster-
format *Los Angeles Times*", was whether having the
number one newspaper in the country was a luxury
the Chandlers, and the city, could still afford.

It was hard, that fall at the *Times*, to sort out exactly
what was going on. A series of shoes had already been
dropped. There had been in January 1989 the instal-
lation of a new editor, someone from outside, someone
whose particular depths and shallows many people
had trouble sounding, someone from the East (actually he was from Tennessee, but his basic training
had been under Benjamin Bradlee at the *Washington
Post*, and around the *Times* he continued to be referred
to, tellingly, as an Easterner), Shelby Coffey III.
There had been some months later the announcement
of a new approach to what had become the *Times'*
Orange County problem, the problem being that a
few miles to the south, in Orange County, the *Times'*
zoned edition had so far been unable to unseat the
Orange County Register, the leading paper in a market
so rich that the *Register* had a few years earlier become
the one paper in the United States with more full-run
advertising linage than the *Times*.
The new approach to this Orange County problem
seemed straightforward enough (the editor of the Orange County edition, at that time Narda Zacchino,

would get twenty-nine additional reporters, an expanded plant, virtual autonomy over what appeared in the *Times* in Orange County, and would report only to Shelby Coffey), although it did involve a new "president", or business person, for Orange County, Lawrence M. Higby, whose particular skills—he was a marketing expert out of Taco Bell, Pepsi, and H. R. Haldeman's office in the Nixon White House, where he had been known as Haldeman's Haldeman—made some people uneasy. Narda Zacchino was liked and respected around the *Times* (she had more or less grown up on the paper, and was married to Robert Scheer), but Higby was an unknown quantity, and there were intimations that not everyone was entirely comfortable with these heightened stakes in Orange County. According to the *Wall Street Journal*, Tom Johnson, the publisher, said in an August 1989 talk to the Washington bureau that the decision to give Narda Zacchino and Lawrence Higby autonomy in Orange County had led to "blood all over the floor" in Los Angeles. He described the situation in Orange County as "a failure of mine", an area in which "I should have done more sooner".

Still, it was September 1989 before people outside the *Times* started noticing the blood, or even the dropped shoes, already on the floor. September was when it was announced, quite unexpectedly, that Tom Johnson, who had been Otis Chandler's own choice as publisher and had in turn picked Shelby Coffey as editor, was moving upstairs to what were described as "broader responsibilities", for example

237

newsprint supply. The publisher's office, it was explained, would now be occupied by David Laventhol, who had spent time at the *New York Herald Tribune* and the *Washington Post*, had moved next to *Newsday* (he was editor, then publisher), had been since 1987 the president of the parent Times Mirror Company, and had achieved, mainly because he was seen to have beat the *New York Times* in Queens with *New York Newsday*, a certain reputation for knowing how to run the kind of regional war the *Los Angeles Times* wanted to run in Orange County. David Laventhol, like Shelby Coffey, was referred to around the office as an Easterner.

Then, on October 11, 1989, there was the format change, to which many of the paper's most vocal readers, a significant number of whom had been comparing the paper favorably every morning with the national edition of the *New York Times*, reacted negatively. It appeared that some readers of the *Los Angeles Times* did not want color photographs on its front page. Nor, it appeared, did these readers want News Highlights or news briefs or boxes summarizing the background of a story in three or four sentences without dependent clauses. A Laguna Niguel subscriber described himself in a letter to the editor as "heartsick". A Temple City reader characterized the changes as "beyond my belief". By the first of December even the student newspaper at Caltech, the *California Tech*, was having a little fun at the *Times'* expense, calling itself the *New, Faster Format Tech* and declaring itself dedicated to "increasing the amount of information on the front page by replacing all stories with pictures". In the lost-and-found classified section of the *Times* itself there appeared, sandwiched among pleas for lost Akitas ("Has Tattoo") and lost Saudi Arabian Airlines ID cards and lost four-carat emerald-cut diamond rings set in platinum ("sentimental value"), this notice, apparently placed by a group of the *Times'* own reporters: *"LA TIMES:* Last seen in a confused state disguised as *USA Today.* If found, please return to Times Mirror Square."

The words *"USA Today"* were heard quite a bit during the first few months of the new, faster format, as were "New Coke" and "Michael Dukakis". It was said that Shelby Coffey and David Laventhol had turned the paper over to its marketing people. It was said that the marketing people were bent on reducing the paper to its zoned editions, especially to its Orange County edition, and reducing the zoned editions to a collection of suburban shoppers. It was said that the paper was conducting a deliberate dumb-down, turning itself over to the interests and whims (less to read, more local service announcements) of the several thousand people who had taken part in the videotaped focus groups the marketing people and key editors had been running down in Orange County. A new format for a newspaper or magazine tends inevitably to suggest a perceived problem with the product, and the insistence with which this particular new format was promoted—the advertising stressed the superior disposability of the new *Times*, how easy it was, how cut down, how little time the reader need spend with it—

convinced many people that the paper was determined to be less than it had been. "READ THIS," *Times* rack cards now demanded. "QUICK."

The architects of the new, faster format became, predictably, defensive, even impatient. People with doubts were increasingly seen as balky, resistant to all change, sulky dogs in the manger of progress. "Just look at this," Narda Zacchino, who as editor of the Orange County edition had been one of the central figures in the redesign, ordered me, brandishing first a copy of that morning's *USA Today* and then one of that morning's *Times*. "Do they look alike? No. They look nothing alike. I know there's been a negative response from within the paper. 'This is *USA Today*,' you hear. Well, look at it. It's not *USA Today*. But we're a newspaper. We want people to read the newspaper. I've been struggling down there for seven years, trying to get people to read the paper. And, despite the in-house criticism, we're not getting criticism from outside. Our response has been very, very good."

Shelby Coffey mentioned the redesign that Walter Bernard had done in 1977 for Henry Anatole Grunwald at *Time*. "They got scorched," he said. "They had thousands of letters, cancellations by the hundreds. I remember seeing it the first time and being jarred. In fact I thought they had lost their senses. They had gone to color. They had done the departments and the type in quite a different way. But it stood up over the years as one of the most successful, maybe *the* most successful, of the redesigns. I think you have to accept as a given that it's going to take six months or a year before people get used to this."

Around the paper, where it was understood that the format change had originally been developed in response to the needs of the Orange County edition, a certain paranoia had taken hold. People were exchanging rumors by computer mail. People were debating whether the Orange County edition should be encouraged to run announcements of local events in column one of page one ("Tonight: Tito Puente brings his Latin Jazz All-Stars to San Juan Capistrano. . . . Puente, a giant among salsa musicians, is a particular favorite at New York's celebrated Blue Note nightclub. Time: 8 P.M. at the Coach House, 33157 Camino Capistrano. Tickets: $19.50. Information: (714) 496-8930") and still call itself the *Los Angeles Times*. People were noticing that the Orange County edition was, as far as that went, not always calling itself the *Los Angeles Times*—that some of its subscription callers were urging telephone contacts to subscribe to "the Orange County *Times*". People were tormenting one another with various forms of the verb "to drive", as in "market-driven" and "customer-driven" and "a lot of people are calling this paper market-driven but it's not, what drives this paper is editorial" and "this paper has different forces driving it than something like *The Nation*". (The necessity for distinguishing the *Los Angeles Times* from *The Nation* was perhaps the most arresting but far from the only straw point made to me in the course of a few days at the *Times*.)

The mood was rendered no less febrile by what

began to seem an unusual number of personnel changes. During the first few days of November 1989, the *Los Angeles Herald Examiner* folded, and a visible number of its columnists and its sports and arts and entertainment writers began appearing immediately in the *Times*. A week or so later, Dennis Britton, who had been, with Shelby Coffey and two other editors, a final contender for the editorship of the *Times* (the four candidates had been asked by Tom Johnson to submit written analyses of the content of the *Times* and of the areas in which it needed strengthening), bailed out as one of the *Times'* deputy managing editors, accepting the editorship of the *Chicago Sun-Times*.

A week after that, it was announced that Anthony Day, the editor of the *Times* editorial pages since 1971, would be replaced by Thomas Plate, who had directed the partially autonomous editorial and op-ed pages for *New York Newsday* and was expected to play a role in doing something similar for Orange County. In the fever of the moment it was easy for some people to believe that the changes were all of a piece, that, for example, Anthony Day's leaving the editorial page had something to do with the new fast read, or with the fact that some people on the Times Mirror board had occasionally expressed dissatisfaction with the paper's editorial direction on certain issues, particularly its strong anti-Administration stand on Central American policy. Anthony Day was told only, he reported, that it was "time for a change", that he would be made a reporter and assigned a beat ("ideas and ideology in the modern world"), and that he would report directly to Shelby Coffey. "There was this strange, and strangely moving, party for Tony last Saturday at which Tom Johnson spoke," a friend at the *Times* wrote me not long after Day was fired. "And they sang songs to Tony—among them a version of 'Yesterday' in which the words were changed to 'Tonyday'. ('Why he had to go, we don't know, they wouldn't say')."

Part of the problem, as some people at the *Times* saw it, was that neither Shelby Coffey nor David Laventhol shared much history with anybody at the *Times*. Shelby Coffey was viewed by many people at the *Times* as virtually unfathomable. He seemed to place mysterious demands upon himself. His manner, which was essentially border Southern, was unfamiliar in Los Angeles. His wife, Mary Lee, was for many people at the *Times* equally hard to place, a delicate Southerner who looked like a lifetime Maid of Cotton but was in fact a doctor, not even a gynecologist or a pediatrician but a trauma specialist, working the emergency room at Huntington Hospital in Pasadena. "You know the golden rule of the emergency room," Mary Lee Coffey drawled the first time I met her, not long after her arrival in Los Angeles. She was wearing a white angora sweater. "Keep 'em alive till eight-oh-five."

Together, Shelby Coffey and David Laventhol, a demonstrated corporate player, suggested a new mood at the *Times*, a little leaner and maybe a little meaner, a little more market-oriented. "Since 1881, the *Los Angeles Times* has led the way with award-winning journalism," a *Times* help-wanted advertisement read around that time. "As we progress into our second century, we're positioned as one of America's largest newspapers. To help us maintain our leadership position, we're currently seeking a Promotion Writer." Some people in the newsroom began referring to the two as the First Street Gangster Crips (the Gangster Crips were a prominent Los Angeles gang, and the *Times* building was on First Street), and to their changes as drive-bys. They were repeatedly referred to as "guys whose ties are all in Washington or New York", as "people with Eastern ideas of what Los Angeles wants or deserves". Shelby Coffey's new editors were called "the Stepford Wives", and Shelby Coffey himself was called, to his face, "the Dan Quayle of journalism". (That this was said by a reporter who continued to be employed by the *Times* suggested not only the essentially tolerant nature of the paper but the extent to which Coffey appeared dedicated to the accommodation of dissent.) During the 1989 Christmas season, a blowup of his photograph, with a red hat pinned above it, appeared in one of the departments at the *Times*. "He Knows When You Are Sleeping," the legend read. "And With Whom."

This question of Coffey and Laventhol being "Easterners" was never far below the surface. "Easterner", as the word is used in Los Angeles, remains somewhat harder to translate than First Street Gangster Crip. It carries both an arrogance and a defensiveness, and has to do not exactly with geography (people who themselves came from the East will quite often dismiss other people as "Easterners") but with a virtually un-crackable complex of attitudes. An Easterner, in the local view, believes that Los Angeles begins and ends on the West Side and is about the movie business. Easterners, moreover, do not understand even the movie business: they come out in January and get taken to dinner at Spago and complain that the view is obscured by billboards, by advertisements for motion pictures, missing the point that advertisements for motion pictures are the most comforting possible view for those people who regularly get window tables at Spago. Easterners refer to Los Angeles as El Lay, as La La Land, as the Left Coast. "I suppose you're glad to be here," Easterners say to Californians when they run into them in New York. "I suppose you can always read the *Times* here," Easterners say on their January visits to Los Angeles, meaning the *New York Times*.

Easterners see the *Los Angeles Times* only rarely, and complain, when they do see it, about the length of its pieces. "They can only improve it," an editor of the *New York Times* said to me when I mentioned that the *Los Angeles Times* had undertaken some changes. He said that the paper had been in the past "unreadable". It was, he said, "all gray". I asked what he meant. "It's these stories that cover whole pages," he said. "And then the story breaks to the next page and keeps going." This was said on a day when, of eight stories on the front page of the *New York Times*, seven broke to other sections. "Who back east cares?" I was asked by someone at the *Los Angeles Times* when I said that I was writing about the changes at the paper. "If this were happening to the *New York Times*, you'd have the *Washington Post* all over it."

When people in Los Angeles talked about what was happening at the *Times*, they were talking about something harder to define, in the end, than any real or perceived or feared changes in the paper itself, which in fact was looking good. Day for day, not much about the *Times* had actually changed. There sometimes seemed fewer of the analytic national pieces that used to appear in column one. There seemed to be some increase in syndicated soft features, picked up with the columnists and arts reviewers when the *Herald Examiner* folded. But the "new, faster-format *Los Angeles Times*" (or, as early advertisements called it, the "new, fast-read *Los Angeles Times*") still carried more words every day than appear in the New Testament. It still carried in the average week more columns of news than the *New York Times* or the *Washington Post*. It still ran pieces at a length few other papers would countenance—David Shaw's January 1990 series on the coverage of the McMartin child-abuse case, for example, ran 17,000 words. The paper's editorials were just as strong under Thomas Plate as they had been under Anthony Day. Its reporters were still filing stories full of details that did not appear in other papers, for example the fact (this was from Kenneth Freed in Panama, January 1, 1990) that nearly 125 journalists, after spending less than twelve hours in

Panama without leaving Howard Air Force Base, where they were advised that there was shooting on the streets of Panama City ("It is war out there," the briefing officer told them), had accepted the Southern Command's offer of a charter flight back to Miami.

The *Times* had begun, moreover, to do aggressive local coverage, not historically the paper's strong point, and also to do frequent "special reports", eight-to-fourteen-page sections, with no advertising, offering wrap-up newsmagazine coverage of, say, China, or Eastern Europe, or the October 1989 Northern California earthquake, or the state of the environment in Southern California. A week or so before Christmas 1989, Shelby Coffey initiated a daily "Moscow Edition", a six-to-eight-page selection of stories from that day's *Los Angeles Times*. This Moscow Edition, which was prepared in Los Angeles, faxed to the *Times* bureau in Moscow, and delivered by hand to some 125 Soviet officials, turned out to be sufficiently popular that the Moscow bureau received a call from the Soviet Foreign Ministry requesting that the *Times* extend its publication to weekends and even to Christmas Day.

"Shelby may be fighting more of a fight against the dumbing-down of the newspaper than we know or he can say," one *Times* editor, who had himself been wary of the changes under way but had come to believe that there had been among some members of the staff an unjustified rush to judgment, said to me. "That the *Times* is still essentially the same paper seems to me so plainly the case as to refute the word 'new' in 'the new, faster-format *Los Angeles Times*'. What small novelty there is would have received very little promotion had it begun as a routine editorial modification. But it didn't originate in editorial discussion. It originated in market research, which was why it got promoted so heavily. The *Times* needed a way to declare Orange County a new ball game, and this was it. But you can't change the paper anywhere without changing it everywhere. And once the *Times* throws the switch, a colossal amount of current seems to flow through the whole system."

In a way the uneasiness had to do with the entire difficult question of "Easterners". It was not that Shelby Coffey was an Easterner or that David Laventhol was an Easterner but that Easterners had been brought in, that there was no Chandler in the publisher's office, no one to whom the *Los Angeles Times* was intrinsically more important than, say, *Newsday*, no one who could reliably be expected to have a visceral appreciation not just of how far the *Times* had come but of how far Los Angeles itself had come, of how fragile the idea of the place was and how easily it could be lost. Los Angeles had been the most idealized of American cities, and the least accidental. Its development had proceeded not from the circumstances of geography but from sheer will, from an idea. It had been General Otis and Harry Chandler who conceived the future of Los Angeles as one of ever-expanding possibility, and had instructed the readers of the *Times* in what was needed to achieve that future. It had been Otis Chandler who articulated this vision by defining the *Times'* sphere of influence as regional, from Santa Barbara to the border and from the mountains to the sea, and who told the readers of the *Times* that this was what they wanted.

What the *Times* seemed to be telling its readers now was significantly different, and was based not on the logic of infinite opportunity proceeding from infinite growth but on the logic of minimizing risk, on corporate logic, and it was not impossible to follow that logic to a point at which what might be best for the *Times* and what might be best for Los Angeles would no longer necessarily coincide. "You talk to people in Orange County, they don't want news of Los Angeles," David Laventhol said one afternoon in late November of 1989. "We did a survey. Ask them what news they want, news from Los Angeles rates very, very low."

We were talking about his sense that Southern California was fragmenting more than it was coalescing, about what one *Times* editor had called "the aggressive disidentification with Los Angeles" of the more recent and more uniformly affluent communities in Ventura and San Diego and Orange counties. This aggressive disidentification with Los Angeles was the reason the Orange County Edition had been made autonomous.

"I spent many years in the New York market, and in many ways this is a more complex market," David Laventhol said. "The *New York Times* and some other papers were traditionally able to connect the entire New York community. It's much tougher here. If anything could bind this whole place together—anything that's important, anything beyond baseball teams—it would probably be the *Times*. But people are looking inward right now. They aren't thinking in terms of the whole region. It's partly a function of transportation, jobs, the difficulty of commuting or whatever, but it's also a function of lifestyle. People in Orange County don't like the West Side of Los Angeles. They don't like the South Side of Los Angeles. They don't like whatever. They're lined up at the county line with their backs to Los Angeles."

Some years ago, Otis Chandler was asked how many readers would actually miss the *Times* were it to stop publishing tomorrow. "Probably less than half," Otis Chandler had said, and been so quoted in his own paper. For reasons that might not have been clear to his market-research people, he had nonetheless continued trying to make that paper the best in the country. During the 1989 Christmas season there was at the *Times*, as there had traditionally been, a party, and a Christmas toast was given, as it had traditionally been, by the publisher. In the past the publishers of the *Times* had stressed the growth of the enterprise, both achieved and anticipated. It had been a good year, David Laventhol said at the 1989 Christmas party, and he was glad it was over.

—1990

NEW YORK

Sentimental Journeys

1

WE KNOW her story, and some of us, although not all of us, which was to become one of the story's several equivocal aspects, know her name. She was a twenty-nine-year-old unmarried white woman who worked as an investment banker in the corporate finance department at Salomon Brothers in downtown Manhattan, the energy and natural resources group. She was said by one of the principals in a Texas oil-stock offering on which she had collaborated as a member of the Salomon team to have done "top-notch" work. She lived alone in an apartment on East 83rd Street, between York and East End, a sublet cooperative she was thinking about buying. She often worked late and when she got home she would change into jogging clothes and at eight-thirty or nine-thirty in the evening would go running, six or seven miles through Central Park, north on the East Drive, west on the less traveled road connecting the East and West Drives at approximately 102nd Street, and south on the West Drive. The wisdom of this was later questioned by some, by those who were accustomed to thinking of the Park as a place to avoid after dark, and defended by others, the more adroit of whom spoke of the citizen's absolute right to public access ("That park belongs to us and this time nobody is going to take it from us," Ronnie Eldridge, at the time a Democratic candidate for the City Council of New York, declared on the op-ed page of the *New York Times*), others of whom spoke of "running" as a preemptive right. "Runners have Type A controlled personalities and they don't like their schedules interrupted," one runner, a securities trader, told the *Times* to this point. "When people run is a function of their lifestyle," another runner said. "I am personally very angry," a third said. "Because women should have the right to run anytime."

For this woman in this instance these notional rights did not prevail. She was found, with her clothes torn off, not far from the 102nd Street connecting road at one-thirty on the morning of April 20, 1989. She was taken near death to Metropolitan Hospital on East 97th Street. She had lost 75 percent of her blood. Her skull had been crushed, her left eyeball pushed back through its socket, the characteristic surface wrinkles of her brain flattened. Dirt and twigs were found in her vagina, suggesting rape. By May 2, when she first woke from coma, six black and Hispanic teenagers, four of whom had made videotaped statements concerning their roles in the attack and another of whom had described his role in an unsigned verbal statement, had been charged with her assault and rape and she had become, unwilling and unwitting, a sacrificial player in the sentimental narrative that is New York public life.

Nightmare in Central Park, the headlines and display type read. *Teen Wolfpack Beats and Rapes Wall Street Exec on Jogging Path. Central Park Horror. Wolf Pack's Prey. Female Jogger Near Death After Savage Attack by Roving Gang. Rape Rampage. Park Marauders Call It "Wilding", Street Slang for Going Berserk. Rape Suspect: "It Was Fun". Rape Suspect's Jailhouse Boast: "She Wasn't Nothing". The teenagers were back in the holding cell, the confessions gory and complete. One shouted "hit the beat" and they all started rapping to "Wild Thing". The Jogger and the Wolf Pack. An Outrage and a Prayer.* And, on the Monday morning after the attack, on the front page of the *New York Post*, with a photograph of Governor Mario Cuomo and the headline *"None of Us Is Safe"*, this italic text: "A visibly shaken Governor Cuomo spoke out yesterday on the vicious Central Park rape: 'The people are angry and frightened—my mother is, my family is. To me, as a person who's lived in this city all of his life, this is the ultimate shriek of alarm.' "

Later it would be recalled that 3,254 other rapes were reported that year, including one the following week involving the near decapitation of a black woman in Fort Tryon Park and one two weeks later involving a black woman in Brooklyn who was robbed, raped, sodomized, and thrown down an air shaft of a four-story building, but the point was rhetorical, since crimes are universally understood to be news to the extent that they offer, however erroneously, a story,

a lesson, a high concept. In the 1986 Central Park
death of Jennifer Levin, then eighteen, at the hands of
Robert Chambers, then nineteen, the "story", extrap-
olated more or less from thin air but left largely un-
corrected, had to do not with people living wretchedly
and marginally on the underside of where they
wanted to be, not with the Dreiserian pursuit of "re-
spectability" that marked the revealed details (Robert
Chambers's mother was a private-duty nurse who
worked twelve-hour night shifts to enroll her son in
private schools and the Knickerbocker Greys), but
with "preppies", and the familiar "too much too
soon".

Susan Brownmiller, during a year spent monitoring
newspaper coverage of rape as part of her research for
Against Our Will: Men, Women and Rape, found, not
surprisingly, that "although New York City police
statistics showed that black women were more frequent victims of rape than white women, the favored
victim in the tabloid headline . . . was young, white,
middle class and 'attractive'." In its quite extensive
coverage of rape-murders during the year 1971, according to Ms. Brownmiller, the *Daily News* published
in its four-star final edition only two stories in which
the victim was not described in the lead paragraph as
"attractive": one of these stories involved an eight-
year-old child, the other was a second-day follow-up
on a first-day story that had in fact described the victim as "attractive". The *Times*, she found, covered
rapes only infrequently that year, but what coverage
they did "concerned victims who had some kind of

middle-class status, such as 'nurse', 'dancer' or 'teacher', and with a favored setting of Central Park".

As a news story, "Jogger" was understood to turn on the demonstrable "difference" between the victim and her accused assailants, four of whom lived in Schomburg Plaza, a federally subsidized apartment complex at the northeast corner of Fifth Avenue and 110th Street in East Harlem, and the rest of whom lived in the projects and rehabilitated tenements just to the north and west of Schomburg Plaza. Some twenty-five teenagers were brought in for questioning; eight were held. The six who were finally indicted ranged in age from fourteen to sixteen. That none of the six had previous police records passed, in this context, for achievement; beyond that, one was recalled by his classmates to have taken pride in his expensive basketball shoes, another to have been "a follower". *I'm a smooth type of fellow, cool, calm, and mellow,* one of the six, Yusef Salaam, would say in the rap he presented as part of his statement before sentencing.

> *I'm kind of laid back, but now I'm speaking so that you know / I got used and abused and even was put on the news. . . .*
> *I'm not dissing them all, but the some that I called.*
> *They tried to dis me like I was an inch small, like a midget, a mouse, something less than a man.*

The victim, by contrast, was a leader, part of what the *Times* would describe as "the wave of young professionals who took over New York in the 1980's", one of those who were "handsome and pretty and educated and white", who, according to the *Times*, not only "believed they owned the world" but "had reason to". She was from a Pittsburgh suburb, Upper St. Clair, the daughter of a retired Westinghouse senior manager. She had been Phi Beta Kappa at Wellesley, a graduate of the Yale School of Management, a congressional intern, nominated for a Rhodes Scholarship, remembered by the chairman of her department at Wellesley as "probably one of the top four or five students of the decade". She was reported to be a vegetarian, and "fun-loving", although only "when time permitted", and also to have had (these were the *Times'* details) "concerns about the ethics of the American business world".

In other words she was wrenched, even as she hung between death and life and later between insentience and sentience, into New York's ideal sister, daughter, Bacharach bride: a young woman of conventional middle-class privilege and promise whose situation was such that many people tended to overlook the fact that the state's case against the accused was not invulnerable. The state could implicate most of the defendants in the assault and rape in their own videotaped words, but had none of the incontrovertible forensic evidence—no matching semen, no matching fingernail scrapings, no matching blood—commonly produced in this kind of case. Despite the fact that jurors in the second trial would eventually mention physical evidence as having been crucial in their bringing guilty verdicts against one defendant, Kevin Richardson, there was not actually much physical evidence at hand. Fragments of hair "similar [to] and consistent" with that of the victim were found on Kevin Richardson's clothing and underwear, but the state's own criminologist had testified that hair samples were necessarily inconclusive since, unlike fingerprints, they could not be traced to a single person. Dirt samples found on the defendants' clothing were, again, similar to dirt found in that part of the park where the attack took place, but the state's criminologist allowed that the samples were also similar to dirt found in other uncultivated areas of the park. To suggest, however, that this minimal physical evidence could open the case to an aggressive defense—to, say, the kind of defense that such celebrated New York criminal lawyers as Jack Litman and Barry Slotnick typically present—would come to be construed, during the weeks and months to come, as a further attack on the victim.

She would be Lady Courage to the *New York Post*, she would be A Profile in Courage to the *Daily News* and *New York Newsday*. She would become for Anna Quindlen in the *New York Times* the figure of "New York rising above the dirt, the New Yorker who has known the best, and the worst, and has stayed on, living somewhere in the middle". She would become for David Dinkins, the first black mayor of New York, the emblem of his apparently fragile hopes for the city itself: "I hope the city will be able to learn a lesson from this event and be inspired by the young woman who was assaulted in the case," he said. "Despite tremendous odds, she is rebuilding her life. What a human life can do, a human society can do as well." She was even then for John Gutfreund, at that time the chairman and chief executive officer of Salomon Brothers, the personification of "what makes this city so vibrant and so great," now "struck down by a side of our city that is as awful and terrifying as the creative side is wonderful". It was precisely in this conflation of victim and city, this confusion of personal woe with public distress, that the crime's "story" would be found, its lesson, its encouraging promise of narrative resolution.

One reason the victim in this case could be so readily abstracted, and her situation so readily made to stand for that of the city itself, was that she remained, as a victim of rape, unnamed in most press reports. Although the American and English press convention of not naming victims of rape (adult rape victims are named in French papers) derives from the understandable wish to protect the victim, the rationalization of this special protection rests on a number of doubtful, even magical, assumptions. The convention assumes, by providing a protection for victims of rape not afforded victims of other assaults, that rape involves a violation absent from other kinds of assault. The convention assumes that this violation is of a nature best kept secret, that the rape victim feels, and would feel still more strongly were she identified, a shame and self-loathing unique to this form of assault;

in other words that she has been in an unspecified way party to her own assault, that a special contract exists between this one kind of victim and her assailant. The convention assumes, finally, that the victim would be, were this special contract revealed, the natural object of prurient interest; that the act of male penetration involves such potent mysteries that the woman so penetrated (as opposed, say, to having her face crushed with a brick or her brain penetrated with a length of pipe) is permanently marked, "different", even—especially if there is a perceived racial or social "difference" between victim and assailant, as in nineteenth-century stories featuring white women taken by Indians—"ruined".

These quite specifically masculine assumptions (women do not want to be raped, nor do they want to have their brains smashed, but very few mystify the difference between the two) tend in general to be self-fulfilling, guiding the victim to define her assault as her protectors do. "Ultimately we're doing women a disservice by separating rape from other violent crimes," Deni Elliott, the director of Dartmouth's Ethics Institute, suggested in a discussion of this custom in *Time*. "We are participating in the stigma of rape by treating victims of this crime differently," Geneva Overholser, the editor of the *Des Moines Register*, said about her decision to publish in February of 1990 a five-part piece about a rape victim who agreed to be named. "When we as a society refuse to talk openly about rape, I think we weaken our ability to deal with it." Susan Estrich, a professor of criminal law at Har-

vard Law School and the manager of Michael Dukakis's 1988 presidential campaign, discussed, in *Real
Rape*, the conflicting emotions that followed her own
1974 rape:

> At first, being raped is something you sim-
> ply don't talk about. Then it occurs to you
> that people whose houses are broken into or
> who are mugged in Central Park talk about
> it *all* the time. . . . If it isn't my fault, why
> am I supposed to be ashamed? If I'm not
> ashamed, if it wasn't "personal", why look
> askance when I mention it?

There were, in the 1989 Central Park attack, specific circumstances that reinforced the conviction that
the victim should not be named. She had clearly been,
according to the doctors who examined her at Metropolitan Hospital and to the statements made by the
suspects (she herself remembered neither the attack
nor anything that happened during the next six
weeks), raped by one or more assailants. She had also
been beaten so brutally that, fifteen months later, she
could not focus her eyes or walk unaided. She had lost
all sense of smell. She could not read without experiencing double vision. She was believed at the time to
have permanently lost function in some areas of her
brain.

   Given these circumstances, the fact that neither the
victim's family nor, later, the victim herself wanted
her name known struck an immediate chord of sym-
pathy, seemed a belated way to protect her as she had
not been protected in Central Park. Yet there was in

this case a special emotional undertow that derived in part from the deep and allusive associations and taboos attaching, in American black history, to the idea of the rape of white women. Rape remained, in the collective memory of many blacks, the very core of their victimization. Black men were accused of raping white women, even as black women were, Malcolm X wrote in *The Autobiography of Malcolm X*, "raped by the slave-master white man until there had begun to emerge a homemade, handmade, brainwashed race that was no longer even of its true color, that no longer even knew its true family names". The very frequency of sexual contact between white men and black women increased the potency of the taboo on any such contact between black men and white women. The abolition of slavery, W. J. Cash wrote in *The Mind of the South*,

> . . . in destroying the rigid fixity of the black at the bottom of the scale, in throwing open to him at least the legal opportunity to advance, had inevitably opened up to the mind of every Southerner a vista at the end of which stood the overthrow of this taboo. If it was given to the black to advance at all, who could say (once more the logic of the doctrine of his inherent inferiority would not hold) that he would not one day advance the whole way and lay claim to complete equality, including, specifically, the ever crucial right of marriage?
>
> What Southerners felt, therefore, was that any assertion of any kind on the part of the Negro constituted in a perfectly real manner

an attack on the Southern woman. What
they saw, more or less consciously, in the
conditions of Reconstruction was a passage
toward a condition for her as degrading, in
their view, as rape itself. And a condition,
moreover, which, logic or no logic, they in-
fallibly thought of as being as absolutely
forced upon her as rape, and hence a condition for which the term "rape" stood as truly
as for the *de facto* deed.

Nor was the idea of rape the only potentially treach-
erous undercurrent in this case. There has historically
been, for American blacks, an entire complex of
loaded references around the question of "naming":
slave names, masters' names, African names, call me
by my rightful name, nobody knows my name; stories, in which the specific gravity of naming locked
directly into that of rape, of black men whipped for
addressing white women by their given names. That,
in this case, just such an interlocking of references
could work to fuel resentments and inchoate hatreds
seemed clear, and it seemed equally clear that some of
what ultimately occurred—the repeated references to
lynchings, the identification of the defendants with
the Scottsboro boys, the insistently provocative repetition of the victim's name, the weird and self-defeating
insistence that no rape had taken place and little harm
been done the victim—derived momentum from this
historical freight. "Years ago, if a white woman said a
Black man looked at her lustfully, he could be hung
higher than a magnolia tree in bloom, while a white

mob watched joyfully sipping tea and eating cookies,"
Yusef Salaam's mother reminded readers of the *Amsterdam News*. "The first thing you do in the United
States of America when a white woman is raped is
round up a bunch of black youths, and I think that's
what happened here," the Reverend Calvin O. Butts
III of the Abyssinian Baptist Church in Harlem told
the *New York Times*. "You going to arrest me now
because I said the jogger's name?" Gary Byrd asked
rhetorically on his WLIB show, and was quoted by
Edwin Diamond in *New York* magazine:

> I mean, she's obviously a public figure, and
> a very mysterious one, I might add. Well,
> it's a funny place we live in called America,
> and should we be surprised that they're up
> to their usual tricks? It was a trick that got
> us here in the first place.

This reflected one of the problems with not naming
this victim: she was in fact named all the time. Everyone in the courthouse, everyone who worked for a
paper or a television station or who followed the case
for whatever professional reason, knew her name. She
was referred to by name in all court records and in all
court proceedings. She was named, in the days immediately following the attack, on some local television stations. She was also routinely named—and this
was part of the difficulty, part of what led to a damaging self-righteousness among those who did not
name her and to an equally damaging embattlement

among those who did—in Manhattan's black-owned newspapers, the *Amsterdam News* and the *City Sun*, and she was named as well on WLIB, the Manhattan radio station owned by a black partnership that included Percy Sutton and, until 1985, when he transferred his stock to his son, Mayor Dinkins.

That the victim in this case was identified on Centre Street and north of 96th Street but not in between made for a certain cognitive dissonance, especially since the names of even the juvenile suspects had been released by the police and the press before any suspect had been arraigned, let alone indicted. "The police normally withhold the names of minors who are accused of crimes," the *Times* explained (actually the police normally withhold the names of accused "juveniles", or minors under age sixteen, but not of minors sixteen or seventeen), "but officials said they made public the names of the youths charged in the attack on the woman because of the seriousness of the incident." There seemed a debatable point here, the question of whether "the seriousness of the incident" might not have in fact seemed a compelling reason to avoid any appearance of a rush to judgment by preserving the anonymity of a juvenile suspect; one of the names released by the police and published in the *Times* was of a fourteen-year-old who was ultimately not indicted.

There were, early on, certain aspects of this case that seemed not well handled by the police and prosecutors, and others that seemed not well handled by the press. It would seem to have been tactically unwise, since New York State law requires that a parent or guardian be present when children under sixteen are questioned, for police to continue the interrogation of Yusef Salaam, then fifteen, on the grounds that his Transit Authority bus pass said he was sixteen, while his mother was kept waiting outside. It would seem to have been unwise for Linda Fairstein, the assistant district attorney in charge of Manhattan sex crimes, to ignore, at the precinct house, the mother's assertion that the son was fifteen, and later to suggest, in court, that the boy's age had been unclear to her because the mother had used the word "minor".

It would also seem to have been unwise for Linda Fairstein to tell David Nocenti, the assistant U.S. Attorney who was paired with Yusef Salaam in a "Big Brother" program and who had come to the precinct house at the mother's request, that he had "no legal standing" there and that she would file a complaint with his supervisors. It would seem in this volatile a case imprudent of the police to follow their normal procedure by presenting Raymond Santana's initial statement in their own words, cop phrases that would predictably seem to some in the courtroom, as the expression of a fourteen-year-old held overnight and into the next afternoon for interrogation, unconvincing:

On April 19, 1989, at approximately 20:30 hours, I was at the Taft Projects in the vicinity of 113th St. and Madison Avenue. I was there with numerous friends. . . . At approximately 21:00 hours, we all (myself and approximately 15 others) walked south on

> Madison Avenue to E. 110th Street, then
> walked westbound to Fifth Avenue. At Fifth
> Avenue and 110th Street, we met up with
> an additional group of approximately 15
> other males, who also entered Central Park
> with us at that location with the intent to rob
> cyclists and joggers . . .

In a case in which most of the defendants had made videotaped statements admitting at least some role in the assault and rape, this less than meticulous attitude toward the gathering and dissemination of information seemed peculiar and self-defeating, the kind of pressured or unthinking standard procedure that could not only exacerbate the fears and angers and suspicions of conspiracy shared by many blacks but open what seemed, on the basis of the confessions, a conclusive case to the kind of doubt that would eventually keep juries out, in the trial of the first three defendants, ten days, and, in the trial of the next two defendants, twelve days. One of the reasons the jury in the first trial could not agree, *Manhattan Lawyer* reported in its October 1990 issue, was that one juror, Ronald Gold, remained "deeply troubled by the discrepancies between the story [Antron] McCray tells on his videotaped statement and the prosecution's scenario":

> Why did McCray place the rape at the res-
> ervoir, Gold demanded, when all evidence
> indicated it happened at the 102 Street cross-
> drive? Why did McCray say the jogger was

raped where she fell, when the prosecution said she'd been dragged 300 feet into the woods first? Why did McCray talk about having to hold her arms down, if she was found bound and gagged?

The debate raged for the last two days, with jurors dropping in and out of Gold's acquittal [for McCray] camp. . . .

After the jurors watched McCray's video for the fifth time, Miranda [Rafael Miranda, another juror] knew it well enough to cite the time-code numbers imprinted at the bottom of the videotape as he rebuffed Gold's arguments with specific statements from McCray's own lips. [McCray, on the videotape, after admitting that he had held the victim by her left arm as her clothes were pulled off, volunteered that he had "got on top" of her, and said that he had rubbed against her without an erection "so everybody would . . . just know I did it".] The pressure on Gold was mounting. Three jurors agree that it was evident Gold, worn down perhaps by his own displays of temper as much as anything else, capitulated out of exhaustion. While a bitter Gold told other jurors he felt terrible about ultimately giving in, Brueland [Harold Brueland, another juror who had for a time favored acquittal for McCray] believes it was all part of the process.

"I'd like to tell Ronnie someday that nervous exhaustion is an element built into the

269

court system. They know that," Brueland says of court officials. "They know we're only going to be able to take it for so long. It's just a matter of, you know, who's got the guts to stick with it."

So fixed were the emotions provoked by this case that the idea that there could have been, for even one juror, even a moment's doubt in the state's case, let alone the kind of doubt that could be sustained over ten days, seemed, to many in the city, bewildering, almost unthinkable: the attack on the jogger had by then passed into narrative, and the narrative was about confrontation, about what Governor Cuomo had called "the ultimate shriek of alarm", about what was wrong with the city and about its solution. What was wrong with the city had been identified, and its names were Raymond Santana, Yusef Salaam, Antron McCray, Kharey Wise, Kevin Richardson, and Steve Lopez. "They never could have thought of it as they raged through Central Park, tormenting and ruining people," Bob Herbert wrote in the *News* after the verdicts came in on the first three defendants.

There was no way it could have crossed their vicious minds. Running with the pack, they would have scoffed at the very idea. They would have laughed.

And yet it happened. In the end, Yusef Salaam, Antron McCray and Raymond Santana were nailed by a woman.

Elizabeth Lederer stood in the courtroom and watched Saturday night as the three were hauled off to jail. . . . At times during the trial, she looked about half the height of the long and lanky Salaam, who sneered at her from the witness stand. Salaam was apparently too dumb to realize that Lederer—this petite, soft-spoken, curly-haired prosecutor—was the jogger's avenger. . . .

You could tell that her thoughts were elsewhere, that she was thinking about the jogger.

You could tell that she was thinking: I did it.

I did it for you.

Do this in remembrance of me: the solution, then, or so such pervasive fantasies suggested, was to partake of the symbolic body and blood of The Jogger, whose idealization was by this point complete, and was rendered, significantly, in details stressing her "difference", or superior class. The Jogger was someone who wore, according to *Newsday*, "a light gold chain around her slender neck" as well as, according to the *News*, a "modest" gold ring and "a thin sheen" of lipstick. The Jogger was someone who would not, according to the *Post*, "even dignify her alleged attackers with a glance." The Jogger was someone who spoke, according to the *News*, in accents "suited to boardrooms", accents that might therefore seem "foreign to many native New Yorkers". In her first appearance on the witness stand she had been subjected, the *Times* noted, "to questions that most people do not have to answer publicly during their lifetimes", principally about her use of a diaphragm on the Sunday preceding the attack, and had answered these questions, according to an editorial in the *News*, with an "indomitable dignity" that had taught the city a lesson "about courage and class".

This emphasis on perceived refinements of character and of manner and of taste tended to distort and to flatten, and ultimately to suggest not the actual victim of an actual crime but a fictional character of a slightly earlier period, the well-brought-up virgin who briefly graces the city with her presence and receives in turn a taste of "real life". The defendants, by contrast, were seen as incapable of appreciating these marginal distinctions, ignorant of both the norms and accoutrements of middle-class life. "Did you have jogging clothes on?" Elizabeth Lederer asked Yusef Salaam, by way of trying to discredit his statement that he had gone into the park that night only to "walk around". Did he have "jogging clothes", did he have "sports equipment", did he have "a bicycle". A pernicious nostalgia had come to permeate the case, a longing for the New York that had seemed for a while to be about "sports equipment", about getting and spending rather than about having and not having: the reason that this victim must not be named was so that she could go unrecognized, it was astonishingly said, by Jerry Nachman, the editor of the *New York Post*, and then by others who seemed to find in this a particular resonance, to Bloomingdale's.

Some New York stories involving young middle-class white women do not make it to the editorial pages, or even necessarily to the front pages. In April 1990, a young middle-class white woman named Laurie Sue Rosenthal, raised in an Orthodox Jewish household and at age twenty-nine still living with her parents in Jamaica, Queens, happened to die, according to the coroner's report from the accidental toxicity of Darvocet in combination with alcohol, in an apartment at 36 East 68th Street in Manhattan. The apartment belonged to the man she had been, according to her parents, seeing for about a year, a minor city assistant commissioner named Peter Franconeri. Peter Franconeri, who was at the time in charge of elevator and boiler inspections for the Buildings Department and married to someone else, wrapped Laurie Sue Rosenthal's body in a blanket; placed it, along with her handbag and ID, outside the building with the trash; and went to his office at 60 Hudson Street. At some point an anonymous call was made to 911. Franconeri was identified only after Laurie Sue Rosenthal's parents gave the police his beeper number, which they found in her address book. According to *Newsday*, which covered the story more extensively than the *News*, the *Post*, or the *Times*,

> Initial police reports indicated that there were no visible wounds on Rosenthal's body. But Rosenthal's mother, Ceil, said

yesterday that the family was told the autopsy revealed two "unexplained bruises" on her daughter's body.

Larry and Ceil Rosenthal said those findings seemed to support their suspicions that their daughter was upset because they received a call from their daughter at 3 A.M. Thursday "saying that he had beaten her up". The family reported the conversation to police.

"I told her to get into a cab and get home," Larry Rosenthal said yesterday. "The next I heard was two detectives telling me terrible things."

"The ME [medical examiner] said the bruises did not constitute a beating but they were going to examine them further," Ceil Rosenthal said.

"There were some minor bruises," a spokeswoman for the Office of the Chief Medical Examiner told *Newsday* a few days later, but the bruises "did not in any way contribute to her death". This is worth rerunning: A young woman calls her parents at three in the morning, "distraught". She says that she has been beaten up. A few hours later, on East 68th Street between Madison and Park avenues, a few steps from Porthault and Pratesi and Armani and Saint Laurent and the Westbury Hotel, at a time of day in this part of New York 10021 when Jim Buck's dog trainers are assembling their morning packs and Henry Kravis's Bentley is idling outside his Park Avenue apartment and the construction crews are clocking in over near the Frick at the multimillion-dollar houses under reconstruction for Bill Cosby and for the owner of The Limited, this young middle-class white woman's body, showing bruises, gets put out with the trash.

"Everybody got upside down because of who he was," an unidentified police officer later told Jim Dwyer of *Newsday*, referring to the man who put the young woman out with the trash. "If it had happened to anyone else, nothing would have come of it. A summons would have been issued and that would have been the end of it." In fact nothing did come of the death of Laurie Sue Rosenthal, which might have seemed a natural tabloid story but failed, on several levels, to catch the local imagination. For one thing she could not be trimmed into the role of the preferred tabloid victim, who is conventionally presented as fate's random choice (Laurie Sue Rosenthal had, for whatever reason, taken the Darvocet instead of a taxi home, her parents reported treatment for a previous Valium dependency, she could be presumed to have known over the course of a year that Franconeri was married and yet continued to see him); for another, she seemed not to have attended an expensive school or to have been employed in a glamour industry (no Ivy Grad, no Wall Street Exec), which made it hard to cast her as part of "what makes this city so vibrant and so great".

In August 1990, Peter Franconeri pled guilty to a misdemeanor, the unlawful removal of a body, and was sentenced by Criminal Court judge Peter Benitez to seventy-five hours of community service. This was neither surprising nor much of a story (only twenty-three lines even in *Newsday*, on page twenty-nine of the city edition), and the case's lenient resolution was for many people a kind of relief. The district attorney's office had asked for "some incarceration", the amount usually described as a "touch", but no one wanted, it was said, to crucify the guy: Peter Franconeri was somebody who knew a lot of people, understood how to live in the city, who had for example not only the apartment on East 68th Street between Madison and Park but a house in Southampton and who also understood that putting a body outside with the trash was nothing to get upside down about, if it was handled right. Such understandings may in fact have been the city's true "ultimate shriek of alarm", but it was not a shriek the city wanted to recognize.

2

PERHAPS THE MOST arresting collateral news to surface, during the first few days after the attack on the Central Park jogger, was that a significant number of New Yorkers apparently believed the city sufficiently well-ordered to incorporate Central Park into their evening fitness schedules. "Prudence" was defined, even after the attack, as "staying south of 90th Street", or having "an awareness that you need to think about planning your routes", or, in the case of one woman interviewed by the *Times*, deciding to quit her daytime job (she was a lawyer) because she was "tired of being stuck out there, running later and later at night". "I don't think there's a runner who couldn't describe the silky, gliding feeling you get running at night," an editor of *Runner's World* told the *Times*. "You see less of what's around you and you become centered on your running."

The notion that Central Park at night might be a good place to "see less of what's around you" was recent. There were two reasons why Frederick Law Olmsted and Calvert Vaux, when they devised their winning entry in the 1858 competition for a Central Park design, decided to sink the transverse roads below grade level. One reason, the most often cited, was aesthetic, a recognition on the part of the designers that the four crossings specified by the terms of the competition, at 65th, 79th, 85th, and 97th streets, would intersect the sweep of the landscape, be "at variance with those agreeable sentiments which we should wish the park to inspire". The other reason, which appears to have been equally compelling, had to do with security. The problem with grade-level crossings, Olmsted and Vaux wrote in their "Greensward" plan, would be this:

> The transverse roads will . . . have to be kept open, while the park proper will be useless for any good purpose after dusk; for experience has shown that even in London, with its admirable police arrangements, the public cannot be assured safe transit through large open spaces of ground after nightfall.

277

> These public throughfares will then re-
> quire to be well-lighted at the sides, and, to
> restrain marauders pursued by the police
> from escaping into the obscurity of the park,
> strong fences or walls, six or eight feet high,
> will be necessary.

The park, in other words, was seen from its conception as intrinsically dangerous after dark, a place of
"obscurity", "useless for any good purpose", a refuge
only for "marauders". The parks of Europe closed at
nightfall, Olmsted noted in his 1882 pamphlet *The
Spoils of the Park: With a Few Leaves from the Deep-laden
Note-books of "A Wholly Unpractical Man"*, "but one surface road is kept open across Hyde Park, and the su-
perintendent of the Metropolitan Police told me that a
man's chances of being garrotted or robbed were, because of the facilities for concealment to be found in
the Park, greater in passing at night along this road
than anywhere else in London."

In the high pitch of the initial "jogger" coverage,
suggesting as it did a city overtaken by animals, this
pragmatic approach to urban living gave way to a
more ideal construct, one in which New York either
had once been or should be "safe", and now, as in
Governor Cuomo's "none of us is safe", was not. It
was time, accordingly, to "take it back", time to "say
no"; time, as David Dinkins would put it during his
campaign for the mayoralty in the summer of 1989, to
"draw the line". What the line was to be drawn against
was "crime", an abstract, a free-floating specter that

could be dispelled by certain acts of personal affirmation, by the kind of moral rearmament that later figured in Mayor Dinkins's plan to revitalize the city by initiating weekly "Tuesday Night Out Against Crime" rallies.

By going into the park at night, Tom Wicker wrote in the *Times*, the victim in this case had "affirmed the primacy of freedom over fear". A week after the assault, Susan Chace suggested on the op-ed page of the *Times* that readers walk into the park at night and join hands. "A woman can't run in the park at an offbeat time," she wrote. "Accept it, you say. I can't. It shouldn't be like this in New York City, in 1989, in spring." Ronnie Eldridge also suggested that readers walk into the park at night, but to light candles. "Who are we that we allow ourselves to be chased out of the most magnificent part of our city?" she asked, and also: "If we give up the park, what are we supposed to do: fall back to Columbus Avenue and plant grass?" This was interesting, suggesting as it did that the city's not inconsiderable problems could be solved by the willingness of its citizens to hold or draw some line, to "say no"; in other words that a reliance on certain magical gestures could affect the city's fate.

The insistent sentimentalization of experience, which is to say the encouragement of such reliance, is not new in New York. A preference for broad strokes, for the distortion and flattening of character and the reduction of events to narrative, has been for well over

279

a hundred years the heart of the way the city presents itself: Lady Liberty, huddled masses, ticker-tape parades, heroes, gutters, bright lights, broken hearts, 8 million stories in the naked city; 8 million stories and all the same story, each devised to obscure not only the city's actual tensions of race and class but also, more significantly, the civic and commercial arrangements that rendered those tensions irreconcilable.

Central Park itself was such a "story", an artificial pastoral in the nineteenth-century English romantic tradition, conceived, during a decade when the population of Manhattan would increase by 58 percent, as a civic project that would allow the letting of contracts and the employment of voters on a scale rarely before undertaken in New York. Ten million cartloads of dirt would need to be shifted during the twenty years of its construction. Four to five million trees and shrubs would need to be planted, half a million cubic yards of topsoil imported, 114 miles of ceramic pipe laid.

Nor need the completion of the park mean the end of the possibilities: in 1870, once William Marcy Tweed had revised the city charter and invented his Department of Public Parks, new roads could be built whenever jobs were needed. Trees could be dug up, and replanted. Crews could be set loose to prune, to clear, to hack at will. Frederick Law Olmsted, when he objected, could be overridden, and finally eased out. "A 'delegation' from a great political organization called on me by appointment," Olmsted wrote in *The*

Spoils of the Park, recalling the conditions under which he had worked:

> After introductions and handshakings, a circle was formed, and a gentleman stepped before me, and said, "We know how much pressed you must be . . . but at your convenience our association would like to have you determine what share of your patronage we can expect, and make suitable arrangements for our using it. We will take the liberty to suggest, sir, that there could be no more convenient way than that you should send us our due quota of tickets, if you will please, sir, in this form, *leaving us to fill in the name*." Here a packet of printed tickets was produced, from which I took one at random. It was a blank appointment and bore the signature of Mr. Tweed.

> As superintendent of the Park, I once received in six days more than seven thousand letters of advice as to appointments, nearly all from men in office. . . . I have heard a candidate for a magisterial office in the city addressing from my doorsteps a crowd of such advice-bearers, telling them that I was bound to give them employment, and suggesting plainly, that, if I was slow about it, a rope round my neck might serve to lessen my reluctance to take good counsel. I have had a dozen men force their way into my house before I had risen from bed on a Sun-

day morning, and some break into my draw-
ing room in their eagerness to deliver letters
of advice.

Central Park, then, for its underwriters if not for
Olmsted, was about contracts and concrete and kick-
backs, about pork, but the sentimentalization that
worked to obscure the pork, the "story", had to do
with certain dramatic contrasts, or extremes, that
were believed to characterize life in this as in no other
city. These "contrasts", which have since become the
very spine of the New York narrative, appeared early
on: Philip Hone, the mayor of New York in 1826 and
1827, spoke in 1843 of a city "overwhelmed with population, and where the two extremes of costly luxury
in living, expensive establishments and improvident
wastes are presented in daily and hourly contrast with
squalid mixing and hapless destruction." Given this
narrative, Central Park could be and ultimately would
be seen the way Olmsted himself saw it, as an essay
in democracy, a social experiment meant to socialize a
new immigrant population and to ameliorate the perilous separation of rich and poor. It was the duty and
the interest of the city's privileged class, Olmsted had
suggested some years before he designed Central
Park, to "get up parks, gardens, music, dancing
schools, reunions which will be so attractive as to
force into contact the good and the bad, the gentleman
and the rowdy".

The notion that the interests of the "gentleman" and
the "rowdy" might be at odds did not intrude: then as

now, the preferred narrative worked to veil actual conflict, to cloud the extent to which the condition of being rich was predicated upon the continued neediness of a working class; to confirm the responsible stewardship of "the gentleman" and to forestall the possibility of a self-conscious, or politicized, proletariat. Social and economic phenomena, in this narrative, were personalized. Politics were exclusively electoral. Problems were best addressed by the emergence and election of "leaders", who could in turn inspire the individual citizen to "participate", or "make a difference". "Will you help?" Mayor Dinkins asked New Yorkers, in a September 1990 address from St. Patrick's Cathedral intended as a response to the "New York crime wave" stories then leading the news. "Do you care? Are you ready to become part of the solution?"

"Stay," Governor Cuomo urged the same New Yorkers. "Believe. Participate. Don't give up." Manhattan borough president Ruth Messinger, at the dedication of a school flagpole, mentioned the importance of "getting involved" and "participating", or "pitching in to put the shine back on the Big Apple". In a discussion of the popular "New York" stories written between 1902 and 1910 by William Sidney Porter, or "O. Henry", William R. Taylor of the State University of New York at Stony Brook spoke of the way in which these stories, with their "focus on individuals' plights", their "absence of social or political implications" and "ideological neutrality", provided "a miraculous form of social glue":

These sentimental accounts of relations between classes in the city have a specific historical meaning: empathy without political
compassion. They reduce the scale of human
suffering to what atomized individuals endure as their plucky, sad lives were re-
counted week after week for almost a decade
. . . their sentimental reading of oppression,
class differences, human suffering, and af-
fection helped create a new language for in-
terpreting the city's complex society, a
language that began to replace the thread-
bare moralism that New Yorkers inherited
from 19th-century readings of the city. This
language localized suffering in particular
moments and confined it to particular occasions; it smoothed over differences because
it could be read almost the same way from
either end of the social scale.

Stories in which terrible crimes are inflicted on innocent victims, offering as they do a similarly sentimental reading of class differences and human
suffering, a reading that promises both resolution and
retribution, have long performed as the city's endor-
phins, a built-in source of natural morphine working
to blur the edges of real and to a great extent insoluble
problems. What is singular about New York, and remains virtually incomprehensible to people who live
in less rigidly organized parts of the country, is the
minimal level of comfort and opportunity its citizens

have come to accept. The romantic capitalist pursuit of privacy and security and individual freedom, so taken for granted nationally, plays, locally, not much role. A city where virtually every impulse has been to stifle rather than to encourage normal competition, New York works, when it does work, not on a market economy but on little deals, payoffs, accommodations, *baksheesh*, arrangements that circumvent the direct exchange of goods and services and prevent what would be, in a competitive economy, the normal ascendance of the superior product.

There were in the five boroughs in 1990 only 581 supermarkets (a supermarket, as defined by the trade magazine *Progressive Grocer*, is a market that does an annual volume of $2 million), or, assuming a population of 8 million, one supermarket for every 13,769 citizens. Groceries, costing more than they should because of this absence of competition and also because of the proliferation of payoffs required to ensure this absence of competition (produce, we have come to understand, belongs to the Gambinos, and fish to the Lucheses and the Genoveses, and a piece of the construction of the market to each of the above, but keeping the door open belongs finally to the inspector here, the inspector there), are carried home or delivered, as if in Jakarta, by pushcart.

It has historically taken, in New York as if in Mexico City, ten years to process and specify and bid and contract and construct a new school; twenty or thirty years to build or, in the cases of Bruckner Boulevard and the West Side Highway, to not quite build a highway. A recent public scandal revealed that a batch of city-ordered Pap smears had gone unread for more than a year (in the developed world the Pap smear, a test for cervical cancer, is commonly read within a few days); what did not become a public scandal, what is still accepted as the way things are, is that even Pap smears ordered by Park Avenue gynecologists can go unread for several weeks.

Such resemblances to cities of the third world are in no way casual, or based on the "color" of a polyglot population: these are all cities arranged primarily not to improve the lives of their citizens but to be labor-intensive, to accommodate, ideally at the subsistence level, since it is at the subsistence level that the work force is most apt to be captive and loyalty assured, a third-world population. In some ways New York's very attractiveness, its promises of opportunity and improved wages, its commitments as a city in the developed world, were what seemed destined to render it ultimately unworkable. Where the vitality of such cities in the less developed world had depended on their ability to guarantee low-cost labor and an absence of regulation, New York had historically depended instead on the constant welling up of new businesses, of new employers to replace those phased out, like the New York garment manufacturers who found it cheaper to make their clothes in Hong Kong or Kuala Lumpur or Taipei, by rising local costs.

It had been the old pattern of New York, supported by an expanding national economy, to lose one kind of business and gain another. It was the more recent error of New York to misconstrue this history of turn-over as an indestructible resource, there to be taxed at will, there to be regulated whenever a dollar could be seen in doing so, there for the taking. By 1977, New York had lost some 600,000 jobs, most of them in manufacturing and in the kinds of small businesses that could no longer maintain their narrow profit margins inside the city. During the "recovery" years, from 1977 until 1988, most of these jobs were indeed replaced, but in a potentially perilous way: of the 500,000 new jobs created, most were in the area most vulnerable to a downturn, that of financial and business services, and many of the rest in an area not only equally vulnerable to bad times but dispiriting to the city even in good, that of tourist and restaurant services.

The demonstration that many kinds of businesses were finding New York expendable had failed to prompt real efforts to make the city more competitive. Taxes grew still more punitive, regulation more Byzantine. Forty-nine thousand new jobs were created in New York's city agencies between 1983 and 1990, even as the services provided by those agencies were widely perceived to decline. Attempts at "reform" typically tended to create more jobs: in 1988, in response to the length of time it was taking to build or repair a school, a new agency, the School Construction Authority, was formed. A New York City school, it was said, would now take only five years to build. The head of the School Construction Authority was to receive $145,000 a year and each of the three vice presidents $110,000 a year. An executive gym, with Nautilus equipment, was contemplated for the top floor of the agency's new headquarters at the International Design Center in Long Island City. Two years into this reform, the backlog on repairs to existing schools stood at 33,000 outstanding requests. "To relieve the charity of friends of the support of a half-blind and half-witted man by employing him at the public expense as an inspector of cement may not be practical with reference to the permanent firmness of a wall," Olmsted noted after his Central Park experience, "while it is perfectly so with reference to the triumph of sound doctrine at an election."

In fact the highest per capita taxes of any city in the United States (and, as anyone running a small business knows, the widest variety of taxes) provide, in New York, unless the citizen is prepared to cut a side deal here and there, only the continuing multiplication of regulations designed to benefit the contractors and agencies and unions with whom the regulators have cut their own deals. A kitchen appliance accepted throughout the rest of the United States as a basic postwar amenity, the in-sink garbage disposal unit, is for example illegal in New York. Disposals, a city employee advised me, not only encourage rats, and "bacteria", presumably in a way that bags of garbage sitting on the sidewalk do not ("Because it is," I was told when I asked how this could be), but also encourage people "to put their babies down them".

On the one hand this illustrates how a familiar urban principle, that of patronage (the more garbage there is to be collected, the more garbage collectors can be employed), can be reduced, in the bureaucratic wilderness that is any third-world city, to voodoo; on the other it reflects this particular city's underlying criminal ethic, its acceptance of graft and grift as the bedrock of every transaction. "Garbage costs are outrageous," an executive of Supermarkets General, which owns Pathmark, recently told *City Limits* about why the chains preferred to locate in the suburbs. "Every time you need to hire a contractor, it's a problem." The problem, however, is one from which not only the contractor but everyone with whom the contractor does business—a chain of direct or indirect patronage extending deep into the fabric of the city—stands to derive one or another benefit, which was one reason the death of a young middle-class white woman in the East 68th Street apartment of the assistant commissioner in charge of boiler and elevator inspections flickered so feebly on the local attention span.

It was only within the transforming narrative of "contrasts" that both the essential criminality of the city and its related absence of civility could become points of pride, evidence of "energy": if you could make it here you could make it anywhere, hello sucker, get smart. Those who did not get the deal, who bought retail, who did not know what it took to get their electrical work signed off, were dismissed as provincials, bridge-and-tunnels, out-of-towners who did not have what it took not to get taken. "Every tourist's nightmare became a reality for a Maryland couple over the weekend when the husband was beaten and robbed on Fifth Avenue in front of Trump Tower," began a story in the *New York Post* during the summer of 1990. "Where do you think we're from, Iowa?" the prosecutor who took Robert Chambers's statement said on videotape by way of indicating that he doubted Chambers's version of Jennifer Levin's death. "They go after poor people like you from out of town, they prey on the tourists," a clerk explained in the West 46th Street computer store where my husband and I had taken refuge to escape three muggers. My husband said that we lived in New York. "That's why they didn't get you," the clerk said, effortlessly incorporating this change in the data. "That's how you could move fast."

The narrative comforts us, in other words, with the assurance that the world is knowable, even flat, and New York its center, its motor, its dangerous but vital "energy". "Family in Fatal Mugging Loved New York" was the *Times* headline on a story following the September 1990 murder, in the Seventh Avenue IND station, of a twenty-two-year-old tourist from Utah. The young man, his parents, his brother, and his sister-in-law had attended the U.S. Open and were reportedly on their way to dinner at a Moroccan restaurant downtown. "New York, to them, was the greatest place in the world," a family friend from Utah was quoted as having said. Since the narrative requires that the rest of the country provide a dramatic contrast to New York, the family's hometown in Utah was characterized by the *Times* as a place where "life revolves around the orderly rhythms of Brigham Young University" and "there is only about one murder a year". The town was in fact Provo, where Gary Gilmore shot the motel manager, both in life and in *The Executioner's Song*. "She loved New York, she just loved it," a friend of the assaulted jogger told the *Times* after the attack. "I think she liked the fast pace, the competitiveness."

New York, the *Times* concluded, "invigorated" the jogger, "matched her energy level". At a time when the city lay virtually inert, when forty thousand jobs had been wiped out in the financial markets and former traders were selling shirts at Bergdorf Goodman for Men, when the rate of mortgage delinquencies had doubled, when 50 or 60 million square feet of office space remained unrented (60 million square feet of unrented office space is the equivalent of fifteen darkened World Trade Towers) and even prime commercial blocks on Madison Avenue in the Seventies were boarded up, empty; at a time when the money had dropped out of all the markets and the Europeans who had lent the city their élan and their capital during the eighties had moved on, vanished to more cheerful venues, this notion of the city's "energy" was sedative, as was the commandeering of "crime" as the city's central problem.

3

THE EXTENT to which the October 1987 crash of the New York financial markets damaged the illu-

JOAN DIDION

sions of infinite recovery and growth on which the city had operated during the 1980s had been at first hard to apprehend. "Ours is a time of New York ascendant," the New York City Commission on the Year 2000, created during the mayoralty of Edward Koch to reflect the best thinking of the city's various business and institutional establishments, had declared in its 1987 report. "The city's economy is stronger than it has been in decades, and is driven both by its own resilience and by the national economy; New York is more than ever the international capital of finance, and the gateway to the American economy."

And then, its citizens had come gradually to understand, it was not. This perception that something was "wrong" in New York had been insidious, a slow-onset illness at first noticeable only in periods of temporary remission. Losses that might have seemed someone else's problem (or even comeuppance) as the markets were in their initial 1987 free-fall, and that might have seemed more remote still as the markets regained the appearance of strength, had come imperceptibly but inexorably to alter the tone of daily life. By April of 1990, people who lived in and around New York were expressing, in interviews with the *Times*, considerable anguish and fear that they did so: "I feel very resentful that I've lost a lot of flexibility in my life," one said. "I often wonder, 'Am I crazy for coming here?' " "People feel a sense of impending doom about what may happen to them," a clinical psychologist said. People were "frustrated", "feeling absolutely desolate", "trapped", "angry", "terrified", and "on the verge of panic".

It was a panic that seemed in many ways specific to
New York, and inexplicable outside it. Even later,
when the troubles of New York had become a common theme, Americans from less depressed venues
had difficulty comprehending the nature of those
troubles, and tended to attribute them, as New Yorkers themselves had come to do, to "crime". "Escape
From New York" was the headline on the front page
of the *New York Post* on September 10, 1990. "Ram-
paging Crime Wave Has 59% of Residents Terrified.
Most Would Get Out of the City, Says Time/CNN
Poll." This poll appeared in the edition of *Time* dated
September 17, 1990, which carried the cover legend
"The Rotting of the Big Apple". "Reason: a surge of
drugs and violent crime that government officials seem
utterly unable to combat," the story inside explained.
Columnists referred, locally, to "this sewer of a city".
The *Times* ran a plaintive piece about the snatch of
Elizabeth Rohatyn's Hermès handbag outside Arca-
dia, a restaurant on East 62nd Street that had for a
while seemed the very heart of the New York everyone now missed, the New York where getting and
spending could take place without undue reference to
having and not having, the duty-free New York; that
this had occurred to the wife of Felix Rohatyn, who
was widely perceived to have saved the city from its
fiscal crisis in the midseventies, seemed to many a
clarion irony.

This question of crime was tricky. There were in
fact eight American cities with higher homicide rates,
and twelve with higher overall crime rates. Crime had
long been taken for granted in the less affluent parts

of the city, and had become in the midseventies, as both unemployment and the costs of maintaining property rose and what had once been functioning neighborhoods were abandoned and burned and left to whoever claimed them, endemic. "In some poor neighborhoods, crime became almost a way of life," Jim Sleeper, an editor at *Newsday* and the author of *The Closest of Strangers: Liberalism and the Politics of Race in New York*, noted in his discussion of the social disintegration that occurred during this period:

> . . . a subculture of violence with complex bonds of utility and affection within families and the larger, "law-abiding" community. Struggling merchants might "fence" stolen goods, for example, thus providing quick cover and additional incentive for burglaries and robberies; the drug economy became more vigorous, reshaping criminal lifestyles and tormenting the loyalties of families and friends. A walk down even a reasonably busy street in a poor, minority neighborhood at high noon could become an unnerving journey into a landscape eerie and grim.

What seemed markedly different a decade later, what made crime a "story", was that the more privileged, and especially the more privileged white, citizens of New York had begun to feel unnerved at high noon in even their own neighborhoods. Although New York City Police Department statistics suggested that white New Yorkers were not actually in

increased mortal danger (the increase in homicides between 1977 and 1989, from 1,557 to 1,903, was entirely among what the NYPD classified as Hispanic,
Asian, and black victims; the number of white murder
victims had steadily declined, from 361 in 1977 to 227
in 1984 and 190 in 1989), the apprehension of such
danger, exacerbated by street snatches and muggings
and the quite useful sense that the youth in the
hooded sweatshirt with his hands jammed in his pockets might well be a predator, had become general.
These more privileged New Yorkers now felt unnerved not only on the street, where the necessity for
evasive strategies had become an exhausting constant,
but in even the most insulated and protected apartment buildings. As the residents of such buildings,
the owners of twelve- and sixteen- and twenty-four-
room apartments, watched the potted ficus trees dis-
appear from outside their doors and the graffiti appear
on their limestone walls and the smashed safety glass
from car windows get swept off their sidewalks, it had
become increasingly easy to imagine the outcome of a
confrontation between, say, the relief night doorman
and six dropouts from Julia Richman High School on
East 67th Street.

And yet those New Yorkers who had spoken to the
Times in April of 1990 about their loss of flexibility,
about their panic, their desolation, their anger, and
their sense of impending doom, had not been talking
about drugs, or crime, or any of the city's more publicized and to some extent inflated ills. These were
people who did not for the most part have twelve- and

sixteen-room apartments and doormen and the luxury of projected fears. These people were talking instead about an immediate fear, about money, about the vertiginous plunge in the value of their houses and apartments and condominiums, about the possibility or probability of foreclosure and loss; about, implicitly, their fears of being left, like so many they saw every day, below the line, out in the cold, on the street.

This was a climate in which many of the questions that had seized the city's attention in 1987 and 1988, for example that of whether Mortimer Zuckerman should be "allowed" to build two fifty-nine-story office towers on the site of what is now the Coliseum, seemed in retrospect wistful, the baroque concerns of better times. "There's no way anyone would make a sane judgment to go into the ground now," a vice president at Cushman and Wakefield told the *New York Observer* about the delay in the Coliseum project, which had in fact lost its projected major tenant, Salomon Brothers, shortly after Black Monday, 1987. "It would be suicide. You're better off sitting in a tub of water and opening your wrists." Such fears were, for a number of reasons, less easy to incorporate into the narrative than the fear of crime.

The imposition of a sentimental, or false, narrative on the disparate and often random experience that constitutes the life of a city or a country means, necessarily, that much of what happens in that city or country will be rendered merely illustrative, a series of set pieces, or performance opportunities. Mayor Dinkins could, in such a symbolic substitute for civic life, "break the boycott" (the Flatbush boycott organized to mobilize resentment of Korean merchants in black neighborhoods) by purchasing a few dollars' worth of produce from a Korean grocer on Church Avenue. Governor Cuomo could "declare war on crime" by calling for five thousand additional police; Mayor Dinkins could "up the ante" by calling for sixty-five hundred. "White slut comes into the park looking for the African man," a black woman could say, her voice loud but still conversational, in the corridor outside the courtroom where, during the summer of 1990, the first three defendants in the Central Park attack, Antron McCray, Yusef Salaam, and Raymond Santana, were tried on charges of attempted murder, assault, sodomy, and rape. "Boyfriend beats shit out of her, they blame it on our boys," the woman could continue, and then, referring to a young man with whom the victim had at one time split the cost of an apartment: "How about the roommate, anybody test his semen? No. He's white. They don't do it to each other."

Glances could then flicker among those reporters and producers and courtroom sketch artists and photographers and cameramen and techs and summer interns who assembled daily at 111 Centre Street. Cellular phones could be picked up, a show of indifference. Small talk could be exchanged with the marshals, a show of solidarity. The woman could then raise her voice: "White folk, all of them are devils, even those that haven't been born yet, they are *devils*. Little *demons*. I don't understand these devils, I guess they think this is *their court*." The reporters could gaze beyond her, faces blank, no eye contact, a more correct form of hostility and also more lethal. The woman could hold her ground but avert her eyes, letting her gaze fall on another black, in this instance a black *Daily News* columnist, Bob Herbert. "You," she could say. "You are a *disgrace*. Go ahead. Line up there. Line up with the white folk. Look at them, lining up for their first-class seats while *my* people are downstairs behind *barricades* . . . kept behind barricades like *cattle* . . . not even allowed in the room to see their sons lynched . . . is that an *African* I see in that line? Or is that a *Negro*. Oh, oh, sorry, shush, white folk didn't know, he was *passing* . . ."

In a city in which grave and disrupting problems had become general—problems of not having, problems of not making it, problems that demonstrably existed, among the mad and the ill and the underequipped and the overwhelmed, with decreasing reference to color—the case of the Central Park jogger provided more than just a safe, or structured, setting in which various and sometimes only marginally related rages could be vented. "This trial," the *Daily News* announced on its editorial page one morning in July 1990, midway through the trial of the first three defendants, "is about more than the rape and brutalization of a single woman. It is about the rape and the brutalization of a city. The jogger is a symbol of all that's wrong here. And all that's right, because she is nothing less than an inspiration."

The *News* did not define the ways in which "the rape and the brutalization of the city" manifested itself, nor was definition necessary: this was a city in which the threat or the fear of brutalization had become so immediate that citizens were urged to take up their own defense, to form citizen patrols or militia, as in Beirut. This was a city in which between twenty and thirty neighborhoods had already given over their protection, which was to say the right to determine who belonged in the neighborhood and who did not and what should be done about it, to the Guardian Angels. This was a city in which a Brooklyn vigilante group, which called itself Crack Busters and was said to be trying to rid its Bedford-Stuyvesant neighborhood of drugs, would before September was out "settle an argument" by dousing with gasoline and setting on fire an abandoned van and the three homeless citizens inside. This was a city in which the *Times* would soon perceive, in the failing economy, "a bright side for the city at large", the bright side being that while there was believed to have been an increase in the number of middle-income and upper-income families who wanted to leave the city, "the slumping market is keeping many of those families in New York".

In this city rapidly vanishing into the chasm between its actual life and its preferred narratives, what people said when they talked about the case of the Central Park jogger came to seem a kind of poetry, a way of expressing, without directly stating, different but equally volatile and similarly occult visions of the same disaster. One vision, shared by those who had seized upon the attack on the jogger as an exact representation of what was wrong with the city, was of a city systematically ruined, violated, raped by its underclass. The opposing vision, shared by those who had seized upon the arrest of the defendants as an exact representation of their own victimization, was of a city in which the powerless had been systematically ruined, violated, raped by the powerful. For so long as this case held the city's febrile attention, then, it offered a narrative for the city's distress, a frame in which the actual social and economic forces wrenching the city could be personalized and ultimately obscured.

Or rather it offered two narratives, mutually exclusive. Among a number of blacks, particularly those whose experience with or distrust of the criminal justice system was such that they tended to discount the fact that five of the six defendants had to varying degrees admitted taking part in the attack, and to focus instead on the absence of any supporting forensic evidence incontrovertibly linking this victim to these defendants, the case could be read as a confirmation not only of their victimization but of the white conspiracy they saw at the heart of that victimization. For the *Amsterdam News*, which did not veer automatically to the radical analysis (a typical issue in the fall of 1990 lauded the FBI for its minority recruiting and the Harlem National Guard for its high morale and readiness to go to the Gulf), the defendants could in this light be seen as victims of "a political trial", of a "legal lynching", of a case "rigged from the very beginning" by the decision of "the white press" that "whoever was arrested and charged in this case of the attempted murder, rape and sodomy of a well-connected, bright, beautiful, and promising white woman was guilty, pure and simple".

For Alton H. Maddox, Jr., the message to be drawn from the case was that the American criminal justice system, which was under any circumstances "inherently and unabashedly racist", failed "to function equitably at any level when a Black male is accused of raping a white female". For others the message was more general, and worked to reinforce the fragile but functional mythology of a heroic black past, the narrative in which European domination could be explained as a direct and vengeful response to African superiority. "Today the white man is faced head-on with what is happening on the Black Continent, Africa," Malcolm X wrote.

> Look at the artifacts being discovered there, that are proving over and over again, how the black man had great, fine, sensitive civilizations before the white man was out of the caves. Below the Sahara, in the places where most of America's Negroes' foreparents were kidnapped, there is being unearthed some of the finest craftsmanship, sculpture and other objects, that has ever been seen by modern man. Some of these things now are on view in such places as New York City's Museum

of Modern Art. Gold work of such fine tol-
erance and workmanship that it has no rival.
Ancient objects produced by black hands
. . . refined by those black hands with results that no human hand today can equal.

History has been so "whitened" by the
white man that even the black professors
have known little more than the most ignorant black man about the talents and rich
civilizations and cultures of the black man of
millenniums ago . . .

"Our proud African queen," the Reverend Al Sharpton had said of Tawana Brawley's mother, Glenda
Brawley: "She stepped out of anonymity, stepped out
of obscurity, and walked into history." It was said in
the corridors of the courthouse where Yusuf Salaam
was tried that he carried himself "like an African
king".

"It makes no difference anymore whether the attack
on Tawana happened," William Kunstler had told
New York Newsday when the alleged rape and torture
of Tawana Brawley by a varying number of white
police officers seemed, as an actual prosecutable crime
if not as a window on what people needed to believe,
to have dematerialized. "If her story was a concoction
to prevent her parents from punishing her for staying
out all night, that doesn't disguise the fact that a lot of
young black women are treated the way she said she
was treated." The importance of whether or not the
crime had occurred was, in this view, entirely resident
in the crime's "description", which was defined by

Stanley Diamond in *The Nation* as "a crime that did not occur" but was "described with skill and controlled hysteria by the black actors as the epitome of degradation, a repellent model of what actually happens to too many black women".

A good deal of what got said around the edges of the jogger case, in the corridors and on the call-in shows, seemed to derive exclusively from the suspicions of conspiracy increasingly entrenched among those who believe themselves powerless. A poll conducted in June of 1990 by the *New York Times* and WCBS-TV News determined that 77 percent of blacks polled believed either that it was "true" or "might possibly be true" (as opposed to "almost certainly not true") that the government of the United States "singles out and investigates black elected officials in order to discredit them in a way it doesn't do with white officials". Sixty percent believed that it was true or might possibly be true that the government "deliberately makes sure that drugs are easily available in poor black neighborhoods in order to harm black people". Twenty-nine percent believed that it was true or might possibly be true that "the virus which causes AIDS was deliberately created in a laboratory in order to infect black people". In each case, the alternative response to "true" or "might possibly be true" was "almost certainly not true", which might have seemed in itself to reflect a less than ringing belief in the absence of conspiracy. "The conspiracy to destroy Black boys is very complex and interwoven," Jawanza Kunjufu, a Chicago educational

303

consultant, wrote in his *Countering the Conspiracy to Destroy Black Boys*, a 1982 pamphlet that has since been extended to three volumes.

> There are many contributors to the conspiracy, ranging from the very visible who are more obvious, to the less visible and silent partners who are more difficult to recognize.
>
> Those people who adhere to the doctrine of white racism, imperialism, and white male supremacy are easier to recognize. Those people who actively promote drugs and gang violence are active conspirators, and easier to identify. What makes the conspiracy more complex are those people who do not plot together to destroy Black boys, but, through their indifference, perpetuate it. This passive group of conspirators consists of parents, educators, and white liberals who deny being racists, but through their silence allow institutional racism to continue.

For those who proceeded from the conviction that there was under way a conspiracy to destroy blacks, particularly black boys, a belief in the innocence of these defendants, a conviction that even their own statements had been rigged against them or wrenched from them, followed logically. It was in the corridors and on the call-in shows that the conspiracy got sketched in, in a series of fantasy details that conflicted not only with known facts but even with each other. It was said that the prosecution was withholding evidence that the victim had gone to the park to meet a drug dealer. It was said, alternately or concurrently, that the prosecution was withholding evidence that the victim had gone to the park to take part in a satanic ritual. It was said that the forensic photographs showing her battered body were not "real" photographs, that "they", the prosecution, had "brought in some corpse for the pictures". It was said that the young woman who appeared on the witness stand and identified herself as the victim was not the "real" victim, that "they" had in this case brought in an actress.

What was being expressed in each instance was the sense that secrets must be in play, that "they", the people who had power in the courtroom, were in possession of information systematically withheld—since information itself was power—from those who did not have power. On the day the first three defendants were sentenced, C. Vernon Mason, who had formally entered the case in the penalty phase as Antron McCray's attorney, filed a brief that included the bewildering and untrue assertion that the victim's boyfriend, who had not at that time been called to testify, was black. That some whites jumped to engage this assertion on its own terms (the *Daily News* columnist Gail Collins referred to it as Mason's "slimiest argument of the hour—an announcement that the jogger had a black lover") tended only to reinforce the sense of racial estrangement that was the intended subtext of the assertion, which was without meaning or significance except in that emotional deep where whites are seen as conspiring in secret to sink blacks in misery. "Just answer me, who got addicted?" I re-

305

call one black spectator asking another as they left the courtroom. "I'll tell you who got addicted, the inner city got addicted." He had with him a pamphlet that laid out a scenario in which the government had conspired to exterminate blacks by flooding their neighborhoods with drugs, a scenario touching all the familiar points, Laos, Cambodia, the Golden Triangle, the CIA, more secrets, more poetry.

"From the beginning I have insisted that this was not a racial case," Robert Morgenthau, the Manhattan district attorney, said after the verdicts came in on the first jogger trial. He spoke of those who, in his view, wanted "to divide the races and advance their own private agendas", and of how the city was "ill-served" by those who had so "sought to exploit" this case. "We had hoped that the racial tensions surrounding the jogger trial would begin to dissipate soon after the jury arrived at a verdict," a *Post* editorial began a few days later. The editorial spoke of an "ugly claque of 'activists' ", of the "divisive atmosphere" they had created, and of the anticipation with which the city's citizens had waited for "mainstream black leaders" to step forward with praise for the way in which the verdicts had brought New York "back from the brink of criminal chaos":

> Alas, in the jogger case, the wait was in vain.
> Instead of praise for a verdict which demonstrated that sometimes criminals are caught

and punished, New Yorkers heard charlatans like the Rev. Al Sharpton claim the case
was fixed. They heard that C. Vernon
Mason, one of the engineers of the Tawana
Brawley hoax—the attorney who thinks
Mayor Dinkins wears "too many yarmulkes"
—was planning to appeal the verdicts . . .

To those whose preferred view of the city was of an
inherently dynamic and productive community ordered by the natural play of its conflicting elements,
enriched, as in Mayor Dinkins's "gorgeous mosaic",
by its very "contrasts", this case offered a number of
useful elements. There was the confirmation of
"crime" as the canker corroding the life of the city.
There was, in the random and feral evening described
by the East Harlem attackers and the clear innocence
of and damage done to the Upper East Side and Wall
Street victim, an eerily exact and conveniently personalized representation of what the *Daily News* had called
"the rape and the brutalization of a city". Among the
reporters on this case, whose own narrative conventions involved "hero cops" and "brave prosecutors"
going hand to hand against "crime" (the "Secret
Agony of Jogger DA", we learned in the *Post* a few
days after the verdicts in the first trial, was that "Brave
Prosecutor's Marriage Failed as She Put Rapists
Away"), there seemed an unflagging enthusiasm for
the repetition and reinforcement of these elements,
and an equally unflagging resistance, even hostility, to
exploring the point of view of the defendants' families

and friends and personal or political allies (or, as they were called in news reports, the "supporters") who gathered daily at the other end of the corridor from the courtroom.

This seemed curious. Criminal cases are widely regarded by American reporters as windows on the city or culture in which they take place, opportunities to enter not only households but parts of the culture normally closed, and yet this was a case in which indifference to the world of the defendants extended even to the reporting of names and occupations. Yusuf Salaam's mother, who happened to be young and photogenic and to have European features, was pictured so regularly that she and her son became the instantly recognizable "images" of Jogger One, but even then no one got her name quite right. For a while in the papers she was "Cheroney", or sometimes "Cheronay", McEllhonor, then she became Cheroney McEllhonor Salaam. After she testified, the spelling of her first name was corrected to "Sharonne", although, since the byline on a piece she wrote for the *Amsterdam News* spelled it differently, "Sharrone", this may have been another misunderstanding. Her occupation was frequently given as "designer" (later, after her son's conviction, she went to work as a paralegal for William Kunstler), but no one seemed to take this seriously enough to say what she designed or for whom; not until after she testified, when *Newsday* reported her testimony that on the evening of her son's arrest she had arrived at the precinct house late because she was an instructor at the Parsons School of Design, did the notion of "designer" seem sufficiently concrete to suggest an actual occupation.

The Jogger One defendants were referred to repeatedly in the news columns of the *Post* as "thugs". The defendants and their families were often said by reporters to be "sneering". (The reporters, in turn, were said at the other end of the corridor to be "smirking".) "We don't have nearly so strong a question as to the guilt or innocence of the defendants as we did at Bensonhurst," a *Newsday* reporter covering the first jogger trial said to the *New York Observer*, well before the closing arguments, by way of explaining why *Newsday*'s coverage may have seemed less extensive on this trial than on the Bensonhurst trials. "There is not a big question as to what happened in Central Park that night. Some details are missing, but it's fairly clear who did what to whom."

In fact this came close to the heart of it: that it seemed, on the basis of the videotaped statements, fairly clear who had done what to whom was precisely the case's liberating aspect, the circumstance that enabled many of the city's citizens to say and think what they might otherwise have left unexpressed. Unlike other recent high visibility cases in New York, unlike Bensonhurst and unlike Howard Beach and unlike Bernhard Goetz, here was a case in which the issue not exactly of race but of an increasingly visible underclass could be confronted by the middle class, both white and black, without guilt. Here was a case that gave this middle class a way to transfer and express what had clearly become a growing and previously inadmissible rage with the city's disorder, with the entire range of ills and uneasy guilts that came to mind in a city where entire families slept in the discarded boxes in which new Sub-Zero refrigerators were delivered, at twenty-six hundred per, to more affluent families. Here was also a case, most significantly, in which even that transferred rage could be transferred still further, veiled, personalized: a case in which the city's distress could be seen to derive not precisely from its underclass but instead from certain identifiable individuals who claimed to speak for this underclass, individuals who, in Robert Morgenthau's words, "sought to exploit" this case, to "advance their own private agendas"; individuals who wished even to "divide the races".

If the city's problems could be seen as deliberate disruptions of a naturally cohesive and harmonious community, a community in which, undisrupted, "contrasts" generated a perhaps dangerous but vital "energy", then those problems were tractable, and could be addressed, like "crime", by the call for "better leadership". Considerable comfort could be obtained, given this story line, through the demonization of the Reverend Al Sharpton, whose presence on the edges of certain criminal cases that interested him had a polarizing effect that tended to reinforce the narrative. Jim Sleeper, in *The Closest of Strangers*, described one of the fifteen marches Sharpton led through Bensonhurst after the 1989 killing of an East New York sixteen-year-old, Yusuf Hawkins, who had come into Bensonhurst and been set upon, with baseball bats and ultimately with bullets, by a group of young whites.

An August 27, 1989, *Daily News* photo of the Reverend Al Sharpton and a claque of black teenagers marching in Bensonhurst to protest Hawkins's death shows that they are not really "marching." They are stumbling along, huddled together, heads bowed under the storm of hatred breaking over them, eyes wide, hanging on to one another and to Sharpton, scared out of their wits. They, too, are innocents—or were until that day, which they will always remember. And because Sharpton is with them, his head bowed, his face showing that he knows what they're feeling, he is in the hearts of black people all over New York.

Yet something is wrong with this picture. Sharpton did not invite or coordinate with Bensonhurst community leaders who wanted to join the march. Without the time for organizing which these leaders should have been given in order to rein in the punks who stood waving watermelons; without an effort by black leaders more reputable than Sharpton to recruit whites citywide and swell the march, Sharpton was assured that the punks would carry the day. At several points he even baited them by blowing kisses . . .

"I knew that Bensonhurst would clarify whether it had been a racial incident or not," Sharpton said by way of explaining, on a recent "Frontline" documentary, his strategy in Bensonhurst. "The fact that I was so controversial to Bensonhurst helped them forget that the cameras were there," he said. "So I decided to help them . . . I would throw kisses to them, and they would go nuts." *Question*, began a joke told in the aftermath of the first jogger trial. *You're in a room with Hitler, Saddam Hussein, and Al Sharpton. You have only two bullets. Who do you shoot? Answer: Al Sharpton. Twice.*

Sharpton did not exactly fit the roles New York traditionally assigns, for maximum audience comfort, to prominent blacks. He seemed in many ways a phantasm, someone whose instinct for the connections between religion and politics and show business was so innate that he had been all his life the vessel for other people's hopes and fears. He had given his first sermon at age four. He was touring with Mahalia Jackson at eleven. As a teenager, according to Robert D. McFadden, Ralph Blumenthal, M. A. Farber, E. R. Shipp, Charles Strum, and Craig Wolff, the *New York Times* reporters and editors who collaborated on *Outrage: The Story Behind the Tawana Brawley Hoax*, Sharpton was tutored first by Adam Clayton Powell, Jr. ("You got to know when to hit it and you got to know when to quit it and when it's quittin' time, don't push it," Powell told him), then by the Reverend Jesse Jackson ("Once you turn on the gas, you got to cook or burn 'em up," Jackson told him), and eventually, after obtaining a grant from Bayard Rustin and campaigning for Shirley Chisholm, by James Brown. "Once, he trailed Brown down a corridor, through a door, and, to his astonishment, onto a stage flooded with spotlights," the authors of *Outrage* reported. "He immediately went into a wiggle and dance."

It was perhaps this talent for seizing the spotlight and the moment, this fatal bent for the wiggle and the dance, that most clearly disqualified Sharpton from casting as the Good Negro, the credit to the race, the exemplary if often imagined figure whose refined manners and good grammar could be stressed and who could be seen to lay, as Jimmy Walker said of Joe Louis, "a rose on the grave of Abraham Lincoln". It was left, then, to cast Sharpton, and for Sharpton to cast himself, as the Outrageous Nigger, the familiar role—assigned sixty years ago to Father Divine and thirty years later to Adam Clayton Powell—of the essentially manageable fraud whose first concern is his own well-being. It was for example repeatedly mentioned, during the ten days the jury was out on the first jogger trial, that Sharpton had chosen to wait out the verdict not at 111 Centre Street but "in the air-conditioned comfort" of C. Vernon Mason's office, from which he could be summoned by beeper.

Sharpton, it was frequently said by whites and also by some blacks, "represented nobody", was "self-appointed" and "self-promoting". He was an "exploiter" of blacks, someone who "did them more harm than good". It was pointed out that he had been indicted by the state of New York in June of 1989 on charges of grand larceny. (He was ultimately acquitted.) It was pointed out that *New York Newsday*, working on information that appeared to have been supplied by federal law-enforcement agencies, had in

January 1988 named him as a federal informant, and that he himself admitted to having let the government tap his phone in a drug-enforcement effort. It was routinely said, most tellingly of all in a narrative based on the magical ability of "leaders" to improve the commonweal, that he was "not the right leader", "not at all the leader the black community needs". His clothes and his demeanor were ridiculed (my husband was asked by *Esquire* to do a piece predicated on interviewing Sharpton while he was having his hair processed), his motives derided, and his tactics, which were those of an extremely sophisticated player who counted being widely despised among his stronger cards, not very well understood.

Whites tended to believe, and to say, that Sharpton was "using" the racial issue—which, in the sense that all political action is based on "using" one issue or another, he clearly was. Whites also tended to see him as destructive and irresponsible, indifferent to the truth or to the sensibilities of whites—which, most notoriously in the nurturing of the Tawana Brawley case, a primal fantasy in which white men were accused of a crime Sharpton may well have known to be a fabrication, he also clearly was. What seemed not at all understood was that for Sharpton, who had no interest in making the problem appear more tractable ("The question is, do you want to 'ease' it or do you want to 'heal' it," he had said when asked if his marches had not worked against "easing tension" in Bensonhurst), the fact that blacks and whites could sometimes be shown to have divergent interests by no means suggested the need for an ameliorative solution. Such divergent interests were instead a lucky break, a ready-made organizing tool, a dramatic illustration of who had the power and who did not, who was making it and who was falling below the line; a metaphor for the sense of victimization felt not only by blacks but by all those Sharpton called "the left-out opposition". *We got the power*, the chants go on "Sharpton and Fulani in Babylon: Volume I, The Battle of New York City", a tape of the speeches of Sharpton and of Leonora Fulani, a leader of the New Alliance Party. *We are the chosen people. Out of the pain. We that can't even talk together. Have learned to walk together.*

"I'm no longer sure what I thought about Al Sharpton a year or two ago still applies," Jerry Nachman, the editor of the *New York Post*, who had frequently criticized Sharpton, told Howard Kurtz of the *Washington Post* in September of 1990. "I spent a lot of time on the street. There's a lot of anger, a lot of frustration. Rightly or wrongly, he may be articulating a great deal more of what typical attitudes are than some of us thought." Wilbert Tatum, the editor and publisher of the *Amsterdam News*, tried to explain to Kurtz how, in his view, Sharpton had been cast as "a caricature of black leadership":

> He was fat. He wore jogging suits. He wore a medallion and gold chains. And the unforgivable of unforgivables, he had processed hair. The white media, perhaps not consciously, said, "We're going to promote this

315

guy because we can point up the ridiculous-
ness and paucity of black leadership." Al
understood precisely what they were doing,
precisely. Al is probably the most brilliant
tactician this country has ever produced . . .

Whites often mentioned, as a clinching argument,
that Sharpton paid his demonstrators to appear; the
figure usually mentioned was five dollars (by November 1990, when Sharpton was fielding demonstrators
to protest the killing of a black woman alleged to have
grabbed a police nightstick in the aftermath of a domestic dispute, a police source quoted in the *Post* had
jumped the payment to twenty dollars), but the figure
floated by a prosecutor on the jogger case was four
dollars. This seemed on many levels a misunderstanding, or an estrangement, or as blacks would say a
disrespect, too deep to address, but on its simplest
level it served to suggest what value was placed by
whites on what they thought of as black time.

In the fall of 1990, the fourth and fifth of the six
defendants in the Central Park attack, Kevin Richardson and Kharey Wise, went on trial. Since this particular narrative had achieved full resolution, or
catharsis, with the conviction of the first three defendants, the city's interest in the case had by then
largely waned. Those "charlatans" who had sought to
"exploit" the case had been whisked, until they could
next prove useful, into the wings. Even the verdicts in

this second trial, coinciding as they did with yet another arrest of John ("The Dapper Don") Gotti, a reliable favorite on the New York stage, did not lead the
local news. It was in fact the economy itself that had
come center stage in the city's new, and yet familiar,
narrative work: a work in which the vital yet belea-
guered city would or would not weather yet another
"crisis" (the answer was a resounding yes); a work, or
a dreamwork, that emphasized not only the cyclical
nature of such "crises" but the regenerative power of
the city's "contrasts". "With its migratory population,
its diversity of cultures and institutions, and its vast
resources of infrastructure, capital, and intellect, New
York has been the quintessential modern city for more
than a century, constantly reinventing itself," Michael
Stone concluded in his *New York* magazine cover
story, "Hard Times". "Though the process may be
long and painful, there's no reason to believe it won't
happen again."

These were points commonly made in support of a
narrative that tended, with its dramatic line of "crisis"
and resolution, or recovery, only to further obscure
the economic and historical groundwork for the situation in which the city found itself: that long unindict-
able conspiracy of criminal and semicriminal civic
and commercial arrangements, deals, negotiations,
gimmes and getmes, graft and grift, pipe, topsoil, concrete, garbage; the conspiracy of those in the know,
those with a connection, those with a rabbi at the
Department of Sanitation or the Buildings Department or the School Construction Authority or Foley

317

Square, the conspiracy of those who believed every-body got upside down because of who it was, it hap-pened to anybody else, a summons gets issued and that's the end of it. On November 12, 1990, in its page-one analysis of the city's troubles, the *New York Times* went so far as to locate, in "public spending", not the drain on the city's vitality and resources it had historically been but "an important positive factor":

> Not in decades has so much money gone for public works in the area—airports, high-ways, bridges, sewers, subways and other projects. Roughly $12 billion will be spent in the metropolitan region in the current fis-cal year. Such government outlays are a healthy counterforce to a 43 percent decline since 1987 in the value of new private con-struction, a decline related to the sharp drop in real estate prices. . . . While nearly every industry in the private sector has been re-ducing payrolls since spring, government hiring has risen, maintaining an annual growth rate of 20,000 people since 1987 . . .

That there might well be, in a city in which the proliferation of and increase in taxes were already driving private-sector payrolls out of town, hardly anyone left to tax for such public works and public-sector jobs was a point not too many people wished seriously to address: among the citizens of a New York come to grief on the sentimental stories told in defense of its own lazy criminality, the city's inevitability remained the given, the heart, the first and last word on which all the stories rested. We love New York, the narrative promises, because it matches our energy level.

—1990